MaiNtENaNt ⁱ⁶

A JOURNAL OF CONTEMPORARY DADA WRITING & ART

PETER CARLAFTES & KAT GEORGES

EDITORS

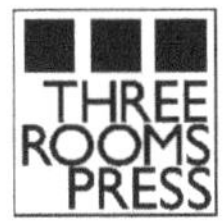

THREE ROOMS PRESS

NEW YORK

WWW.THREEROOMSPRESS.COM

EACH BOOK BORN IN GREENWICH VILLAGE

**MAINTENANT: A JOURNAL OF CONTEMPORARY DADA WRITING & ART
ISSUE 16**

Editors
Peter Carlaftes & Kat Georges

Design & Production
KG Design International

Inspiration
Arthur Cravan

ON THE COVER:
"DEFLATING EARTH"
Acrylic on canvas, 36 x 36 inches
CHUCK CONNELLY
©Copyright Chuck Connelly

A key figure among the New York-based Neo-expressionist painters, alongside artists such as Julian Schnabel and Jean-Michel Basquiat, Chuck Connelly's work is collected by major institutions across the United States. In the late 1990s, Connelly returned to his native Philadelphia where he continues to live and work. Since his early successes, Connelly has been portrayed in film by Martin Scorcese (Nick Nolte's character in *New York Stories* (1989) was based on Connelly) and was the subject of a 2008 HBO documentary.

Special thanks to Mary Rose Manspeaker, Kaitlyn Kinnard, and Ashlyn Petro, all the contributors, and everyone who supports this journal.

ISBN: 978-1-953103-22-2   ISSN 2333-2034   TRP-097

MAINTENANT: A JOURNAL OF CONTEMPORARY DADA WRITING & ART
is published annually by Three Rooms Press, New York, NY

Current and back issues of MAINTENANT are available at www.threeroomspress.com/shop.

For submission details, visit www.threeroomspress.com.

For inquiries about obtaining the MAINTENANT series for your educational or cultural institution archives, shop, or classroom, please email editor@threeroomspress.com.

Distributed by Publishers Group West (www.pgw.com)

INTRODUCTION: NYET ZERO

Creative pursuits have a funny way of aligning with reality. When we began to collect contributions for MAINTENANT 16, our theme, "NYET Zero," was intended to lay the groundwork for an artistic power grab using DADA—in the form of original art, poetry, and writing aimed at exposing the hypocrisy of the engine-idle rich on recycled paper. Our goal: change the "now" with art and thought. Otherwise, the future has NOTENTIAL. When the corporate powers that be control all of the energy resources, Art Becomes A Necessity!!! Or as Tristen Tzara put it in his Dada Manifesto, "Dada Dada Dada, a roaring of tense colors, and interlacing of opposites and of all contradictions, grotesques, inconsistencies: LIFE!"

All this was before the start of war in Ukraine. Once again, we see the continuation of eminent destruction, horror, cruelty, and terror inherent in all wars. Opposition to war was and is at the core of the ongoing DADA movement, and our MAINTENANT series continues to emphasize this urgent pursuit.

In MAINTENANT 16's "NYET Zero" theme we now find multiple layers of purpose: exposing both threats to individuals, countries, and an entire planet. We create to inspire imagination; through imagination the world has a chance at a future of actual peace—and, of equal importance—a future, period.

—Peter Carlaftes and Kat Georges, editors

CONTENTS

MaiNtENaNt[16]

ORCHID SPANGIAFORA

WYNCOTE, PENNSYLVANIA

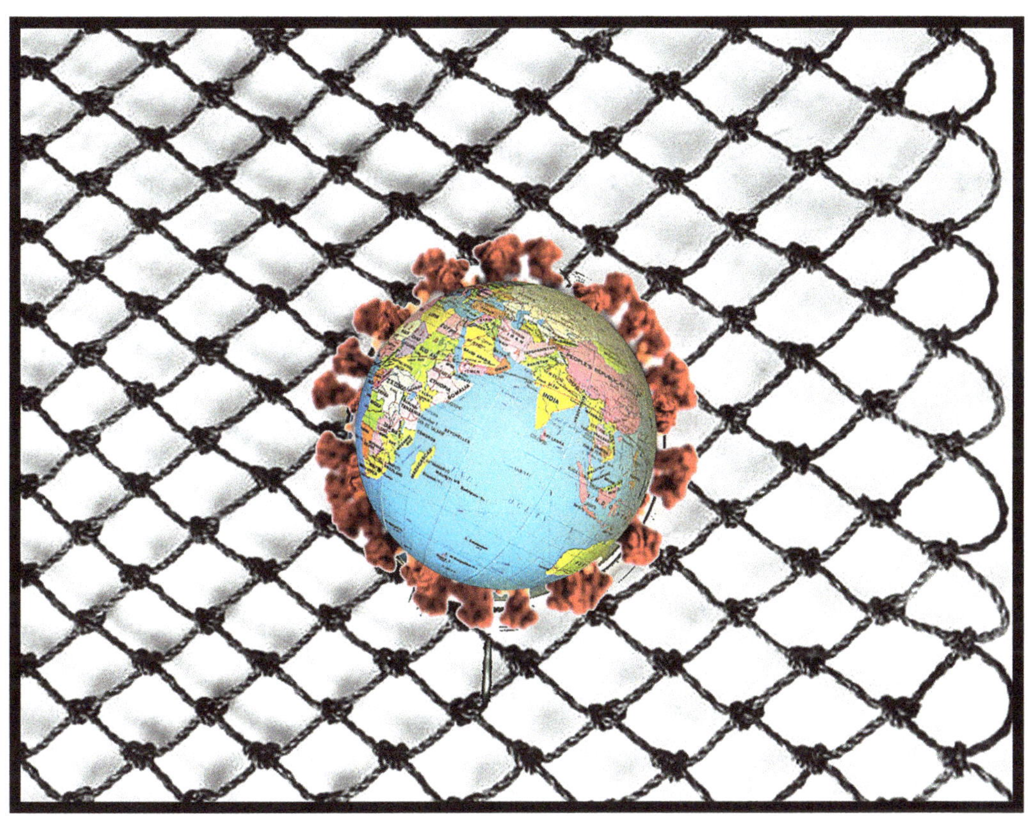

STATE OF THE WORLD

Digital collage, 1459 x 1111 pixels

CHRISTINE SLOAN STODDARD

BROOKLYN, NEW YORK

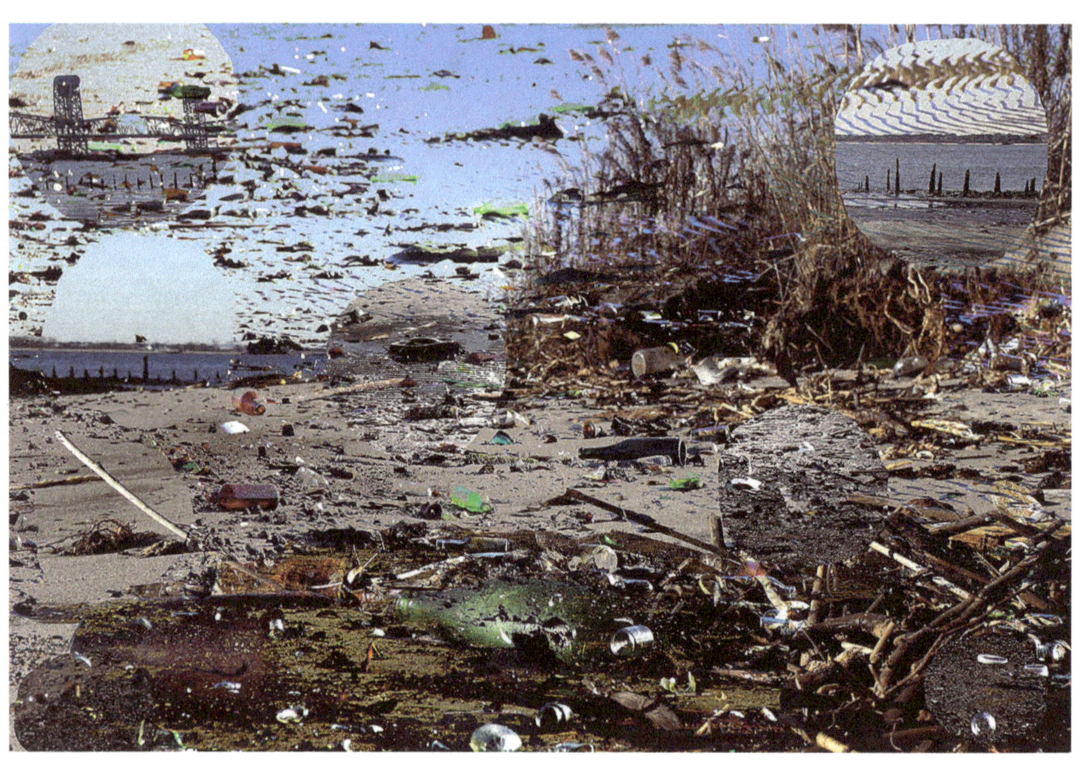

BACK THEN (RESPONSE)

Digital, dimensions variable

AIMEE HERMAN

BOULDER, COLORADO

DITCH THE PLASTICS

FAQ

Do you charge for shipping?
Unidentified caller from the planet NPR explains that
tiny red and blue synthetic fibers
which can cause rashes to those unused to comfort
can backbend out of pockets too quickly
to keep track of

Do you ship outside the U.S.?
Mr. McHarrison, elementary history teacher, said if you walk too closely to
the edge of the earth, you will find
(I wasn't listening)

How fragile are your materials?
Treatment can be outsourced but
there is no cure

Can I track my order?
37.3012 ° N, 81.6909° W

Can I change my mind?
A global emergency of brain cells uncovered by most health insurance
bigwigs.

Where are your products made?
My mother told me
she refuses to share her recipes
so it might be best
you hire someone with taste buds
that know how to speak up
to translate the coordinates
of her ingredients.

How do I apply for a discount?
Take off
all of
your clothes

What if I am not satisfied?
There is a pill for that.

Can I speak to a human?
Richard Brautigan once said,
"it's so nice/
          to wake up in the morning/
all alone"

          & also
if you sew a thousand glossolalia heartbeats together / you will
forget
          what you were hoping for

MARK GLISTA

NEW YORK, NEW YORK

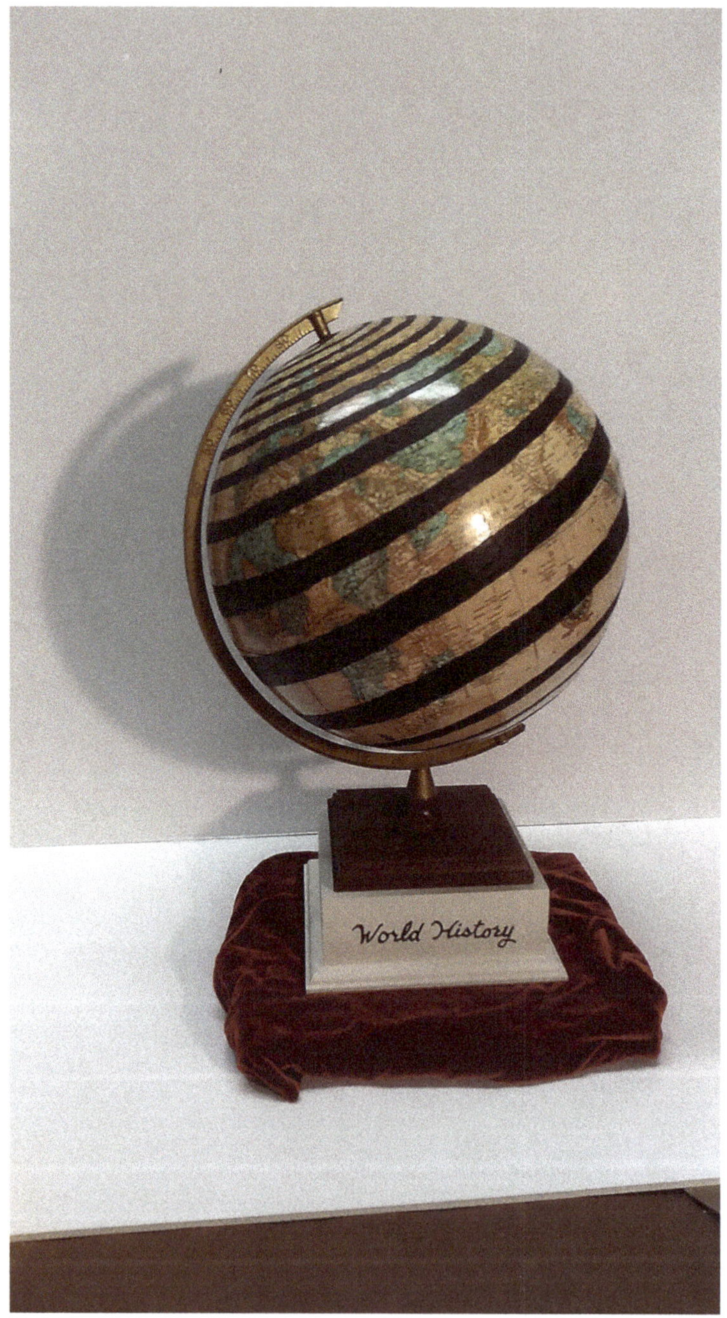

WORLD HISTORY

Wood and ink, 18 × 12 inches

MARILYN STABLEIN

PORTLAND, OREGON

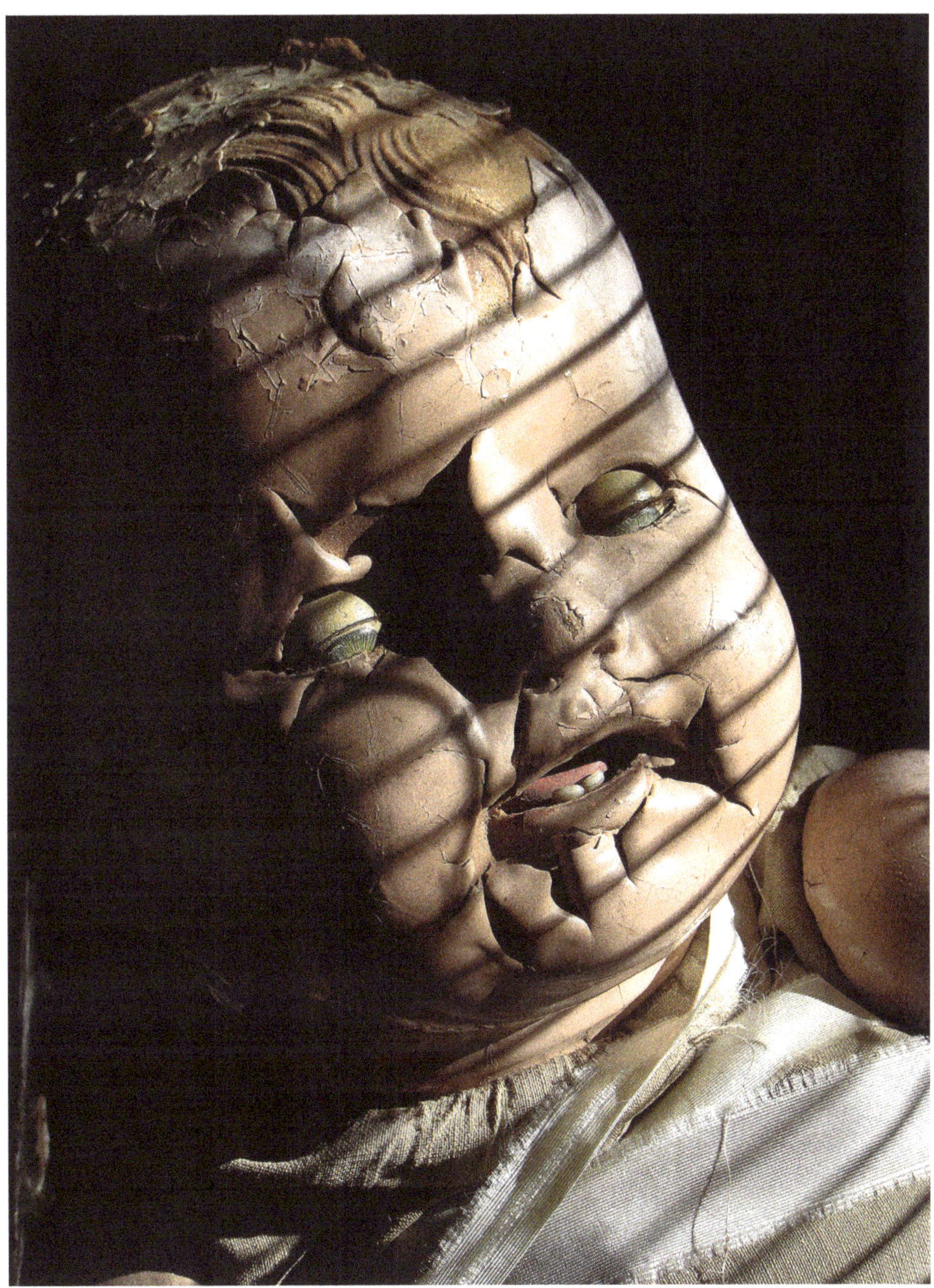

TOXIC FUMES KILL

Color portrait photograph of a decrepit, peeling, chipped, and cracked, eco-devasted vintage doll head,
2448 x 3264 pixels

VOLODYMYR BILYK

ZHYTOMYR, UKRAINE

ніц чиниться.—
ненастанне пусте
розносить скроні...

трощ: небо здійнялось.
дибиться з розпуки:

нізвідкіль — шарп навскоси;
— нута недоладна,
вгрузає жартома.

захват почуття. —
безсило скніє...

шал: шморг
— дзизь;
батожить відтінь —

тупотіння вал:
вивершив намір —
випружується . . .

никне незбагнутим.

*poem written hours before war started.
pretty much sums up everything i felt up to
this point and what i felt just five hours later
when i was leaving kyiv in haste.*

PAWEŁ KUCZYŃSKI

POLICE, POLAND

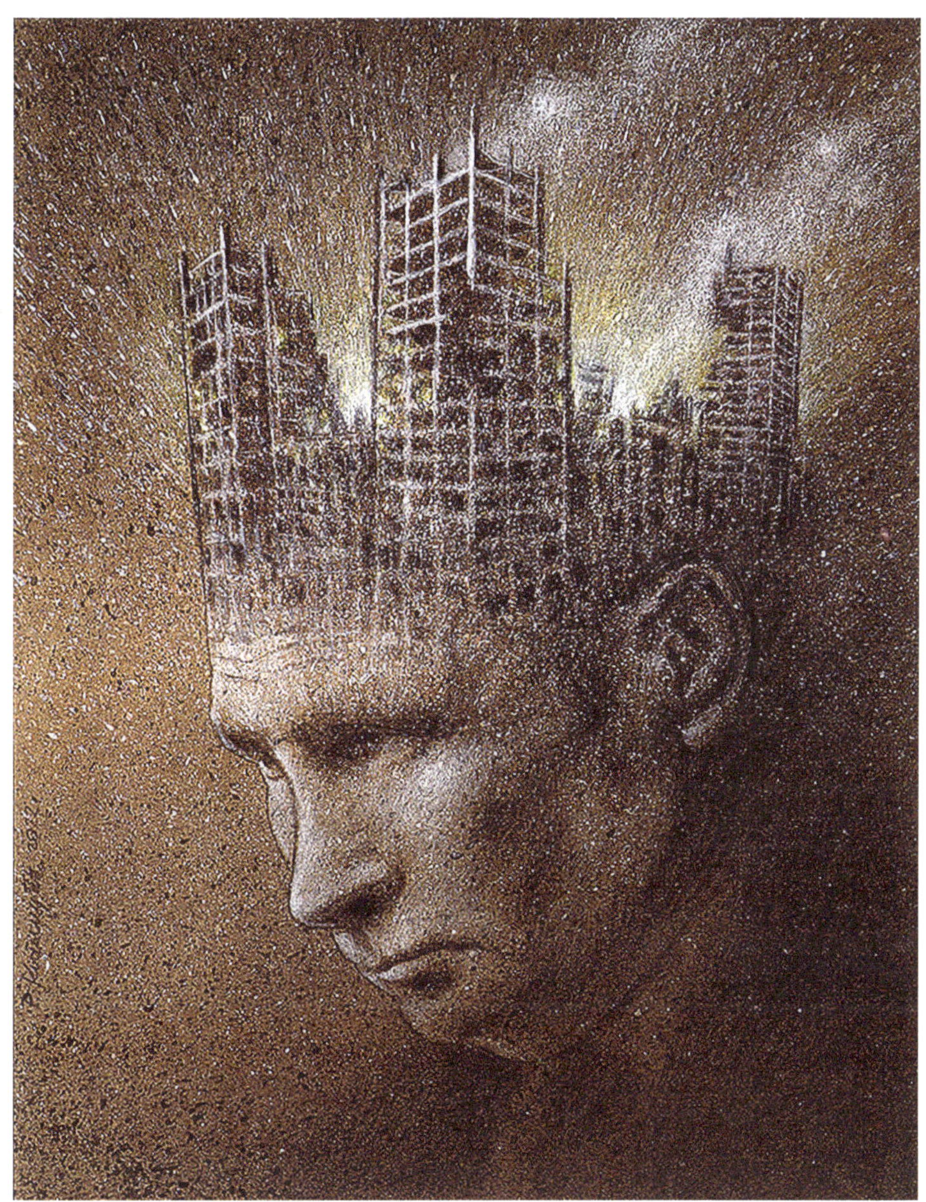

CROWN

LAYLAH DeLAUTRÉAMONT

LAS VEGAS, NEVADA

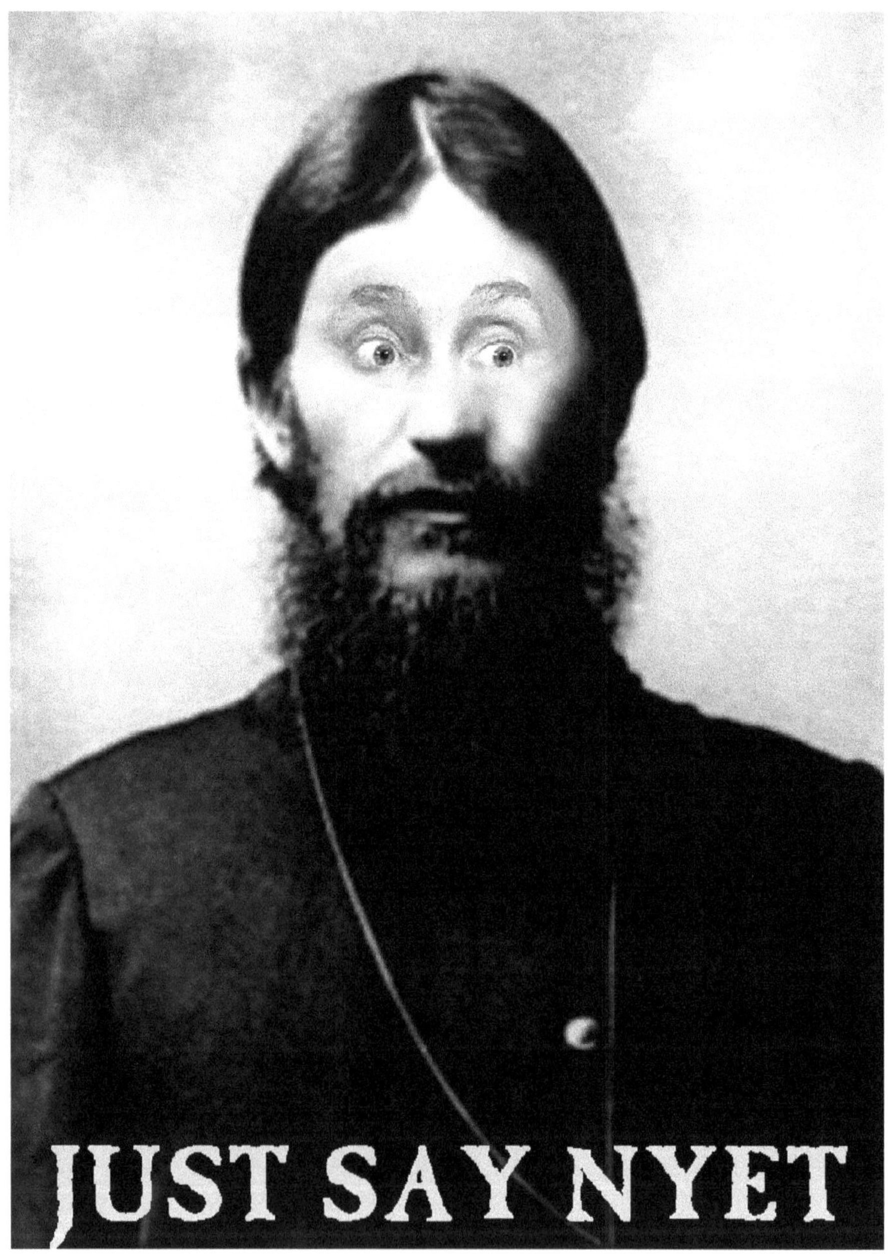

RAZZPUTIN

Photo collage

ROGER CONOVER

FREEPORT, MAINE

FOR VLADIMIR PUTIN

We who you call beautiful
Are not your animals.

We who you call animals
Will never be pets of yours.

We who you call Nazis
Have no name for you.

We see you now
For how you war.

We hold mirrors
And round-trip tickets:

Back
To Ukraine.

We who you call sexy
Are not yours to rape.

You fucked with us
And made a ruin.

The damage is permanent
To your face.

KAREN NEUBERG

BROOKLYN, NEW YORK

THIS POEM DOESN'T WANT TO TALK ABOUT THE WAR

Who?

We, said

        the industrialists

        the politicians

        the lobbyists

        the capitalists

        the deniers

        the totalitarians

        the oligarchs

        the fascists

We killed

the future.

And who'll toll the bells?

No one, said

the wind.

No one will be left to toll the bells.

SILVIO SEVERINO

CORK, IRELAND

Digital collage

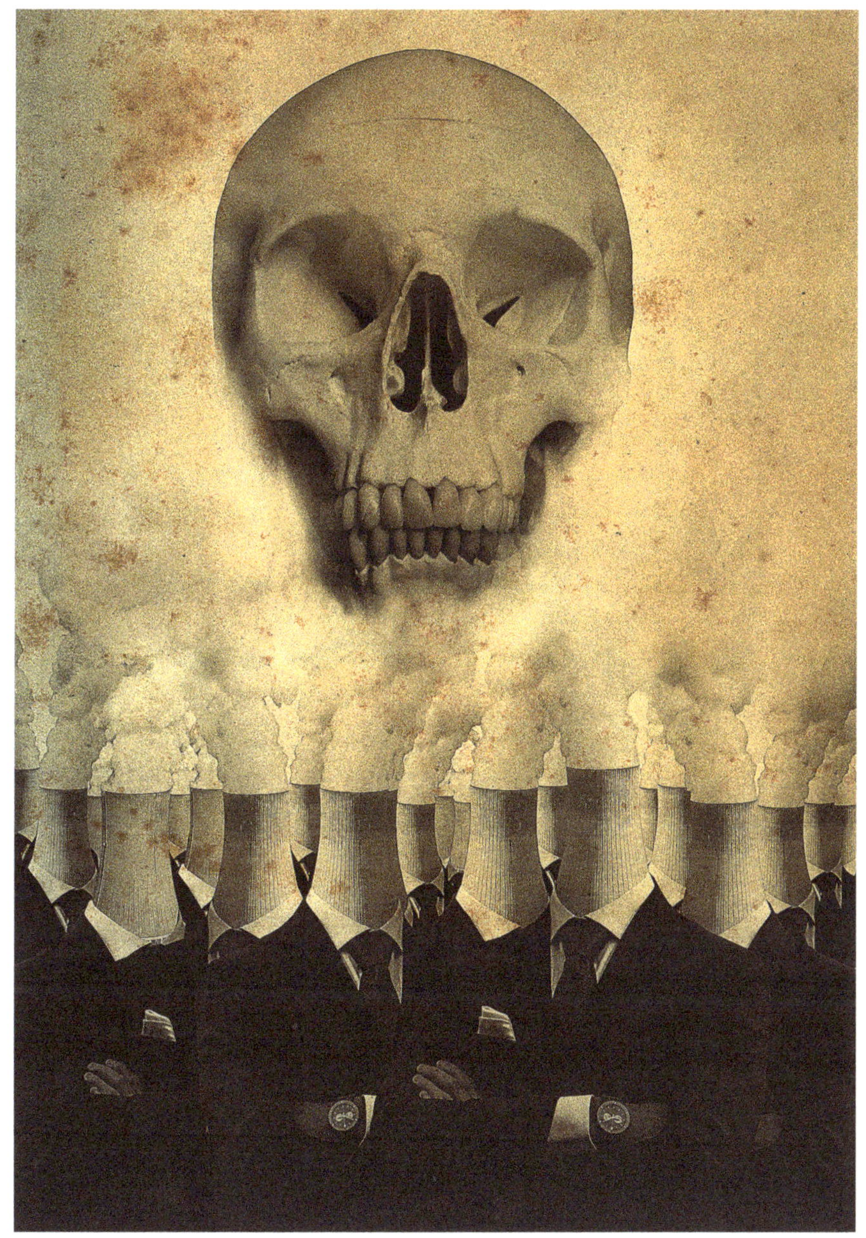

OLIGARCHS!

Digital collage

RENAAT RAMON

BRUGES, BELGIUM

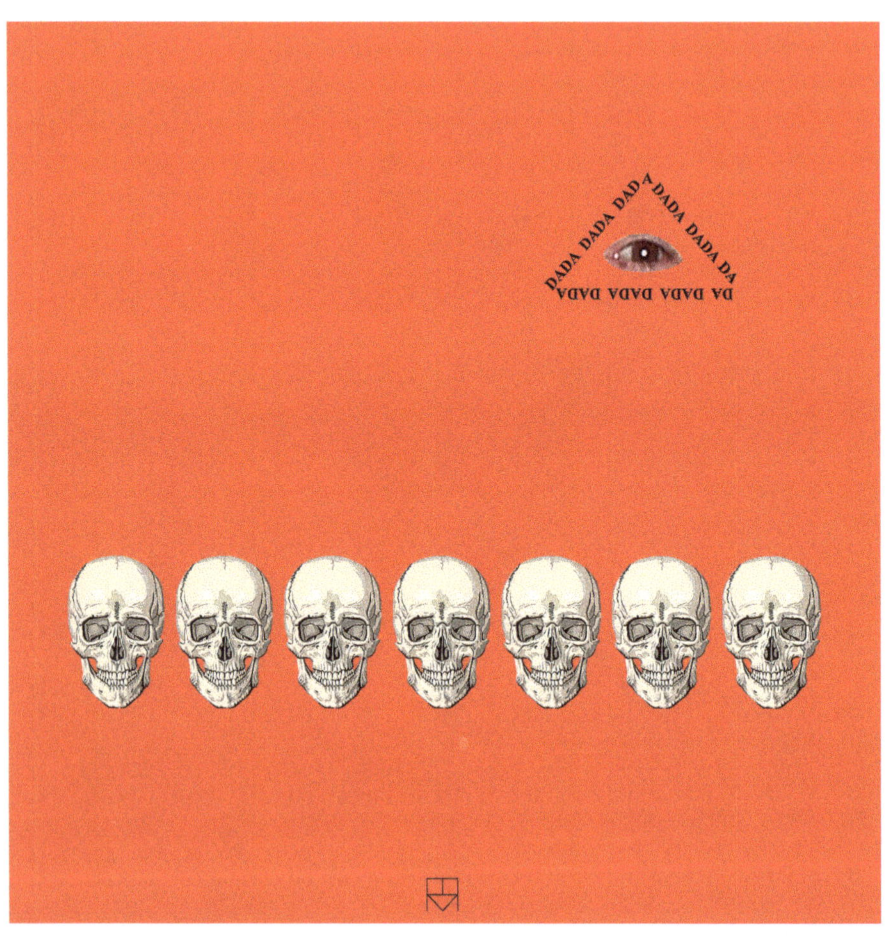

NYET ZERO – YAY DADA

YOUSSEF ALAOUI

SAN LUIS OBISPO, CALIFORNIA

AND THE DREAD THEREFORE

Da! Da! Razz!
Forgot Z joke.

Nyet Zero. Dada Adeen.

Zero One equals choke of holding laughter.

Adeen is Dada. Nyet is Zero.

Eight Raz. Rest Zero. Red no Dead
Horny hammer. Poppy sickle.

There is no Da in Nyet.

No aDeen in Zero.

And the Dread Therefore
DAlexis de Tocqueville, DAmockracy in Amerika, 1835

And the dread therefore always to conceive
privileges are imperfect, so fugitive

Straining to pursue or to have a sufficient
many scanty they never losing enough to satisfy it

When the freedom widely taste for these retain gratifications
of the gratifications and education

American poor, when he, exertion, together and
fortunes spring destroyed and subdivided

And they share of physical pleasures — but not
procure them without apprehension, Americans are confounded

Them that of world haunts distinctions of ranks so delightful, so
the imagination comforts of the Up; those who

Possess them desire of hereditary in them without
acquiring the diffused, the never indulge property the rich

ANDREI CODRESCU

BROOKLYN, NEW YORK

A PANDEMIC CAROUSEL

INEXPLICABLE INCORRIGIBLE INEXPLICABLE UNTREATABLE

I will now leave the pandemic glass doghouse to riot in Mr. Rogers neighborhood. Blush, and that was youth worthy of all the adjectives above. Then there was "dissonance" meaning money. A gentle man Ted Berrigan did not want to hurt artists but he saw that even greedy bastards will bow to art if not to discipline and all-consuming disregard for health by noting in parentheses and capitals (GET THE MONEY) to mean a cry for mommy to notice the shiny quality of print. The paucity of things in my commie youth was transparent so we looked each day through it to see what was on the other side of soldiers with their rifles turned toward us the curious but there weren't enough soldiers to block our sight.

Our thoughts were not about things but art.
Things were flattered but they weren't music.
When things are flattered they turn seductive.
They turn into music and nudity.
The industrial pretended to quench our appetites emptied of social utility.
Mocking laughter filled the republics of jokes.
Objects and thoughts got along like family
separated only by borders of music and textiles.
Some things like wooden forks and spoons saw
themselves as patrons of younger steel ladles
espresso makers nonstick pans and fireworks
that broadcast dylan the beatles stones janis
keats blake ginsberg corso berrigan warhol.
We prefered escape over boredom and death.
A lot of my friends died trying to escape
so we don't really know how boring
is the afterlife, postmortem capitalism is incognito.
We will now compare communism the ideology
with Covid the virus to see if the pandemic jail
and the political jail of the police differ.
We find they do and declare virus the winner!
But wait! A third competitor enters the ring:
Carnival! According to Carnival, this virus
is treatable but ideology is forever and the only
eternal cure is revolution.

BIBIANA PADILLA MALTOS

WESTMINSTER, CALIFORNIA

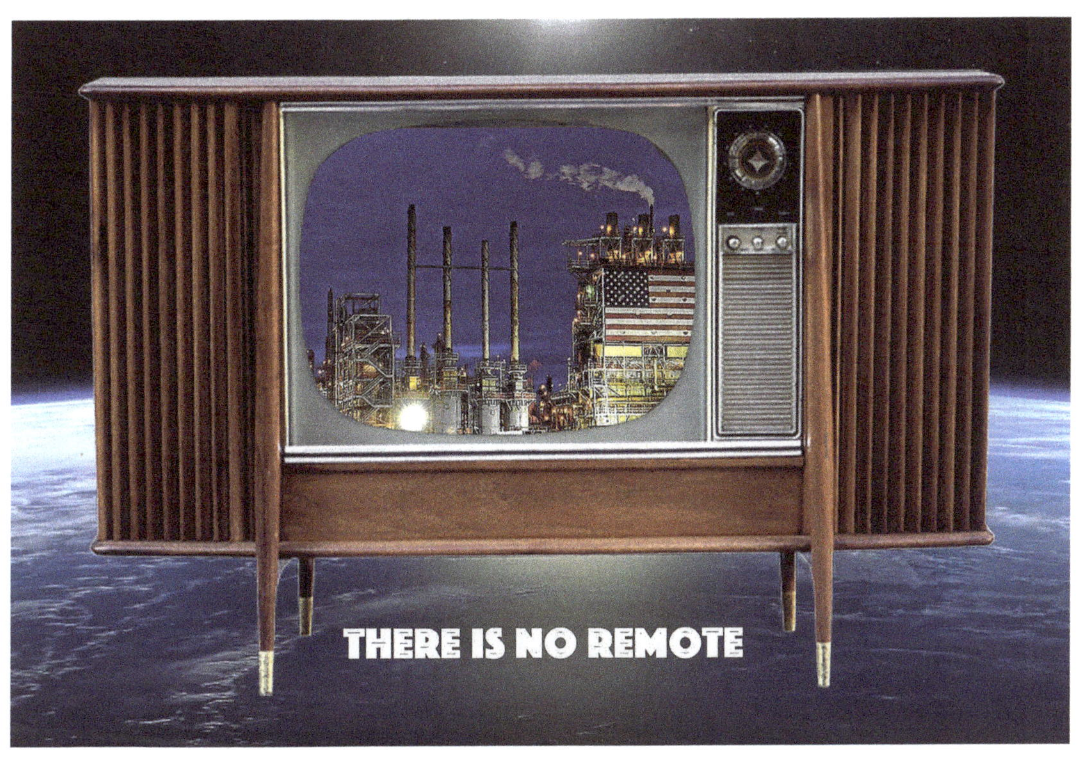

THERE IS NO REMOTE

Digital collage, 6 X 4 inches

AMY BASSIN & MARK BLICKLEY

LONG ISLAND CITY, NEW YORK

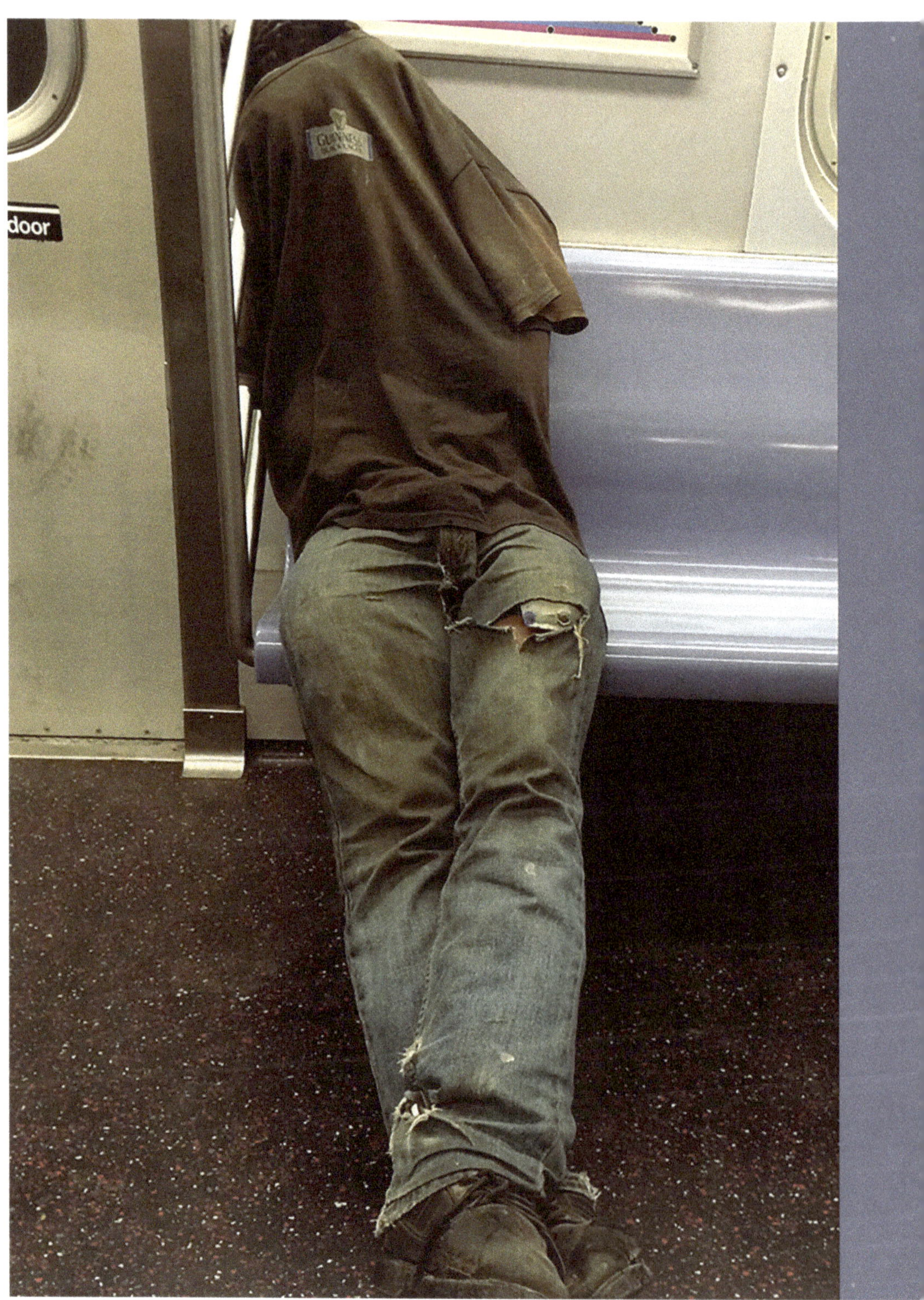

HEADS-UP DREAM FOR PEACE

I resent when beheading videos go viral and zombie apocalypses top viewer entertainment lists as it makes it much too easy for them to ignore the walking dead sharing a subway ride on way to a final destination that proves being heads up simply exposes one as too easy a target regardless of the helmet I first wear in boot camp when angry drill sergeants scream at me during squadron maneuvers to pull my head out of my ass so I don't kill my buddies because of a lack of concentration though I was concentrating real hard when Happy Jack took two shots to the head that exploded his Chicago style ghetto humor all over my face and flak jacket dripping down inside sand coated combat boots that allow me to walk away and proclaim heads you lose but tales you win if you're alive and able to speak of them to a passenger audience who bury their heads in smart phone images and sounds to avoid their neighbor's headless pain of surrender seated alone across the aisle where no one else sits to coax a face from my torn and stained civilian clothes while the train chugs to the South Ferry final stop where a whiff of rusty river replaces my body odor and signals a free boat ride that promises freedom when midway to Staten Island it glides past the Statue of Liberty and I plunge towards the crowned Lady who will read my DD214 safely wrapped in protective plastic and pinned to my pants pocket along with instructing letter that will guide me towards my very own plot of land in lovely Virginia where I can sleep with silent brothers and sisters and share a peace my grateful government will mark and preserve with a uniformly crafted and informative headstone...

JOEL ALLEGRETTI
FORT LEE, NEW JERSEY

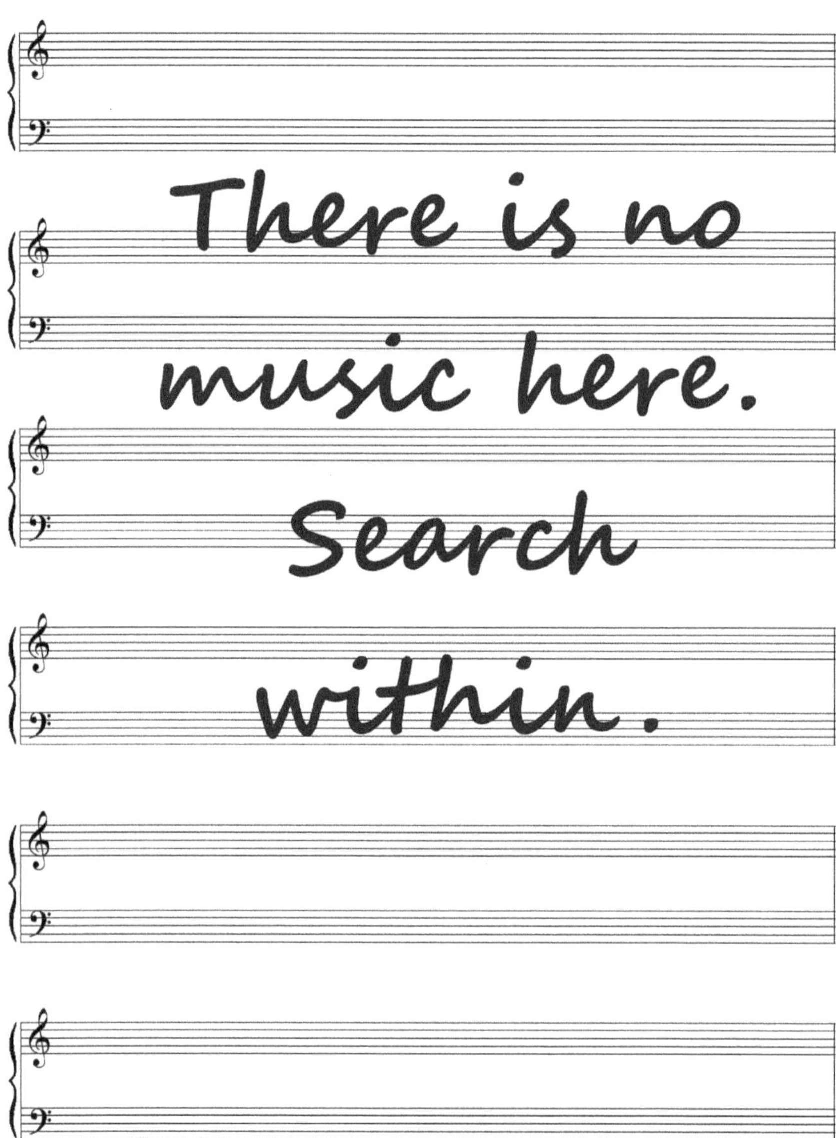

THERE IS NO MUSIC HERE

Manuscript paper and text

THOMAS STOLMAR
SAN FRANCISCO, CALIFORNIA

SILENCE

———   ,   …
           .
———   .
               ,   ,   .

———   ,   ,   .
———,   ,   .
———   …
      ,   .
(————-   .)

———   ,   ,   ‖   .
         .   .
———

         ——   .

———   ‖   —,
———,   ——   ,   .
———   .

(… ‑ ‑ ‑ … ‖ … ‑ ‑ ‑ …)

Special attention was paid to ensure
quiet punctuation only, so as not to
disturb the perfect cadence or
disrupt meanings, etc.
… Just go skiing &
forget about the
Ukrainian
masacre?
Can I?
SOS.

SANTIAGO AMAYA

OAKLAND, CALIFORNIA

META-IRONY

Weatherman says tomorrow's heat is gonna be a
Record breaker
Everyone's got their own version of the story

I used up all of my sick days staring at the tv
Sinking into the couch watching the summer rot
with a teacher's salary worth of ketamine

Flipping the channel to see if the game is on
which celebrities overdosed today
And which country is getting carpet bombed in the name of freedom

I spend my weekends buying up property in the Metaverse
With the money I made from NFTs of
hair dye running down Rudy Giuliani's face

Found god in virtual reality
Rigging the darwinian lottery
And livestreaming the end of the world

Tiptoeing around the Anthropocene Extinction
Sustaining myself on the sludge of war
Edging on the possibility of nuclear armageddon

When I finally crawl out of my hole
I start my daily routine, wipe the dried blood from my nose
And walk towards the liquor store

Junkies pile up in the corner
With spines that stick out like metal girders
Buckling in the sun

I check up on them every once in awhile
with clean needles in hand and a spoonful of tar
watching their black veins sing the blues

Life is as easy as American politics
Ignore all your real problems
And let everyone else deal with the consequences

At the end of every day
I go back home and I turn on the tv
I stumble across a documentary of the Trinity Test as it is ending

Now for the news
Congress approves trillion dollar war budget
Weatherman says tomorrow's heat is gonna be a
Record breaker

RAYMOND PETTIBON

NEW YORK, NEW YORK

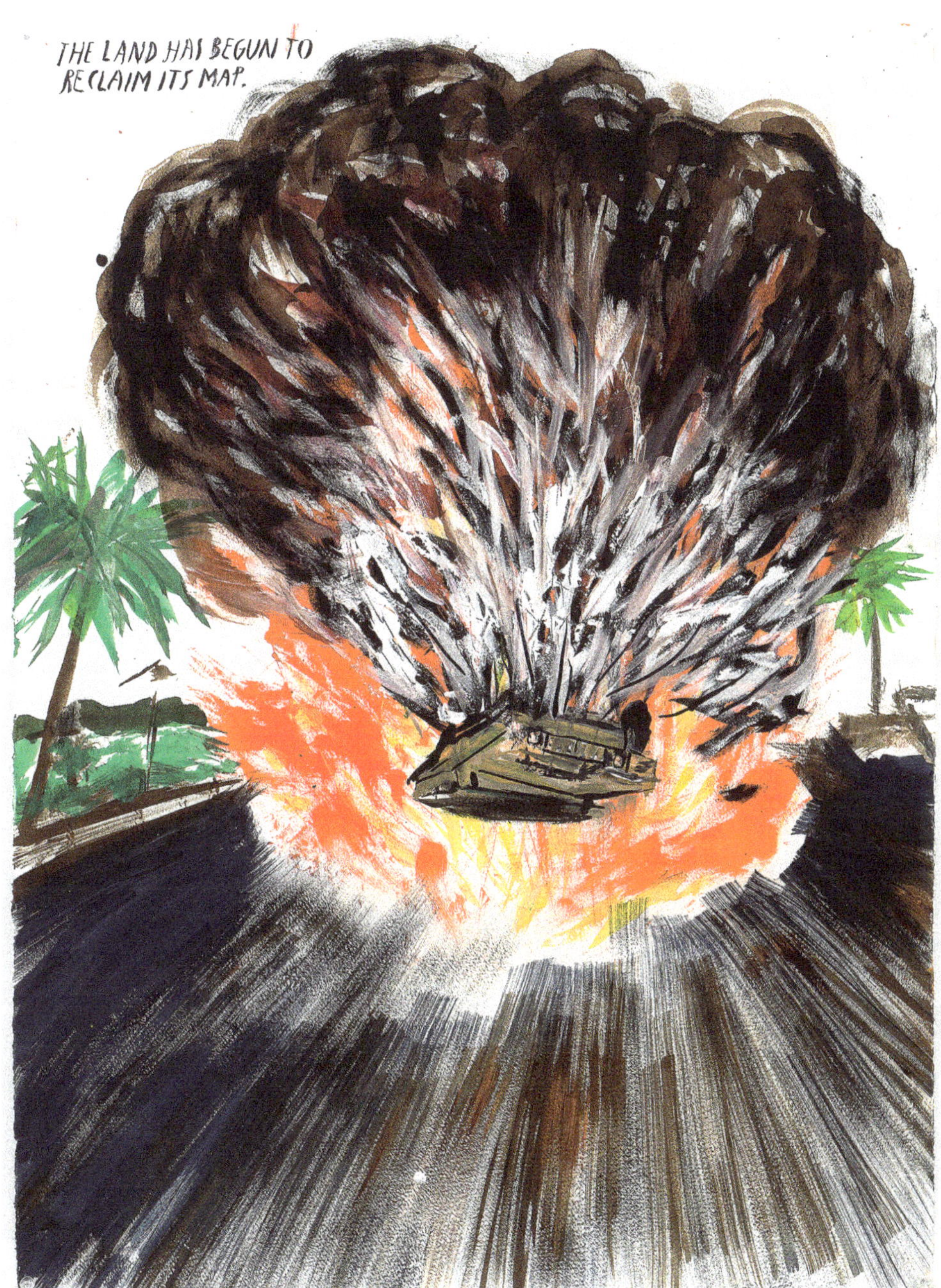

NO TITLE (THE LAND HAS...)

Pen, ink and gouache on paper, 29 1/2 x 22 1/4 inches (74.9 x 56.5 cm)

CHARLES PLYMELL
CHERRY VALLEY, NEW YORK

"SPACE STEPS INTO THE JEWELED INDIFFERENCE"

I was driving back to Wichita from Oregon in
    my 1953 Buick Roadmaster Rivera

I bought almost new in Hollywood. I was on
    the Rt. through Ely, Nevada

where there was a good Basque restaurant
    across tracks.

They had a jug of wine & bread on the table as
    soon as one sat down.

They herded sheep in those parts.

Driving alone, it was pitch black. If I turned off
    car lights, I couldn't see my hand in front
    of me.

There it was: The traditional mother ship, long
    cigar shaped with illuminations alongside

where the traditional saucer shaped craft flew
    out. The hairs on my neck stood up

as they maneuvered. I put the Buick to the floor
    over a hundred mph,

but they weren't after me and disappeared in
    "space steps."

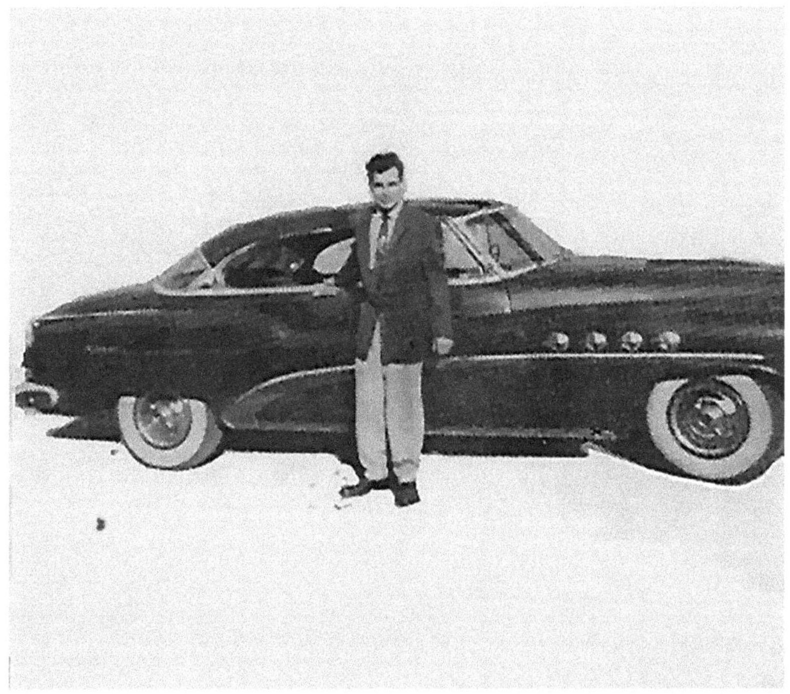

Here's the photo of my Buick that raced the saucers! —C.P.

PHILIPPE MARCADE

BOLOGNA, ITALY

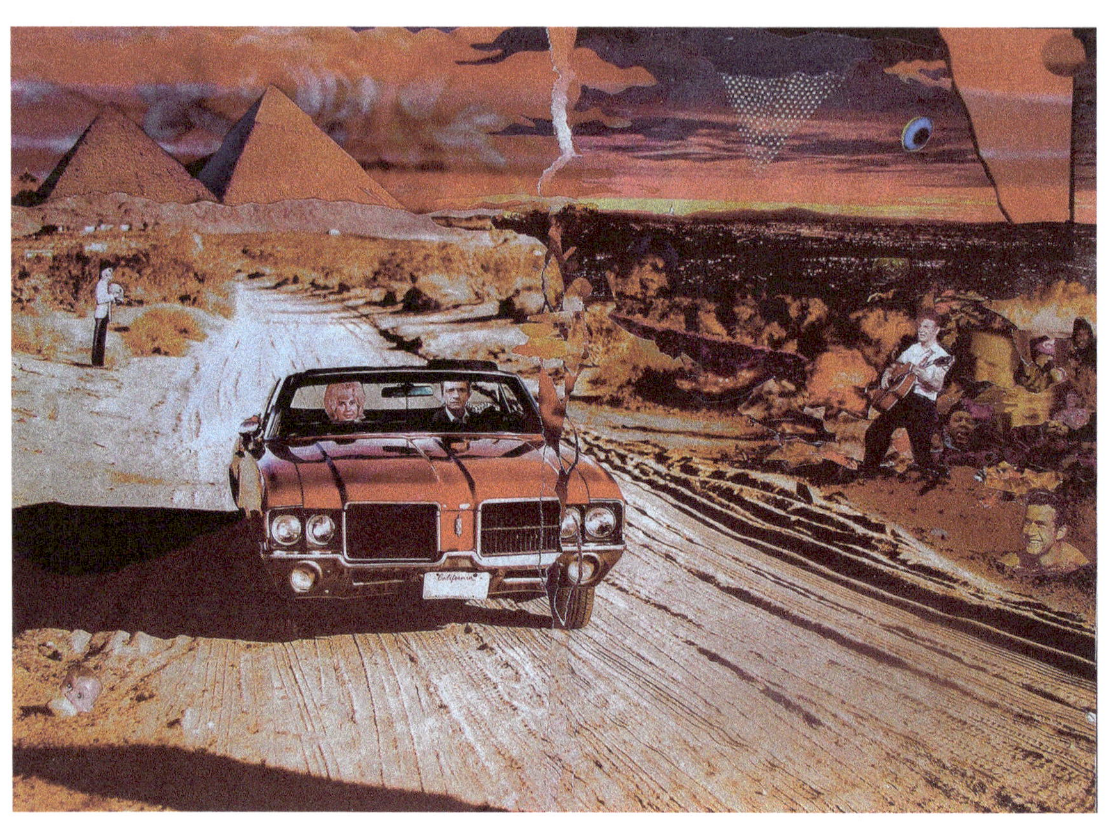

ON THE ROAD TO ROUEN

Collage, paper, glue, 30 x 40 cm

THURSTON MOORE

LONDON, UNITED KINGDOM

NEW YEAR'S DAY

Burning bridge fell on top of ice cold mirror

Cracked to reveal the grin of

God's only daughter the smart

Whip of sense waiting with enlightened

Patience for the clock to shout

Rock n roll will never lie

GERARD MALANGA

HUDSON, NEW YORK

I believe I have found the missing link between animals and civilized man,
Konrad Lorenz wrote. *It is us.*

NUTRIA, OR LUTRA, MYOCASTOR COYPUS

Audubon would have fallen in love with you, as would Way Teale.

As would Nuttal, Lorenz, and Jedediah Smith.

You are a kindly character, yet untamed, defined

by ferocious winds and clouds, by tidepools, bogs.

Today you're hunted mercilously.

You're doing what you can,

God-given as with any birds or lowly creatures gathering.

It's not you who wreak the havoc

but the ghostly genocide.

You are the scapegoat.

Man is the "Judas" nutria. Beware the scent.

It's not for naught

your pelt is sought.

Man still plays the old man shaman game

mockingly, connivingly.

Beware the scent.

Even in your demise

may your ghosts thrive.

Nature wins out in the end.

Who will mourn the timber wolf, the Japanese wolf,

the red fox and the gray fox?

Who will mourn the tyger tyger burning bright?

Who will mourn those soundings in the night?

Who mourns the Bison of the Plains?

The cougar in its lair? The soaring albatross?

Only you will mourn you

by the mere wisp of your brow, your loving eyes.

Who will mourn the ghost of man?

MIKE WATT

SAN PEDRO, CALIFORNIA

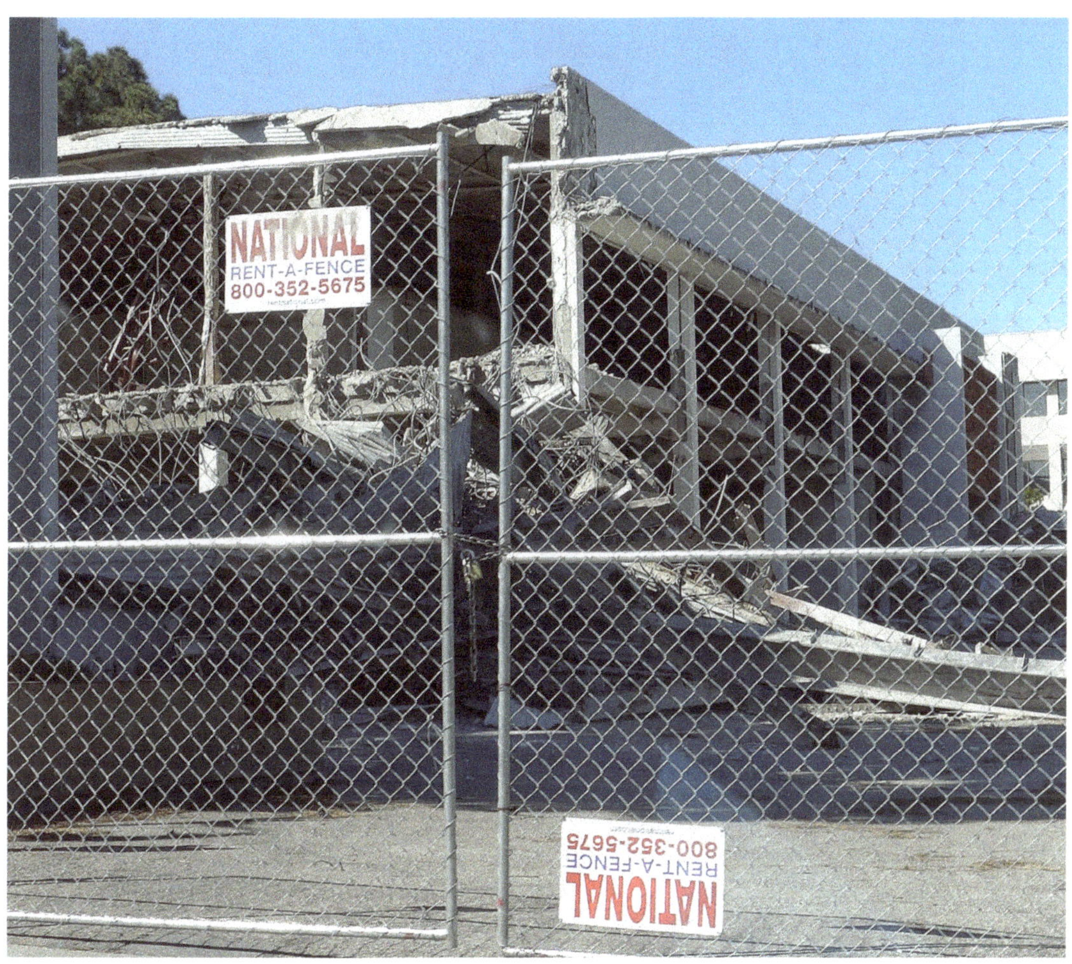

FORMER COURTHOUSE IN DOWNTOWN SAN PEDRO

Digital photo

LAURIE STEELINK & JEFF FARR

SAN PEDRO, CALIFORNIA & NEW YORK, NEW YORK

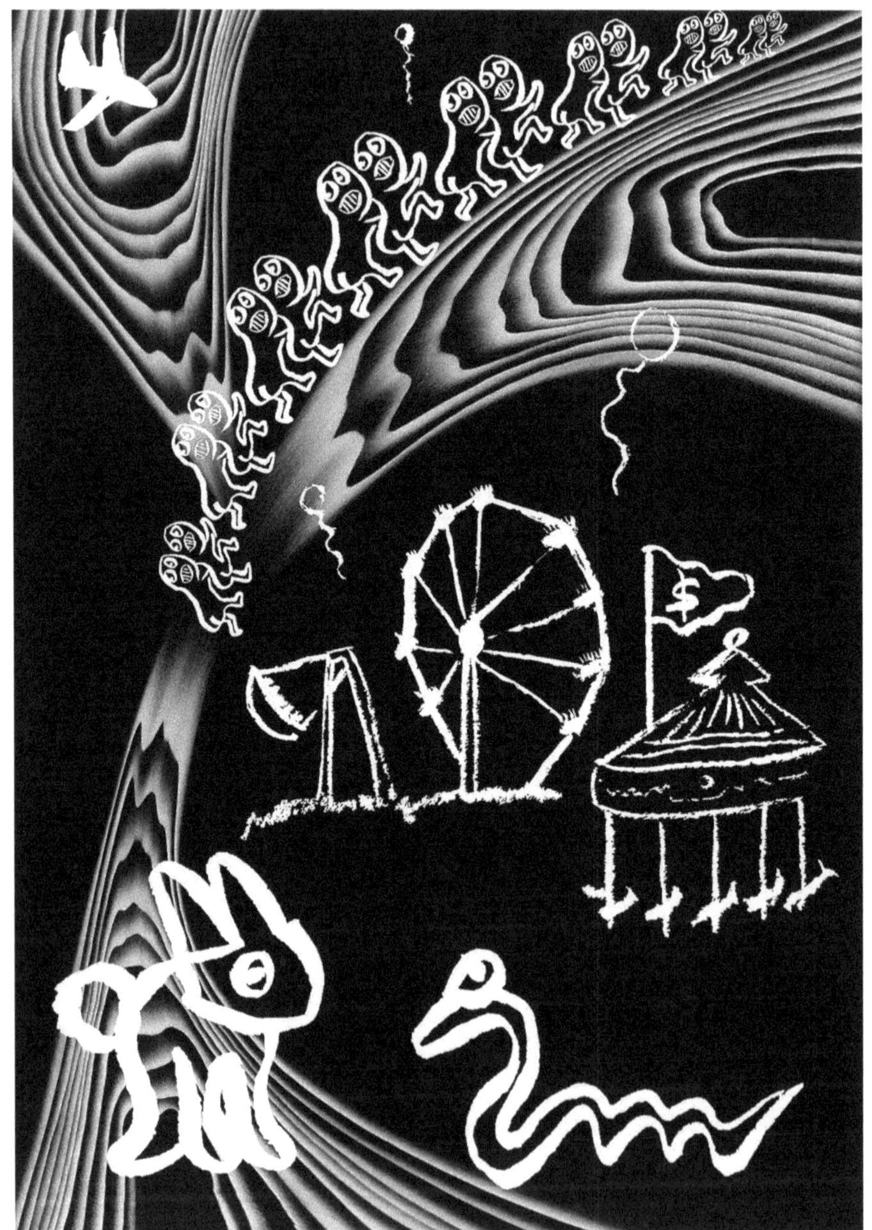

TO BE DETERMINED

Digital image, 7 x 5 inches

FRED MARCHANT

ARLINGTON, MASSACHUSETTS

APPLE SAUCE

"Your poem brings us / into the world"
—Eugène Guillevic

mine says leave
    me alone but
they come round
    with apple sauce
and a spoon
    so light it could
be plastic but is
    a thin metal
that adds its taste
    to the spoonful
whereon two pills
    needed to bring
me back to life
    rest and wait for
me to open wide,
    pills in pleasing
violet, meaning
    they are extended
release so saith
    the good nurse
and i say back
    i am trying not
to cry and just
    want to go back
to sleep, go back
    to my dream
which is now
    the best part
of my day
    almost every night

MARK HOEFER

SAN DIEGO, CALIFORNIA

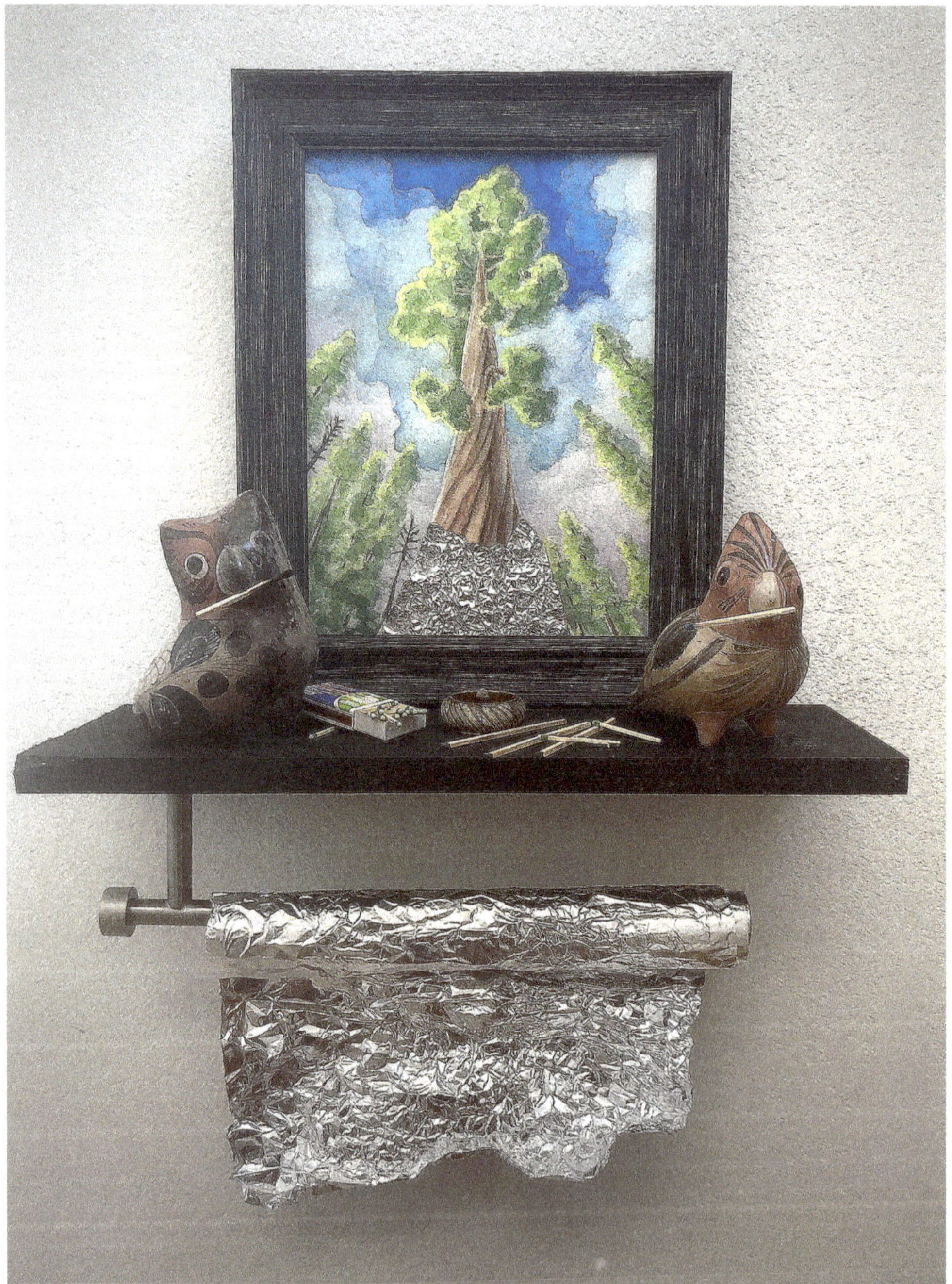

CARBON OFFSET CREDIT—CURSES FOILED AGAIN!

Watercolor, foil, and bric-a-brac, 18 x 24 inches

A. D. WINANS

SAN FRANCISCO, CALIFORNIA

THOUGHTS ON THE CALIFORNIA DROUGHT

I sit here feeling like a used car

one part after the other failing me

the drought laughs at the masses

teases them with a light drizzle

forest fires burning out of control

tornado's leveling towns

hurricanes in and out of season

poisoned air courting asthma-stricken children

corporate greed wed to bought politicians

the planet their private playground

my room a dust garden

dances with my respiratory system

corona virus sweeps the world

mutates like a mythical sea monster

working class men and women puppets

caught up in a money-making machine

that grinds them up like a sausage maker

I take refuge in a sea of poems

ride the waves to a distant shore

the peace of solitude rides my veins

like a steamship treading calm waters

the garden of my mind is still green

poetry seeds wait for planting in fertile soil

no drought or politician can kill

KATHLEEN FLORENCE

THOUSAND ISLANDS, ONTARIO, CANADA

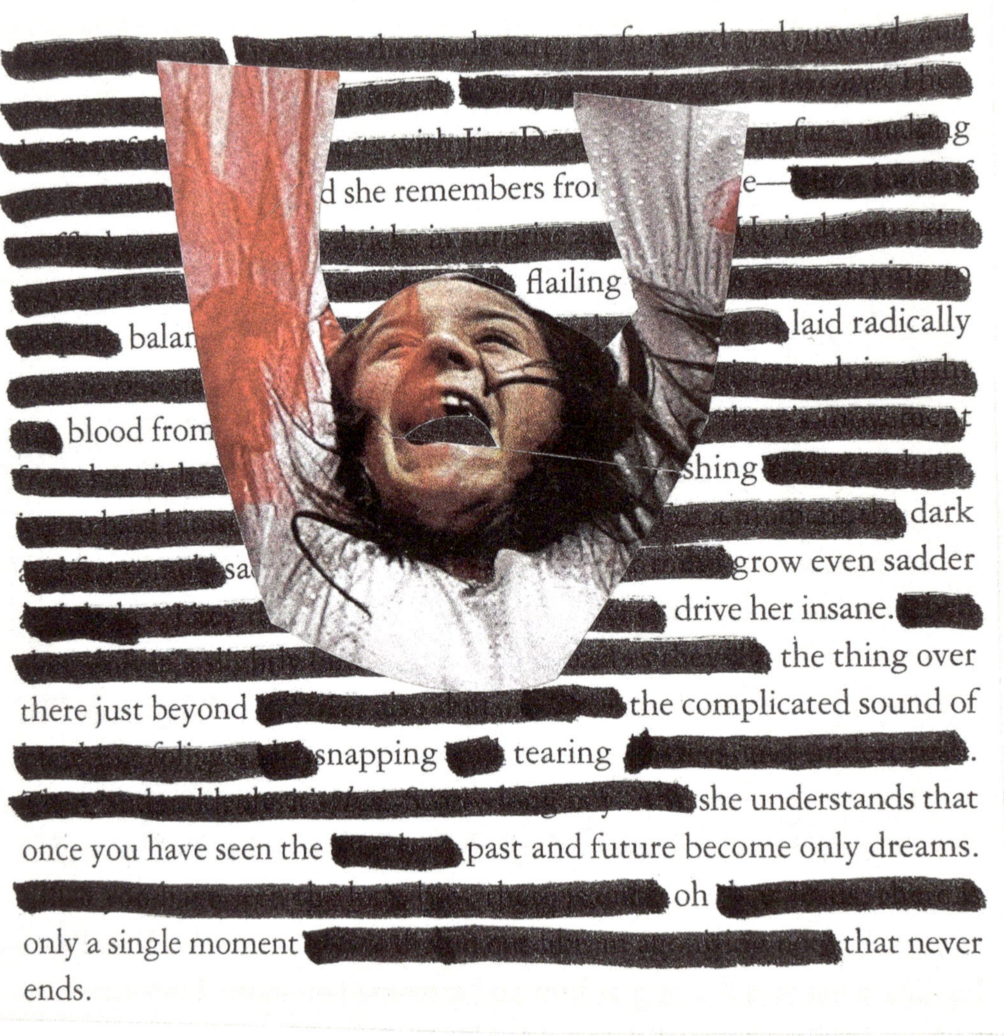

LUNG READING

Collage and ink, 6 x 5 inches

MAW SHEIN WIN

EL CERRITO, CALIFORNIA

THOUGHT LOG 21

Mastering the art of doing nothing.

She dreamt that we were wearing matching pinafores & attending an event that started with the letter M.

Three of my close friends have fallen in the last three weeks.

A group of devoted volunteers are knitting below the skin of my abdomen.

Kerfuffle, skedaddle, paradiddle.

The ovarian cyst was defrosted for the biopsy.

Cinnabar, Carmine, Cordovan.

What is it? Is it? It?

Two children hawk objects on the lawn: wild daisies, toothpicks wetly painted, a neck brace.

We are 100% committed to hope at this moment.

Myometrium, puerperium, endometrium.

My brother's neighbor ripped down his decorative flower boxes & hummingbird feeder.

Drill down into metaphor making.

King Dong, Lemon Oreos, unwashed scrubs.

Cutie Thunderstomp upstairs annoys & amuses us.

Enter the zero rodeo.

WILLIAM SEATON

GOSHEN, NEW YORK

LING

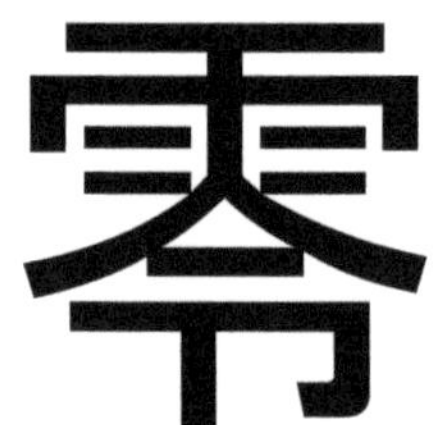

líng

zero; nought

líng

a hard rain falls through the top half of the character

battering the roof of the phonetic below

till one can scarcely see

líng

to wither and fall / to wither

nothing

CSABA PAL

BUDAPEST, HUNGARY

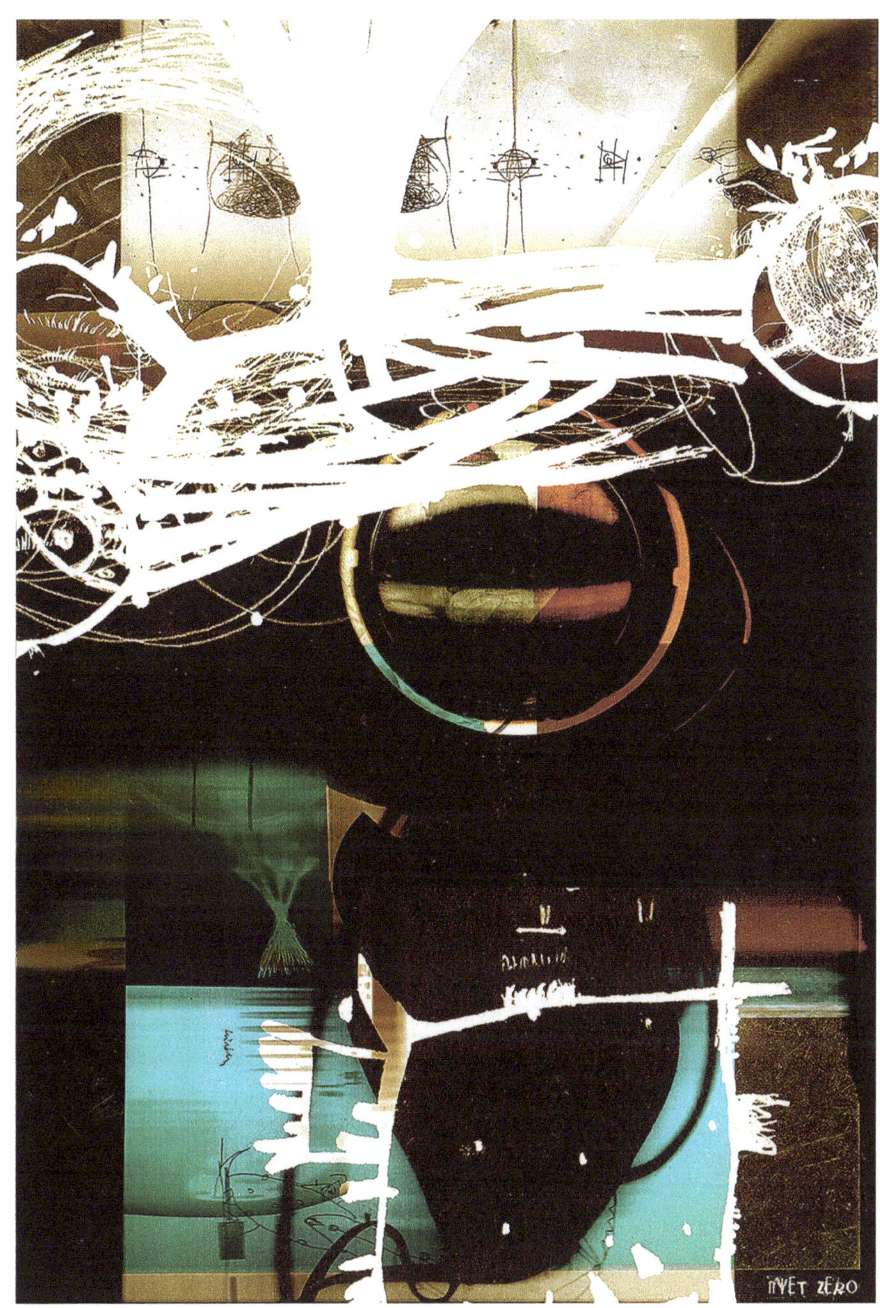

NYET ZERO

Digital print, A4, 21 x 29.7 cm

SYPORCA WHANDAL

BUDAPEST, HUNGARY

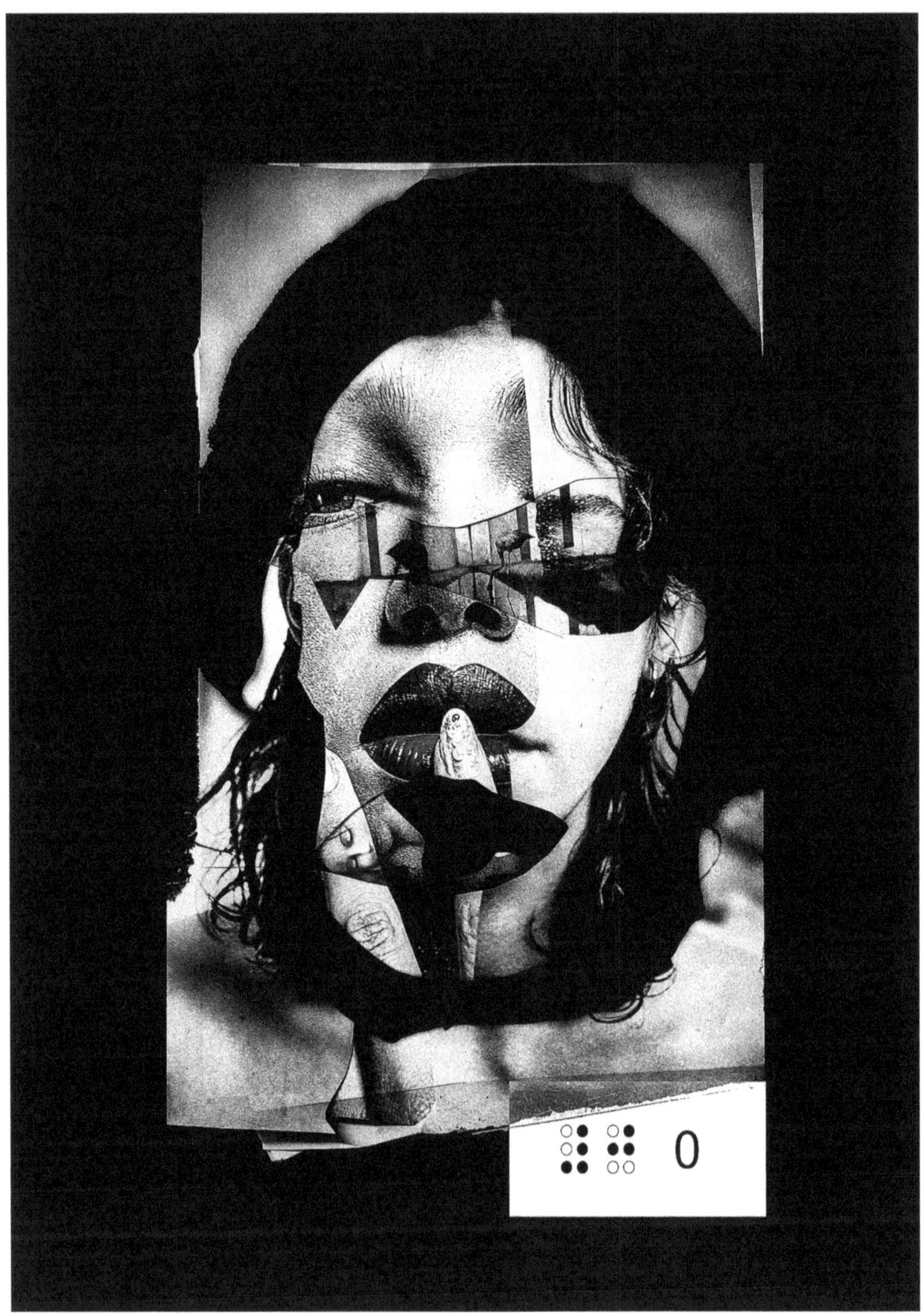

0

Photo-based mixed media, 21 x 29 cm

JANE LeCROY

NEW YORK, NEW YORK

I am nothing. You are nothing. Each one of us was dealt a rough hand, each person on every continent with varying capabilities and means. Every flower too, and all the fish, and butterflies, each one dealt such a rough hand, coming from nothing. The chance of existing almost zero, and then precarious, brief, existence. The needs of living things just keep renewing, they'll never be done drinking water or peeing or eating or shitting, fucking, masturbating, are you fucking masturbating again? The needs just go go go, processing things, putting them in, changing them, pushing them out. The thoughts become things, things become thoughts, we forget, we lose, it all dissipates and amasses. The masses come together to dance and mate and sing and swarm and murmurate and they come apart and fall to pieces to peace, peace to war. War leaves nothing, a big empty hole where there was a home, cities rise by digging holes in the land, the city falls in war, to rubble and dust, to become a memory, a ghost that haunts and makes another war, a sickness from nothing, it's always something, the nothing. The ruin is real, nothing is real, we see the nothing destroy lives and leave a hole, a whole lot of death and piles of nothing rolling through history, barbaric, it is history, a big Oh! A letter like a hole, an O, a capital O, the Capitol to a hole, zero 0, so many zeros amount to nothing. One nothing the same as another nothing, you, me, them, it, all, it all comes, it all comes to nothing, nothing comes and keeps coming a whole of nothing, rolling. Nothing, is just a word. We make nothing with the idea of nothing, it's ours, our words did it. There was not nothing before the word nothing. Words inert as glass, they have no impact but you can see through them and they can distort the surface so you see othering things, words can hold things the way glass does and shatter, so fast they become useless sharp dust and shards and when they are broken they can hurt and then are they inert? Glass and words, one is abstract, and one is of the physical realm, which is more real? It doesn't matter, nothing matters, except for every little thing like each eyelash, each blade of grass, each grain of sand and dust, dust, dust, fossils and seeds and clouds and music and coal and graphite. I cry every day to wash my eyes, they get so dirty from seeing all, and in a blink it's gone, 0, nothing, like it was never even there and I laugh and laugh to clear my lungs and it's not funny and so funny and sad and terrible and wonderful and beautiful it all comes and cancels each other out, the great equilibrium of extremes, Whitman was always telling us about it, his lists and list and long sentences of everything and nothing and how they're the same, the multitudes. I used to dream about my lover every night for years and years and then he moved far away into a different time zone and he wasn't in my dreams anymore and he wasn't in my days but the remnants of his actions and the evidence were all around it is nothing it is everything. It comes back to oh, zero, O, 0, o, O, 0, O, o oh nothing oh O, 0, o, O, 0, O, 0, o, O, 0, o, O, O, 0, o, 0, O, o ooze zeros ooze oh it's nothing, nothing at all.

HEIDE HATRY

NEW YORK, NEW YORK

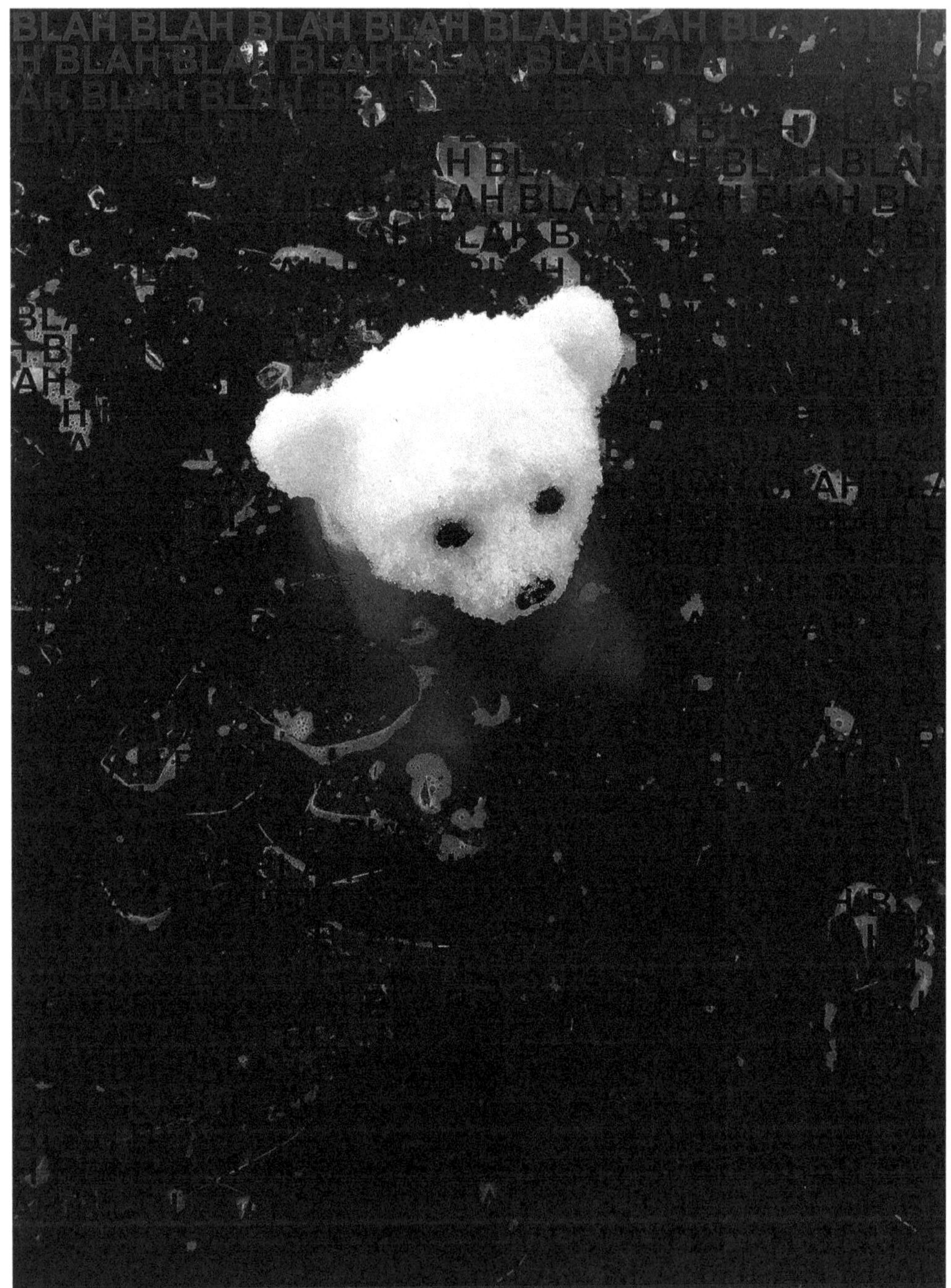

BLAH BLAH BLAH

Photograph of snow, black kitchen sponges, black tape, candies, and wire, 12 x 18 inches

JESPER HASSELTOFT

COPENHAGEN, DENMARK

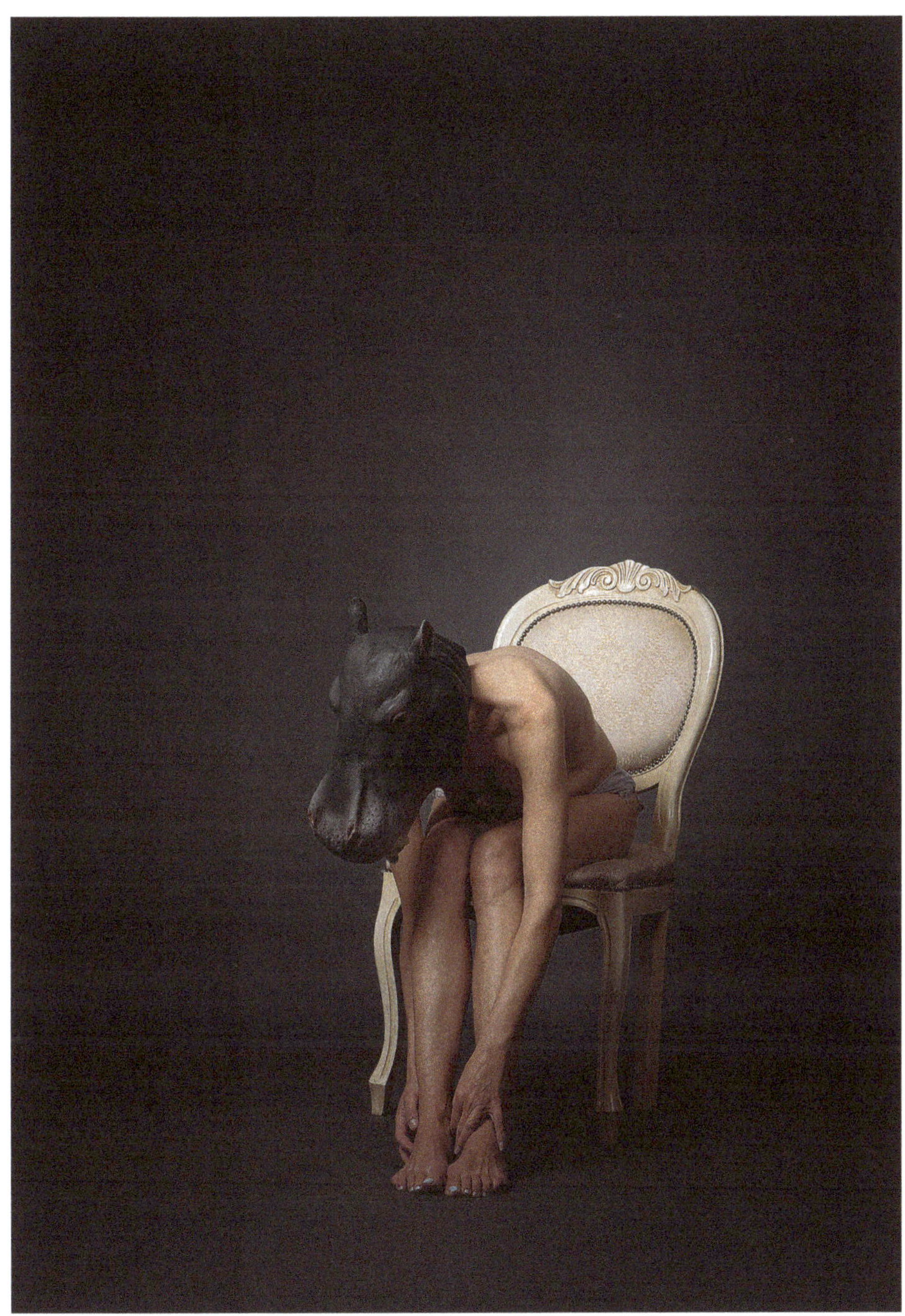

GIRAFFE AND HIPPOPOTAMUS 1

Photograph giclée print, A1

S.A. GRIFFIN

LOS ANGELES, CALIFORNIA

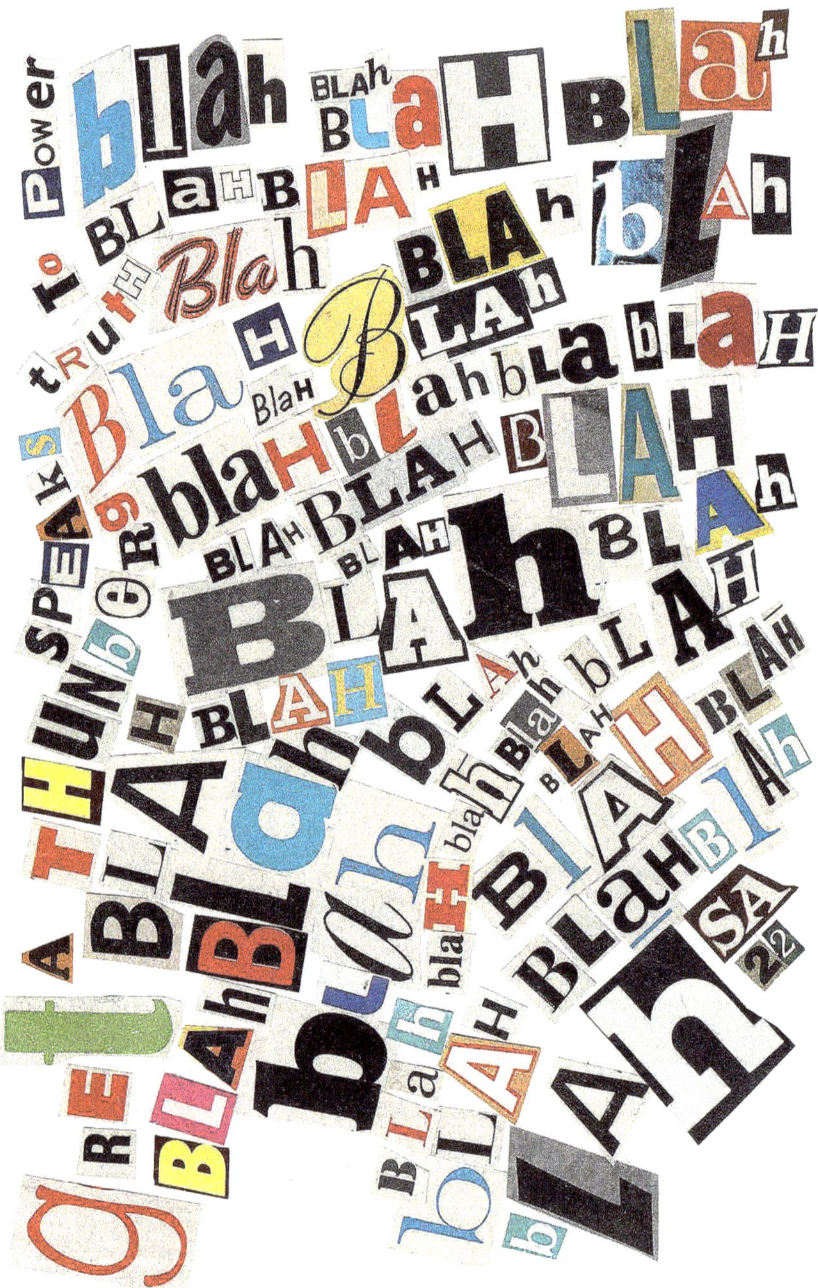

GRETA THUNBERG SPEAKS TRUTH TO POWER

Collage

RUGGERO MAGGI

MILAN, ITALY

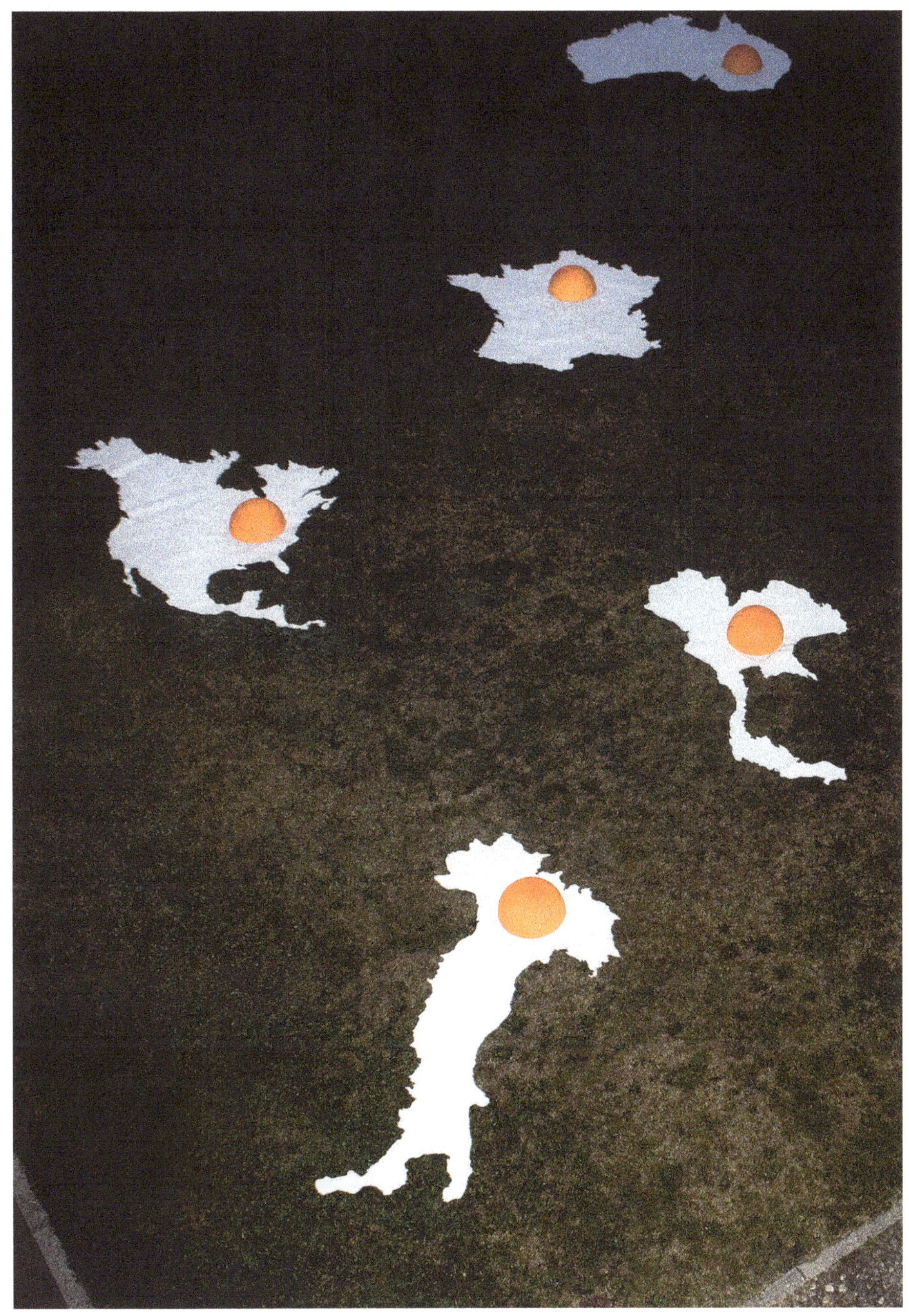

ECCE OVO

Site-specific installation, variable sizes

GIORGIA PAVLIDOU

LOS ANGELES, CALIFORNIA

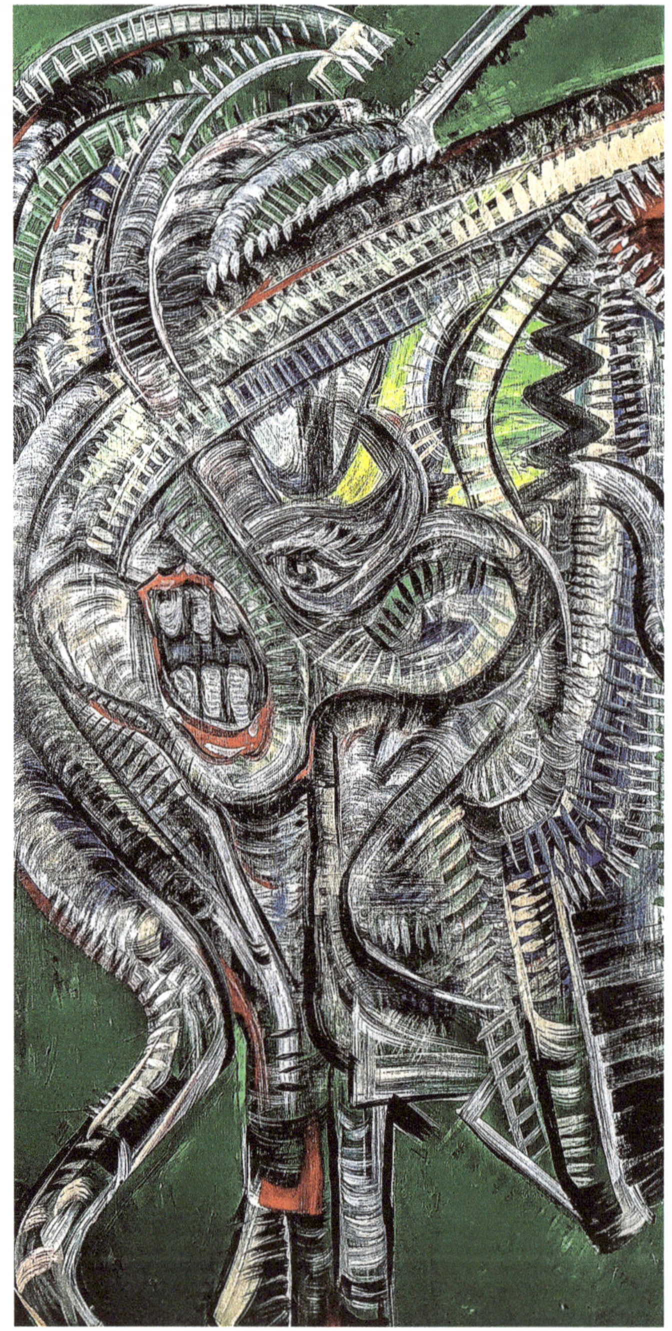

BURGLAR OF LANGUAGE

Acrylic on wood panel, 48 x 24 inches

FORK BURKE

BIEL-BIENNE, SWITZERLAND

LIVE BEYOND

This color of time
A universe is drawn in circles
folds like fire   itself back from itself
I am the bread I have made
I am the egg of the world   buried egg
swallow air the sky and the blue
What rises lives

guard nest

                    I spotted I   the to the

        cry itself season
style gods of Speak   was that wound

This dream will not be prepared
amputate all desire to be at peace

Ancestors birthing through sacred time which unites
concepts are family roots   Our through future

        multitudes   birthed gods
language split   the split taught you

What does our sound worship
play drum brain
        word contains previous experiences

The   is storied human

                    I I the the itself that

Evil can`t tie it`s own shoes   Hands glued to the wheel
    time keepers   death through you

how words nest

ANOEK VAN PRAAG

ARDEN, NORTH CAROLINA

NET ZERO

00000
Zero zip zilch
Nada none niks
Zero emissions
Many countries
Many promises
Multi million
Pledges net zero
Blah blah blah
To save us
From catastrophe

0 0 0 0
The world is at war
With others and ourselves
Some looking for light
In the darkest darkness
or love amidst hate
the earth is on fire
I put my fear behind a wall
So I can think
All answers got lost

000
Electrify everything
Eliminate cars
Extinguish tyranny
Emissions of negativity
Epic

00
Transform transcend
Tremble terrified
Tsunamis of despair
Treaties made
Trust the process
Net zero

0

DENISE SILK-MARTELLI

LOWER HUTT, NEW ZEALAND

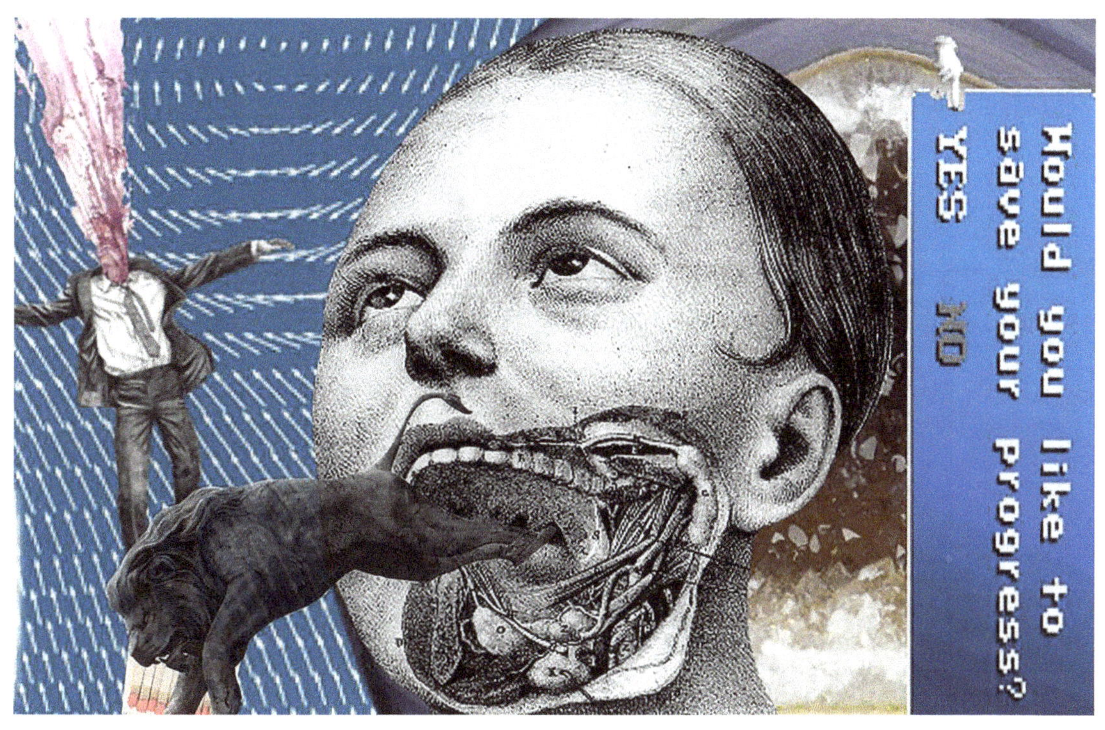

SHOUT

Digital collage

BERTHOLDUS SIBUM

ZWOLLE, NETHERLANDS

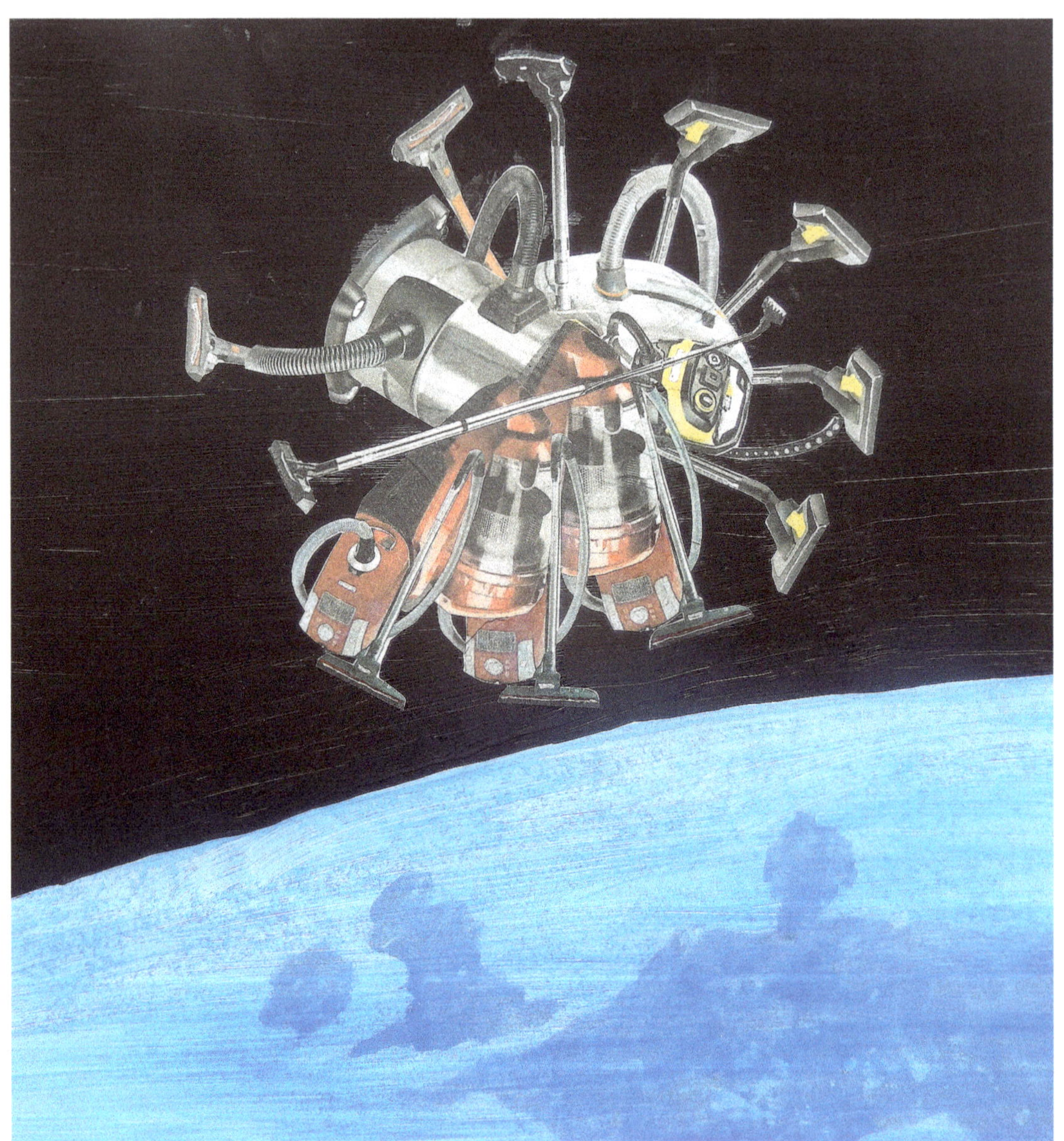

CO$_2$ CLEAN SATELITE

Handmade collage on paper, acrylic painting, 350 x 320 mm

ROBERT C. FORD

NEW YORK, NEW YORK

HAIL TO THE GAS-POWERED LEAF-BLOWERS

31% omission + 41% deflection + 59% exaggeration

Bake into a 360-degree pie chart

Until all assets are frozen

Eventually the spreadsheets

Ran out of memory and developed leaks

No longer could soiled baby diapers

Be classified as Brut cologne sales

Icebergs were liberated

With blow torch enthusiasm

The Maldives took a dive

and disappeared

However, nocturnal emissions

Continued unabated

Until one day butt-plugged cows

Exploded into supernovas

And it rained hamburgers

For forty days and forty nights

MARK KOSTABI

NEW YORK, NEW YORK

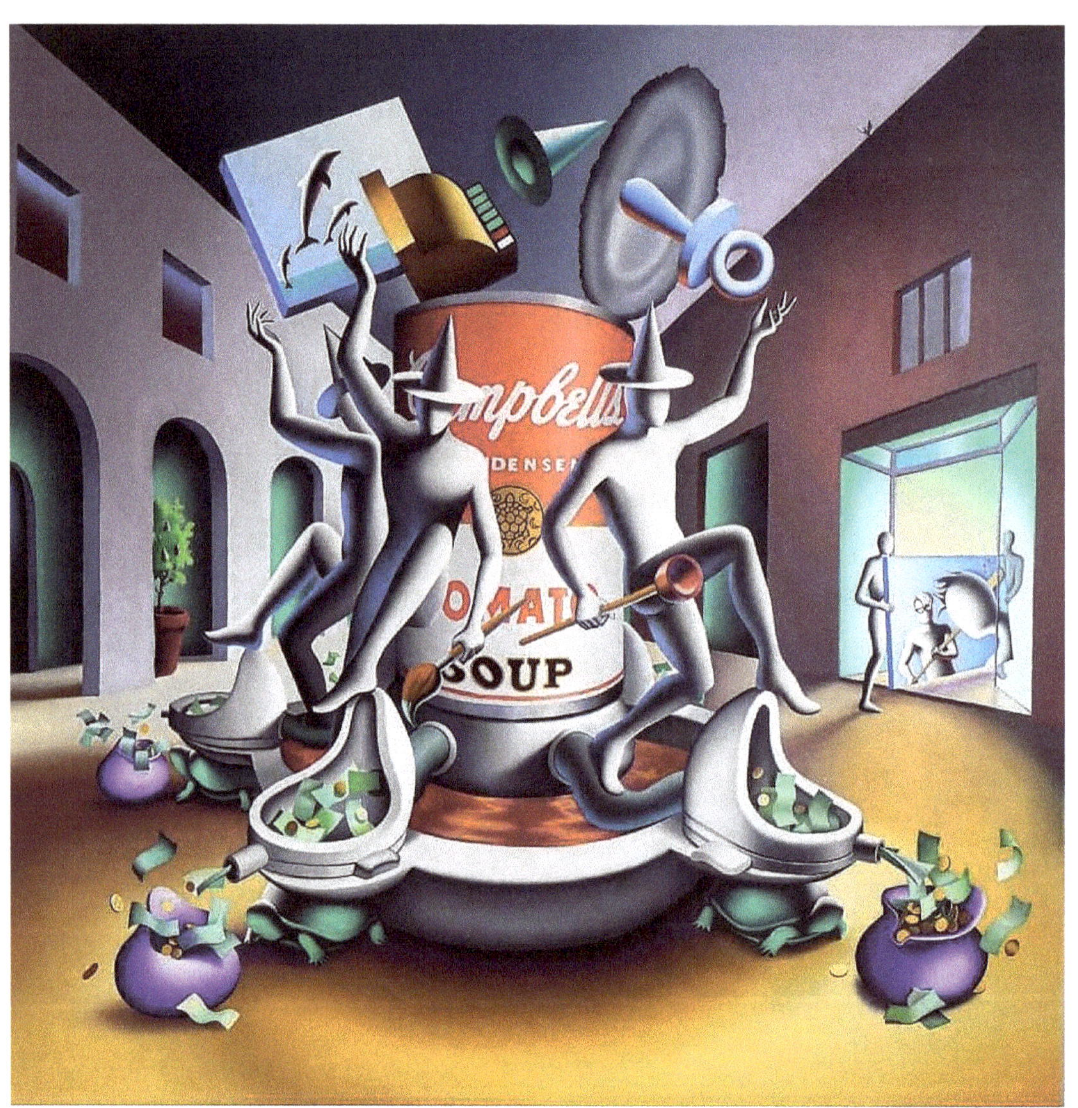

IDEAS ARE DRIPS FROM A MELTING BRAIN

Painting

KOFI FOSU FORSON

NEW YORK, NEW YORK

MY DINNER WITH LAWRENCE SAUVIGNON BLANC

Damned at the foot of the table, all I saw was hell on fire
His hair flaming red, matching suit, red-rimmed glasses
Bordeaux as a mood setter; watching as he stood, poured
Sat to a Beef Stroganoff plate, knife, fork, paper napkin

Outside snow knee-deep, temperature minus some degrees
Wind at a many miles per hour, automobiles frozen, invisible
Train I took left stranded; I walked, eyes tortured by hail storm

Floor to ceiling glass windows overlook a valley overcome
Music is Ravel; a sound system so clear, beyond perfection

What would he desire, but a black intellectual across from him
Done nothing to save the whales; ecologically far from green
Rides motorcycles inter-continentally; vacations at Burning Man

Conversations rotate around theories on sunbathing in the nude
Erogenous zones titillated, heightened from the waves echoing
He once was a Polar Bear, swam dangerous waters on a cold day

WES RICKERT

LANSDOWNE, ONTARIO, CANADA

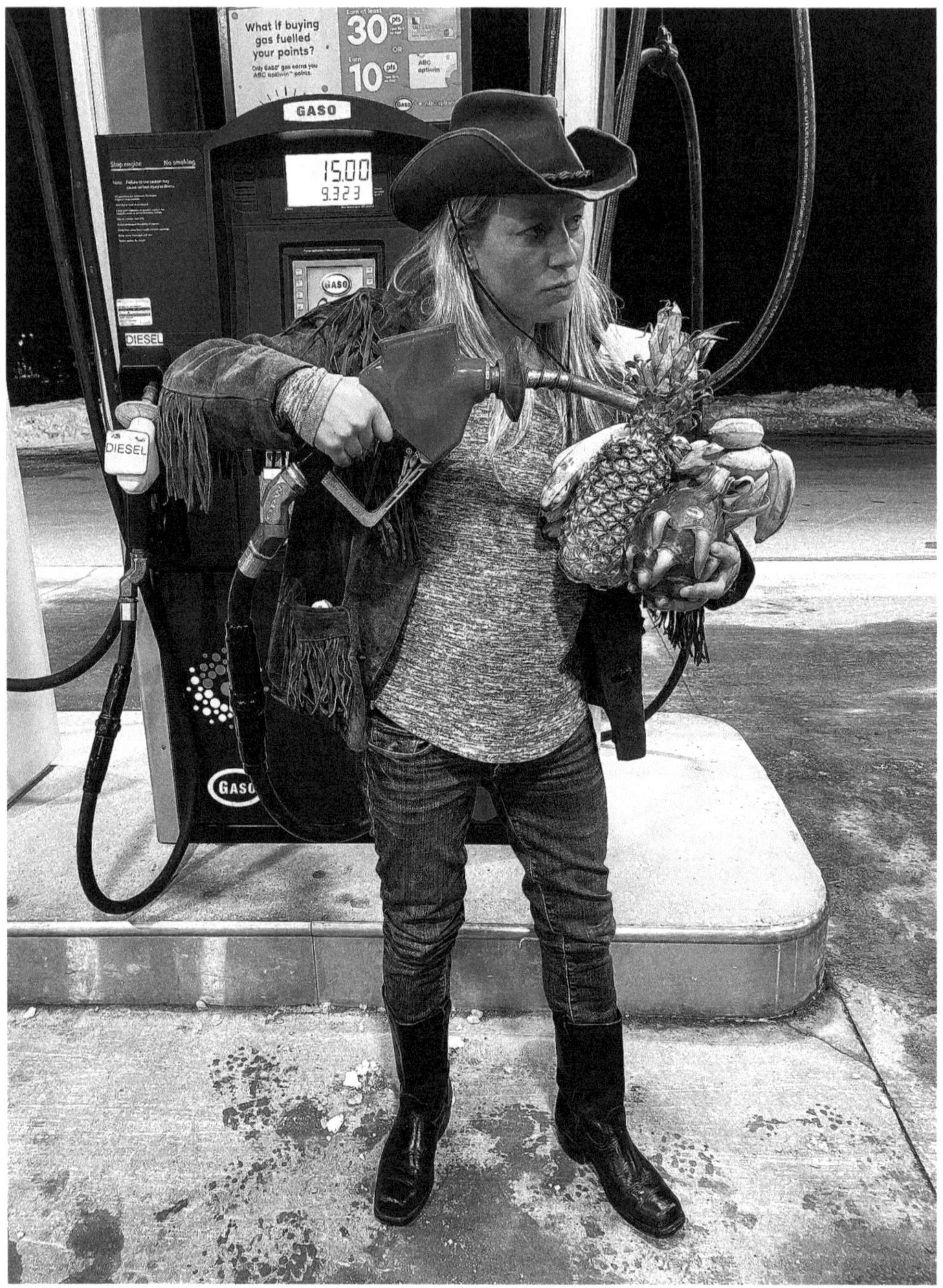

FRESH FROM THE TROPICS

iPhone photo, 3024 x 4032 pixels

RICHARD LORANGER

OAKLAND, CALIFORNIA

ACTION TIME

She gets in the car. The car is an explosion. Not to worry, her teacher told her, it's a controlled explosion. It doesn't hurt anything and gets you where you're going. The microbes disagree, but they are also explosions. Her cells are explosions. Biology an explosion bound by exosphere. An explosion of gasses. An explosion of culture. Car culture exploding into action. Get

        me

          some

              action, she thinks. She guns the car, over-revs and floors it, peels street, yanks the wheel and goes into a slide. The continuous controlled explosion screams through her cells. The car bears down on the cheering crowd, mass of flesh explodes in scream a cellular response. Most of that flesh will live past the moment but the exploding exploding takes cells, takes gasses, takes screaming microbes as cells explode, molecules scream and are gone and the air itself dies with them. Just a little, tho, and who can see it anyway. Gotta get some action.

GUSTAVO GÓMEZ-MEJÍA

TOURS, FRANCE

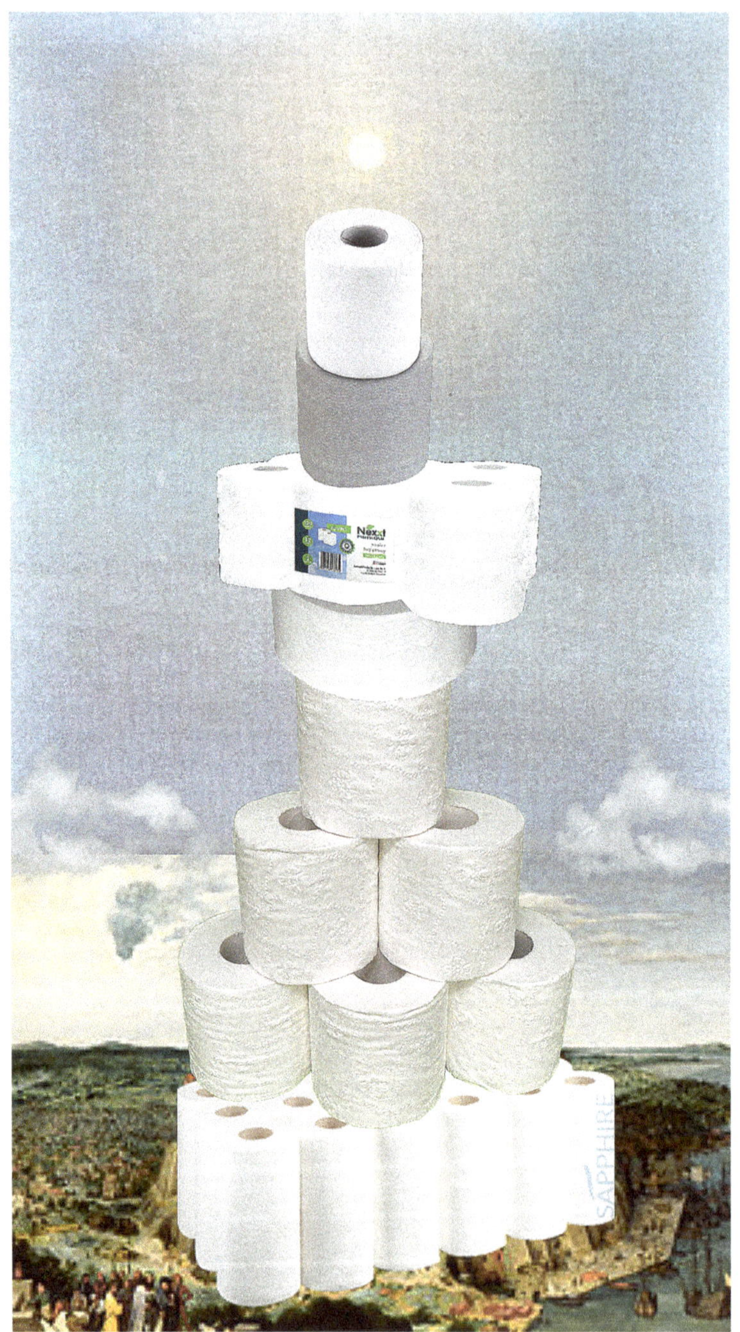

BABEL HIGIÉNICO

Digital collage, 3862 x 2172 pixels

ELANCHARAN GUNASEKARAN

SINGAPORE, SINGAPORE

NOT YET ZERO

I look down at my notes, these men seem to be saying otherwise, speaking of a great future, a defining moment for humanity, more lies, more lies, I look down at my notes, I see my feet, I think these men are bullshitting us, sitting on satin seats, clothed in the finest regalia, given the highest of honors, oh the decorum, oh the money spent, look at these men and women and staring at these men and women in awe, in such mad ways we look up to them, and what have they done for us, what will they do for us, when the world turns to ash and skies are forever grey and waters are forever black will they come forward and save us all, would they skydive from their ivory towers and protect us from civilization-eating wildfires, I look down at my notes, I see my feet, I see the shoes I wear, and I think to myself, I should slap myself for coming to this place, to even listen to this propaganda, I think I should slap one of these men with my shoe, I reach down, I pick a feet, I pick a shoe, I aim and I throw, it lands squarely in the mouth of a man who was going on and on about integrity and pride and ricochets into another woman and man who seem to have something going on under the table, they look at me, the man assaulted shouts and guards grab me, manhandle me, drag me off my feet from my chair and throw me out of the hall, they spew hate and vulgarities, what more can they do, the world had ended inside of that hall, but out here, there was hope on the streets, people I could count on, so, not yet, it was not yet the end as we know it, perhaps some kind of hope lingered in my soul, it was not yet down to zero, maybe, fight back we might.

BECKY FAWCETT

GOXHILL, UNITED KINGDOM

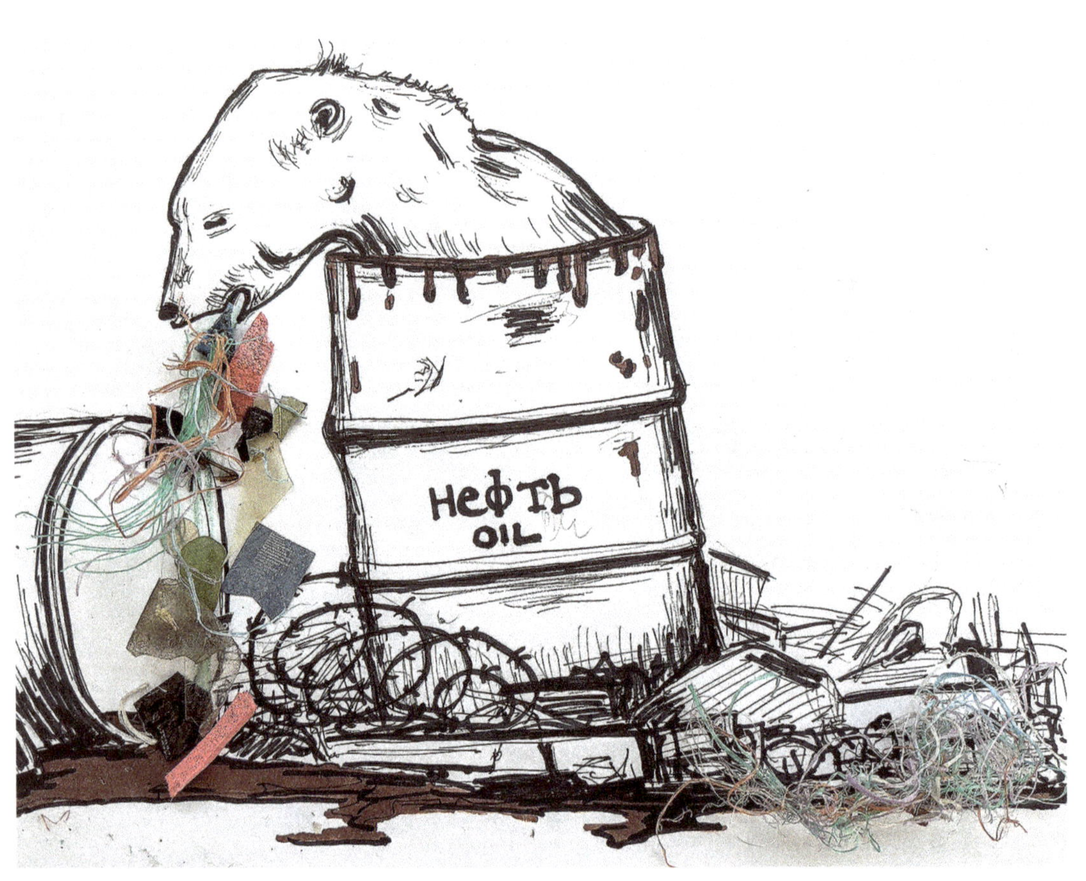

POLAR BEAR HABITAT

Ink and plastic waste collage

ALISON ROSS

ATLANTA, GEORGIA

THE BUBBLE BATH AT THE END OF THE WORLD

In the bubble bath at the end of the world, I fill the tub with boiling hot water, in preparation for hell.

In the apocalyptic ablution, I cleanse myself of all transgressions using only the highest quality or-ganic soaps and paraben-free foam bath powder. That way, just in case I am accidentally accepted into heaven's overflow lobby, the record will show that I cared, however superficially, about planet earth. And that I lived cleanly, sans sin.

In the douche of doom, I read the poems of Emily Dickinson. She could not stop for death, but I kindly stopped for her verse before death rudely stopped for me.

In *el ultimo baño de espuma*, I watch the world go down the drain.

Mr. Bubble's goofy grin morphs into a wicked cackle, echoing across the checkered tiles in the bathroom of the universe.

PAUL SIEGELL

WILLOW GROVE, PENNSYLVANIA

ANNOUNCER

Like a crocodile cloaked in a campfire,
our gathering guarantees no safety.

The wind creaks the overhead sign on its wire.

An area man looks at an area map—
A prehistoric whale graveyard in the desert.

Never underestimate the anxiety of time
it takes to implement a frozen cactus.

Or a spear of marshmallows in the snow—

Like a polar bear in a sleeping bag,
it's after the end of the world: Be chill.

ANA-MARIA GUTA

CONSTANTA, ROMANIA

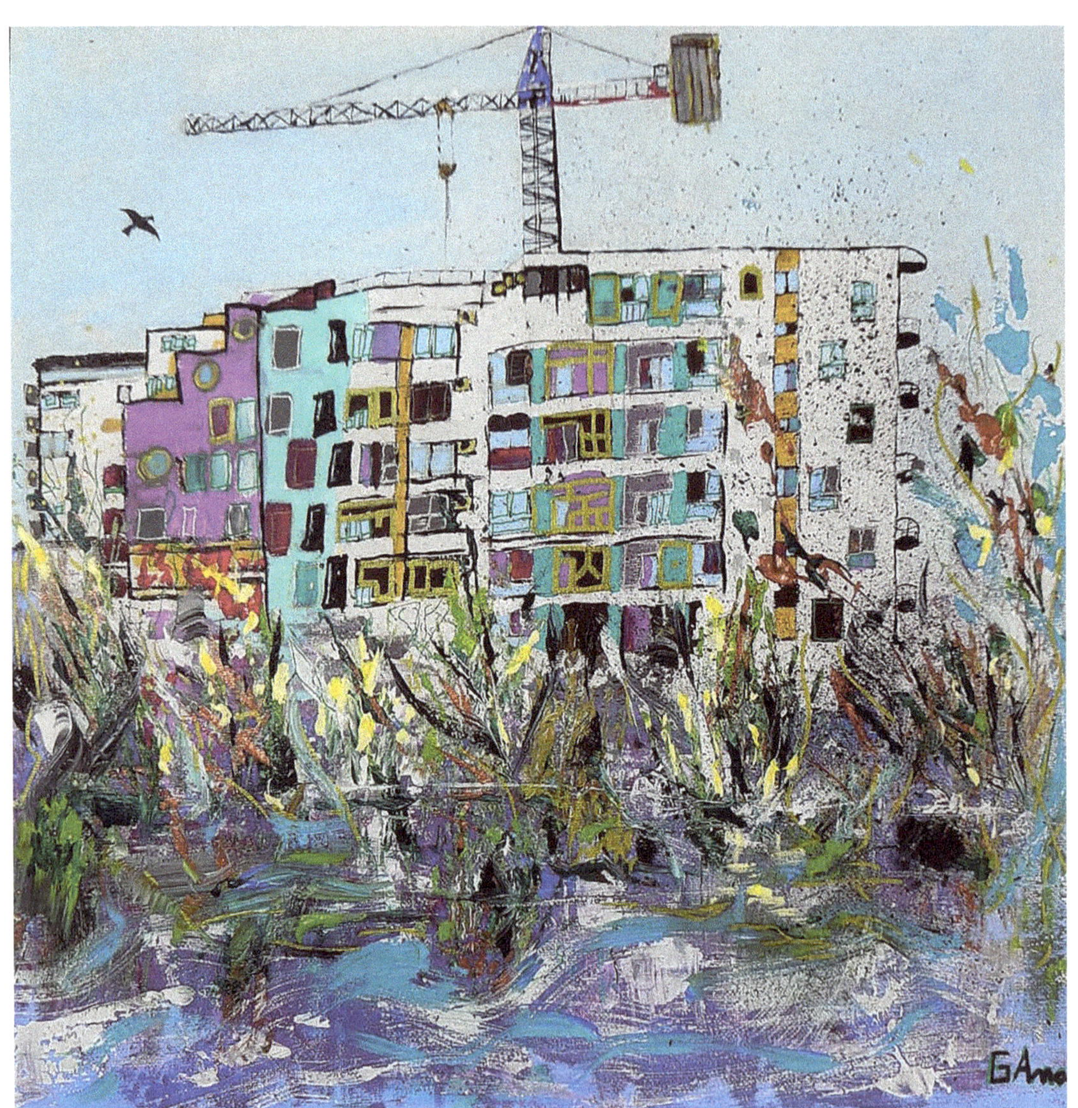

INTRUSION

Acrylic and marker on canvas panel, 40 x 40 cm

MARY ROSE MANSPEAKER

BROOKLYN, NEW YORK

MOBIUS

Today, I think maybe everyone in New York is interesting. They all just go about their days. You know, like on TV. The truth is I've been windowless so long I'm imagining them all anyway. I can't sleep because I have to keep them alive. Because the TV & our brain run on electric current. Maybe if has a little more warmth. After the season closes. What if because you died

Anyway, the air's been cold I think. & bakeries keep churning out their steam just like the manholes. I walk overtop of them so I can feel alive again, just for a moment. If it's not too much effort. Something like finally hanging the painting just right.

I've heard it's all in the angles. That's how my body meets the ground. What if we held hands. Today, I think maybe someone.

Something's been bothering me about days. Or maybe it's all been about bodies. Overtop the seasons, churning out our steam. The truth is I'm a better window. The doors no longer separate one hour from the next.

Today we're set in a bakery. What if everything was served cold. That's an interesting conflict, I think. Because we'll no longer need electricity.

Why the heart
steams. If it's too much
moment.

Anyway, the streets
just keep churning
out our lives.

MATHIAS JANSSON

ÅKARP, SWEDEN

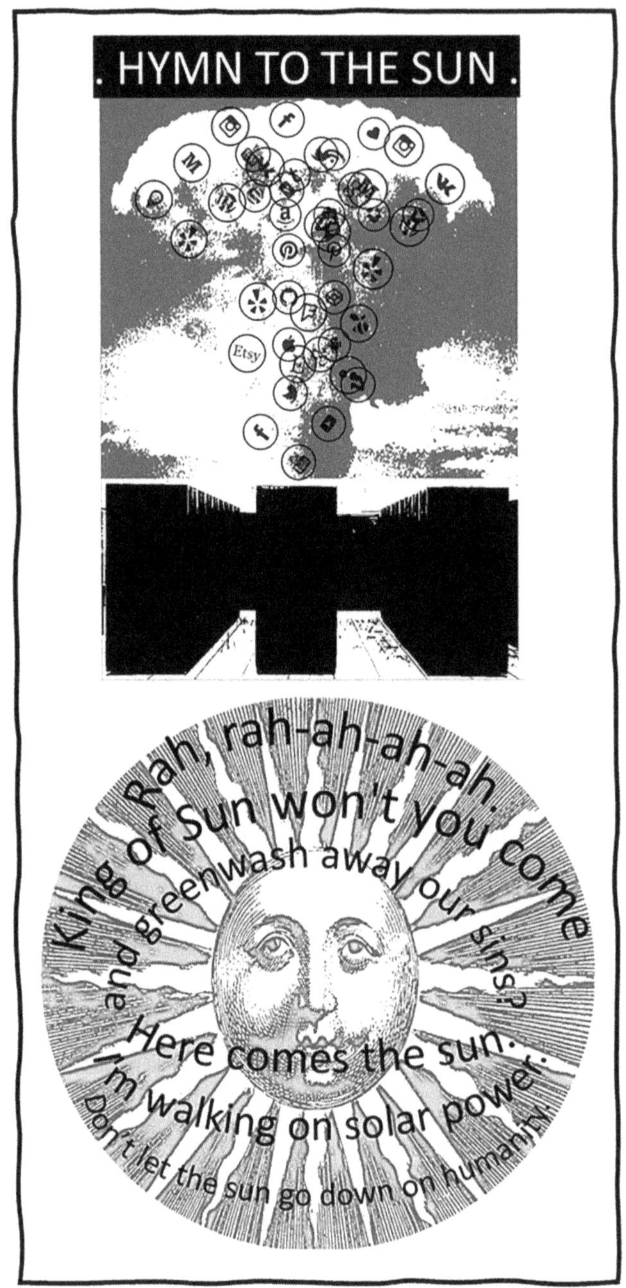

HYMN TO THE SUN

Digital collage, 720 x 1280 pixels

MIKE M. MOLLETT & MICHAEL LANE BRUNER

LOS ANGELES, CALIFORNIA & LAS VEGAS, NEVADA

NUMBER TWENTY-TWO

What to make of the messy cadavers, strewn about the playing fields, with the heroisms of death and defeat the exact equal of life and victory? In our hyperinflation, the games and the dances are for most of us long overdue, or long gone, long over and gone elsewhere.

Fearing life and death and the incomprehensibly infinite, our atoms shared with everyone, our souls left to ourselves with substance we might imagine. What's a soul to do in this place and its violence? What's expected on the next day, and the next, apparently forever?

Fishing for relief is what the addict says, no matter how clean. Listen, for example: "Oh ignorant kings of the universe, a mirrored endless rain falling makes a lot of sense. Its wild rhythms layering blankets all over the place of fields and rooftop thinking, orchestrally layered, pilgrims dancing, so many tunes recalled, locked in again and wetting the body. Just look at them! Don't try to count. But listen to the rush . . . ahhhhhh."

FRIE J. JACOBS

ZOERSEL, BELGIUM

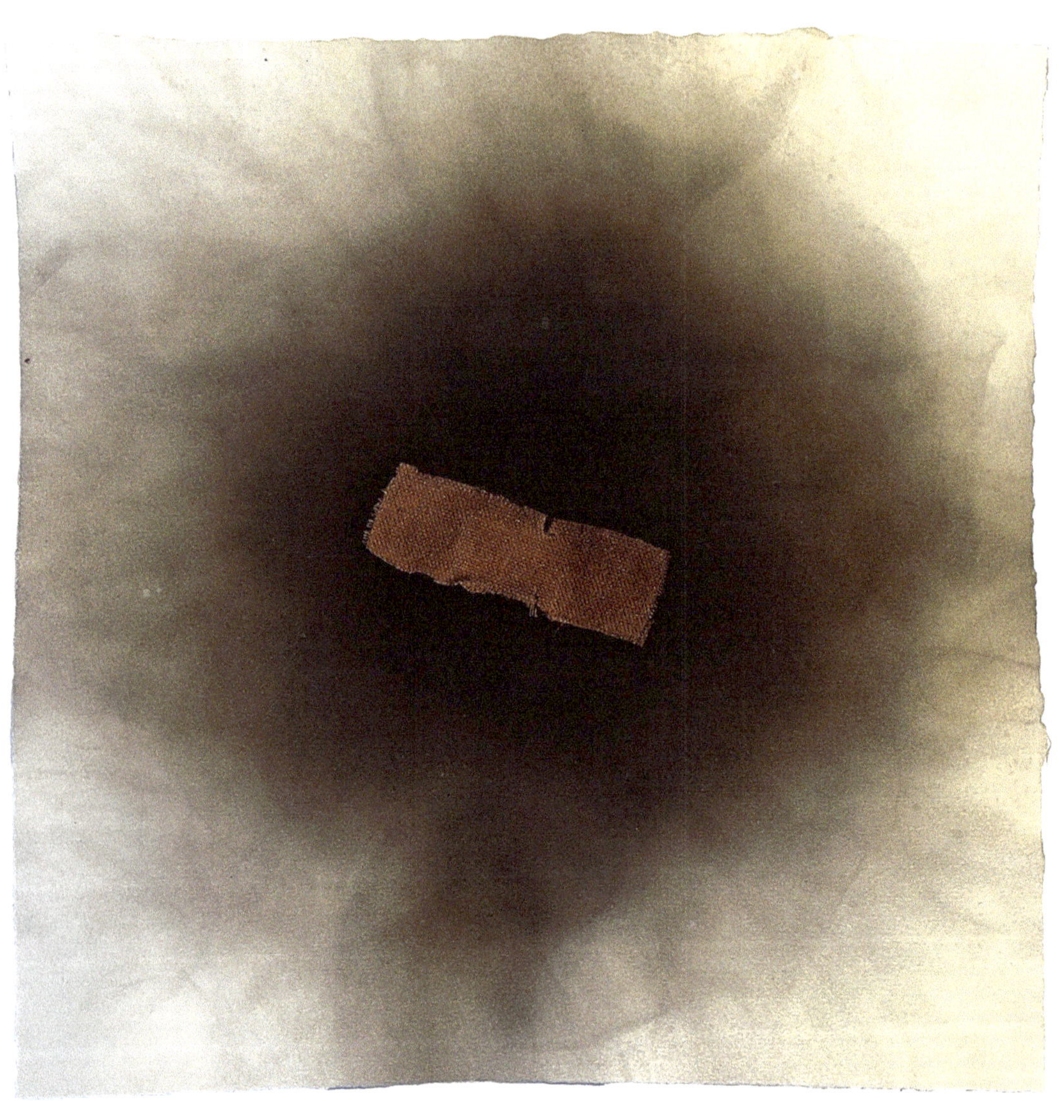

OUCH

Fire (soot) and Band-Aid on paper, 9.45 x 9.45 inches

ZYGIMANTAS KUDIRKA

VILNIUS, LITHUANIA

GLOBAL WARNING

Sorry, I can't think about climate right now.
Although the climate did change after Russia started the bloody invasion
of Ukraine.
And we can already witness the catastrophic impacts of this climate
change.

Sorry, can't think about greenhouse gas emissions,
while Russia calls this brutal occupation just "a mission."

Sorry, can't think about decarbonization,
while Russia calls this invasion of Ukraine denazification.
All I can pray for is deescalation.

Sorry, can't think of intense heat and storms,
while there's intense shelling and bullet storms.

Sorry, can't think about wildfires and heavy flooding,
while there's civilians under heavy fire and refugees flooding Europe.
Sorry, can't think about Kyoto Protocol,
all I can think about right now is the Budapest Memorandum,
which was cynically betrayed by Russia.

And if you really need arguments that include actual ecological impact—
an armored division of the army can use as much as 600,000 gallons of
fuel a day.

Indeed, tireless Ukrainians have some renewable inner energy to fight back
the intruders.
Indeed, sanctions may send Russia to pre-industrial levels.
But there's definitely something else to be done.

I really do care to the depths of my heart about the issue of global warming,
but this thing happening right now is Global Warning.

GIOVANNI FONTANA

ALATRI, ITALY

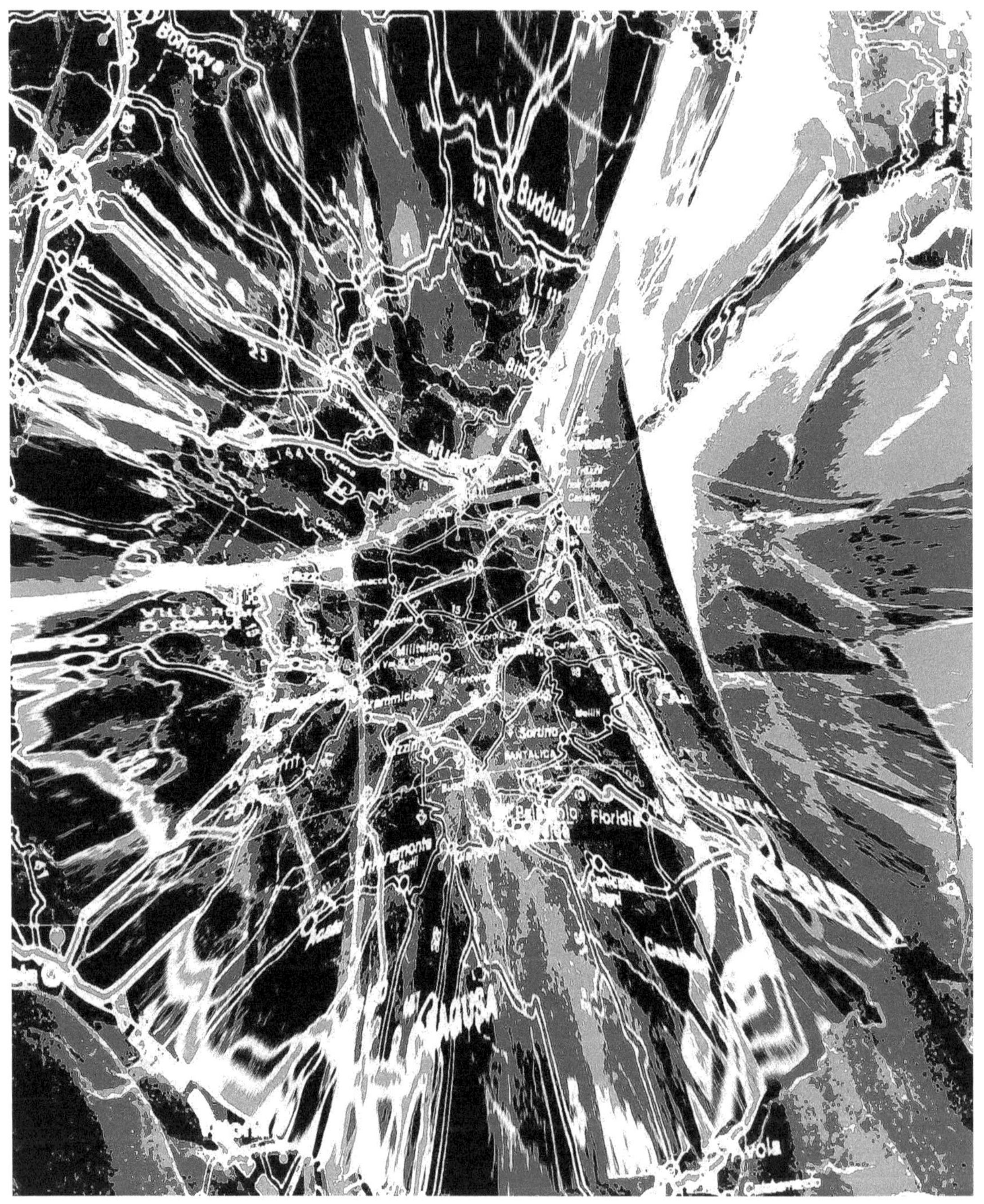

ZERO DAWN: HORIZON NYET

Digital image printed on paper, 21 x 25.16 cm

RICHARD MODIANO

MAR VISTA, CALIFORNIA

BURN IT DOWN/BURN IT UP

To say that the signals have fallen on the deaf ears of

the ruling classes of this world would be an understatement.

They are not perturbed by the odor from the blazing trees.

They do not worry at the sight of islands sinking

They do not run from the roar of the approaching hurricanes

Their fingers never need touch the stalks from withered harvests

Their mouths do not become sticky and dry after a day with nothing to drink.

To appeal to their reason and common is futile.

Their commitment to the endless accumulation of capital wins out every time.

After the past three decades, there can be no doubt that

the ruling classes are constitutionally incapable of responding to the catastrophe

in any other way than by expediting it

of their own accord, under their inner compulsion,

they can do nothing but burn their way to the end.

And so we are still here.

We are still perfectly, immaculately peaceful.

There are more of us now, by orders of magnitude.

There is another pitch of desperation in our voices; we talk of extinction and no future.

And still business continues very much as usual.

What then must be done?

Damage and destroy new CO2-emitting devices.

Put them out of commission, pick them apart, demolish them, blow them up.

Let the capitalists who keep on investing in the fire know that their properties will
     be trashed.

What is the crime of blowing up a pipeline compared with the crime of operating one?

JERRY T. JOHNSON
NEW YORK, NEW YORK

TOXICITY

my eyes water and burn every time you open

your mouth at a press conference or in a news

interview or during one of your filibusters.

like fumes of mixing bleach and ammonia

your words are toxic.

it's known that cyanide smells like bitter almonds.

membranes my nostrils swell from irritation your

deceit, your false claims, irritation your incessant

misrepresentation. I gag and puke, your words stink,

your words are the bitter almond.

salmon and trout choke and float in sad, murky

waters disturbed by waste pissed from lies.

birds plunge from the sky while flying

in bad air cooked by your burning smokestacks

that puff your loony, vitriolic broadcasts.

you scoff at global warming, you enable

irresponsible factories, you cut funding to

control emissions, you take the stage and

ridicule all the warnings and all the danger

signs you tear down. you are the toxic,

you are the perpetuating lie, you are the

toxicity in a toxic, toxic, toxic world.

ABIGAIL FRANKFURT

NEW YORK, NEW YORK

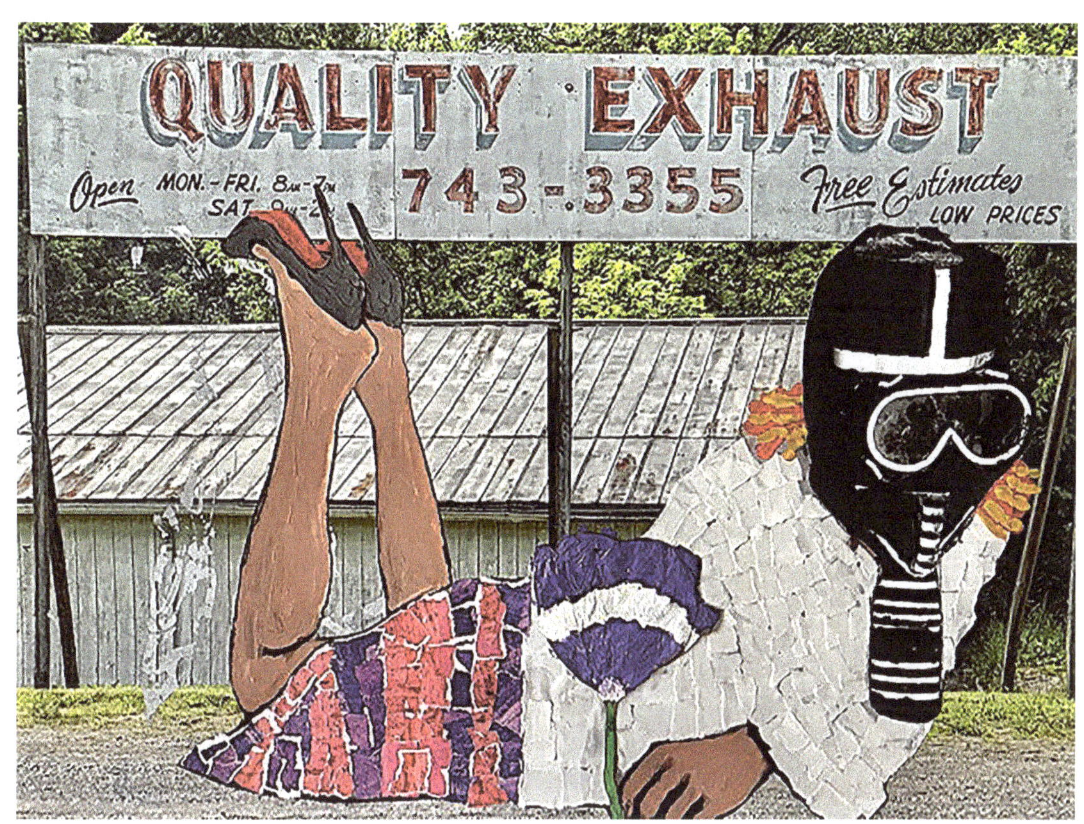

CHEMICAL WEAPON

Collage, torn paper, lost and found magazines, acrylic paint and gouache, matte gel, 30 x 19 inches

GABRIEL DON & HEATHER DAWISH

NEW YORK, NEW YORK & DUBAI, UNITED ARAB EMIRATES

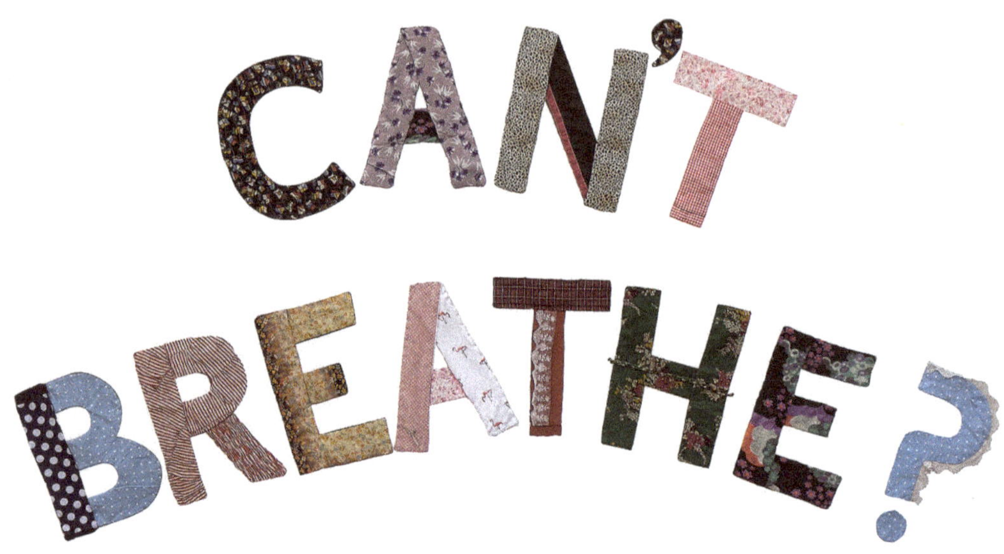

CAN'T BREATHE?

Old clothes and cotton thread, 48 x 96 inches

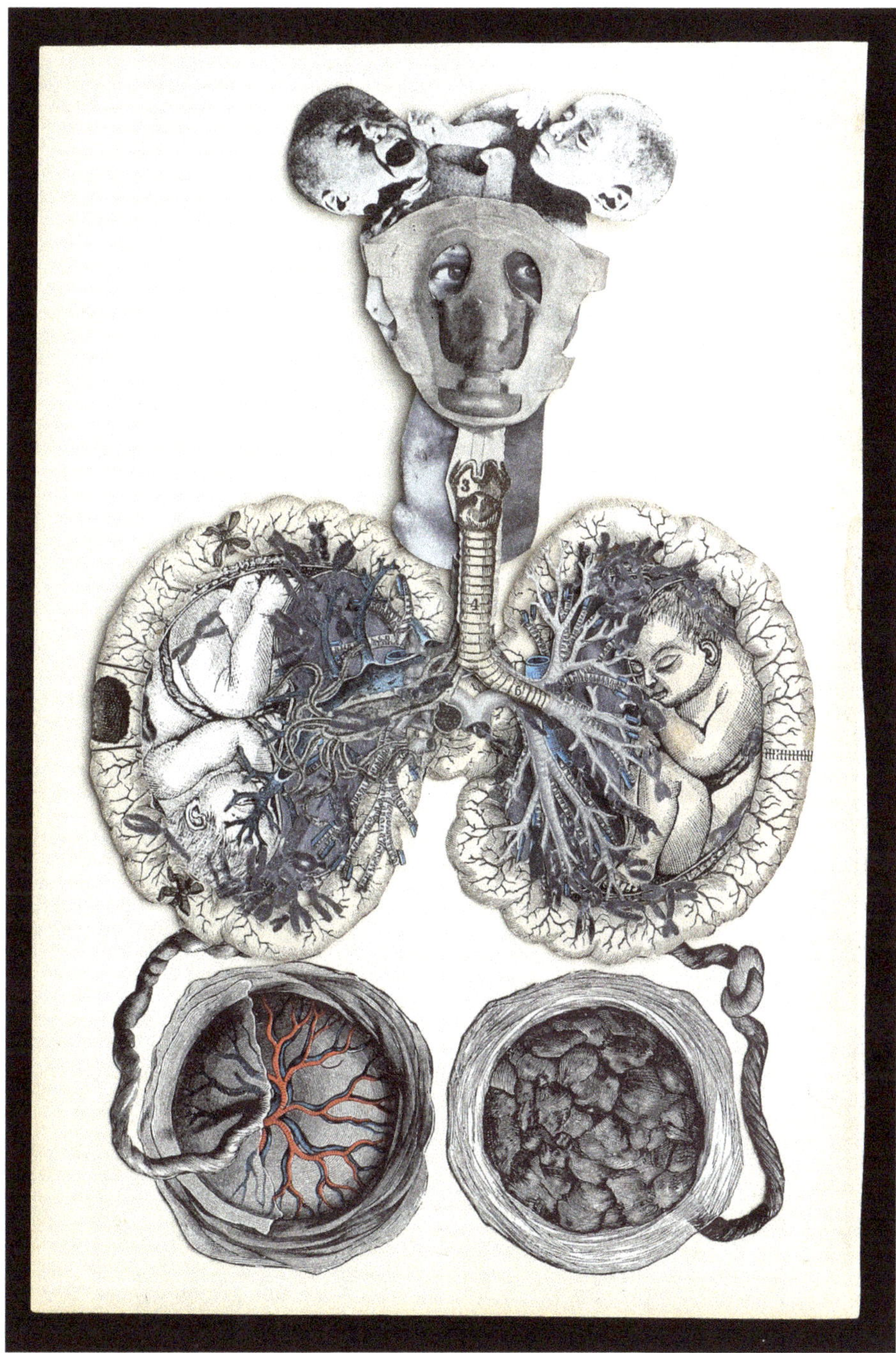

BREATHE DEEPLY

Hand cut paper collage, three dimensional, vintage book paper

HAL CITRON

NEW YORK, NEW YORK

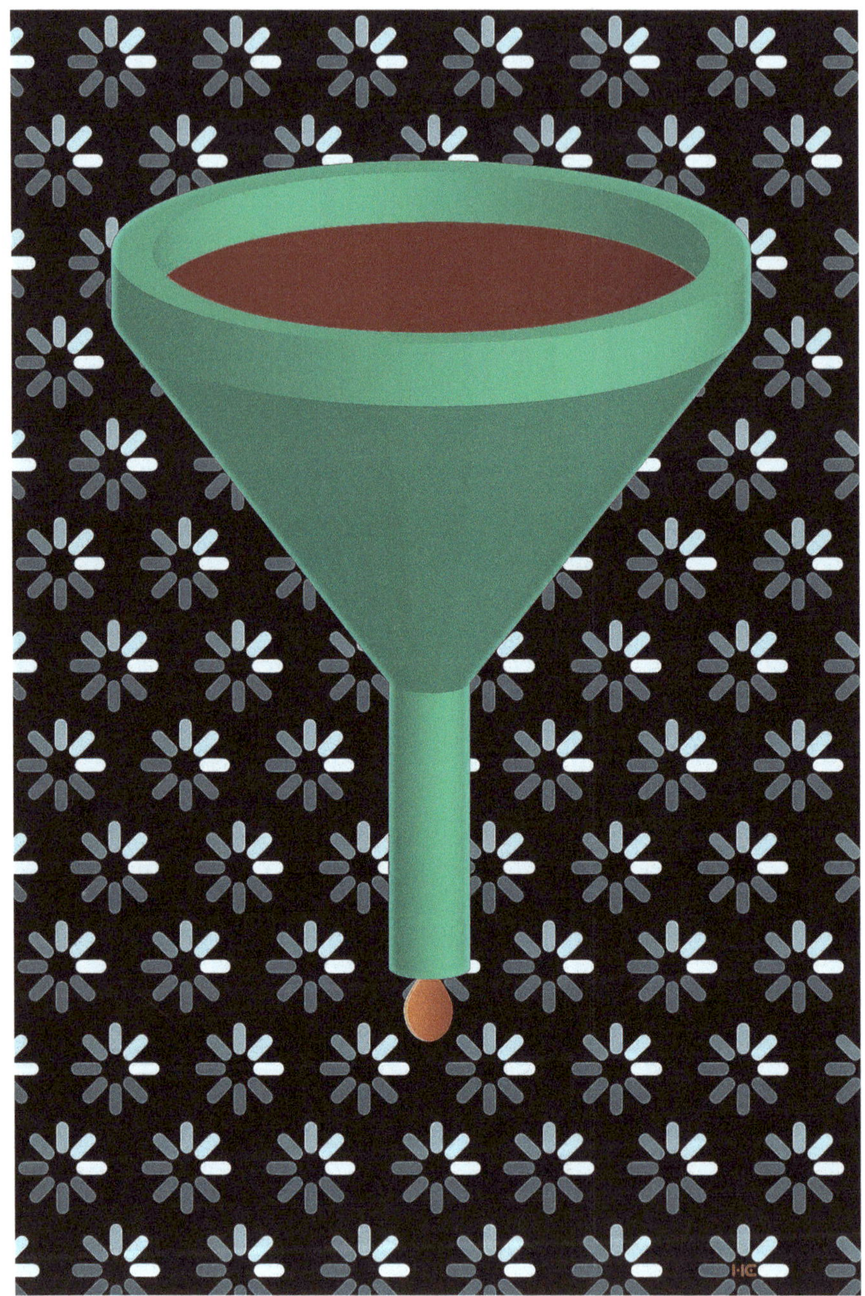

OUT OF TIME

.jpg format; 7200 x 9000 pixels

ELENI KOURTI

NEW YORK, NEW YORK

IT ALWAYS COMES IN PLASTIC

Then I get some food
it always comes in plastic
wonton soup in plastic
I don't throw it out,
I keep it with me
I don't want some whale to eat it
I keep it in my apartment
just the plastic trash mind you
the rest I take down
I'm not a hoarder
just worried
I don't want my plastic to go in the ocean
I'll keep it all here – till I die I guess
in ancient times they buried people with their favorite daily objects
I shall be buried with a bunch of plastic cups
I use them every day
top of the sushi container in my mouth
I'll be discovered thousands of years later
as who I truly was
not a poet, an artist, a noblewoman
I'll just be trash, which is the truth
perhaps, everybody is trash now
everything, we create is trash now
was looking inside a bin the other day
and saw my face
bottle of Evian, couple of straws
like I was in an art gallery
the rest was empty space

HARRY E. NORTHUP

WOODLAND HILLS, CALIFORNIA

MEDITATION ON A FLOWER

A freeway flower grows in death

A savior flower in isolation

Revolving flower sits by freeway

Waiting to die flower in pleasant place

Time of aging life limited flower

Flower in hand no longer young

Being displaced flower, motel flower

Vigilant flower, obsessed & lost

Foreign flower, unknown & blessed

When time itself has no accountability

A flower given gets no reply

Flower accepted, desire discounted

Where wide freeways separate,

Connect memories with departed love

A time never contained again

Flower death, flower body removed

A kneeling, faith removed — where

Apple eaten, desire peeled, naked

Seen, rescued with forever patience

A listening for one word understood

JESSE McCLOSKEY

NEW YORK, NEW YORK

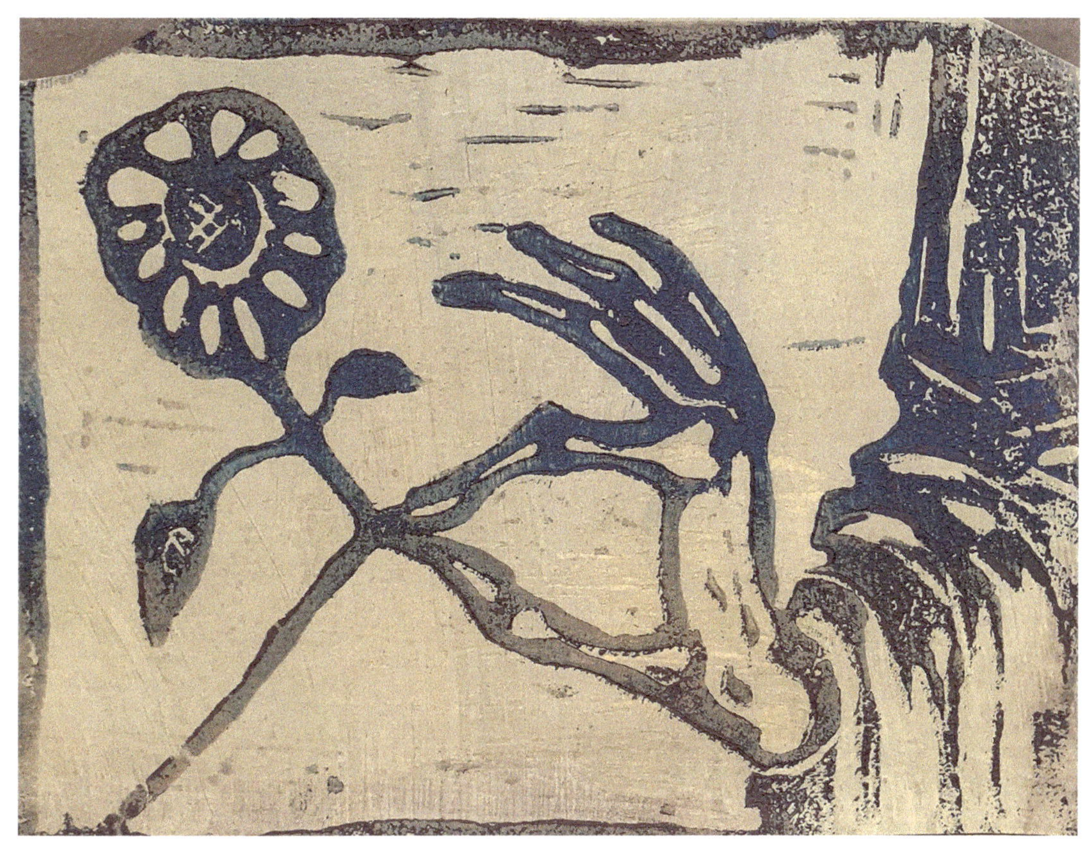

FLOWER IN TROUBLE

Mixed media under block print, 7 x 5 inches

JULIAN MITHRA

OAKLAND, CALIFORNIA

HAS THE GLACIAL AGE COME AGAIN?

Due to *anti-volcanic* activity, Earth's boiling heart

panics with cold. Prominences frost

an *expanding ice cake*. "Make a wish, Crystal!"

Antarctica gobbles the sea and tentacles floes

to *Gibraltar, Folkestone, and Yokohama*. Livestream

glaciation. At a "glacial pace" now means "relatively quickly."

Earth, *in a blue funk* from a bad breakup,

plumes her uterine steam and vulval slick

into space. "Don't the comets deserve a bacchanal?"

Interplanetary hot tubs fill with magma, seducing meteors.

Meanwhile, back on pangaea, the *sinister growth* thickens.

Ice-bridges eliminate ships. Sled-dogs evolve sentience.

Coal mines reopen. Lumberjills grace lifestyle mags.

Earth gets off to crystal parthenogenesis, lattice

bondage, shibari icicles. It makes her hot to voyeur

on humans gripped in the clutches of a *supersaturate*

solution. She envies iceberg's *latent superstition* that

absolute zero completely cleanses desire. If only she'd dig

her heels in, get it together, drag to a halt and park

in one spot, kneeling before Sun.

The italics are sampled from A Thousand Degrees Below Zero
by Murray Leinster (1919)

LUCY JANE BLEDSOE

ANTARCTICA

VIA BERKELEY, CALIFORNIA

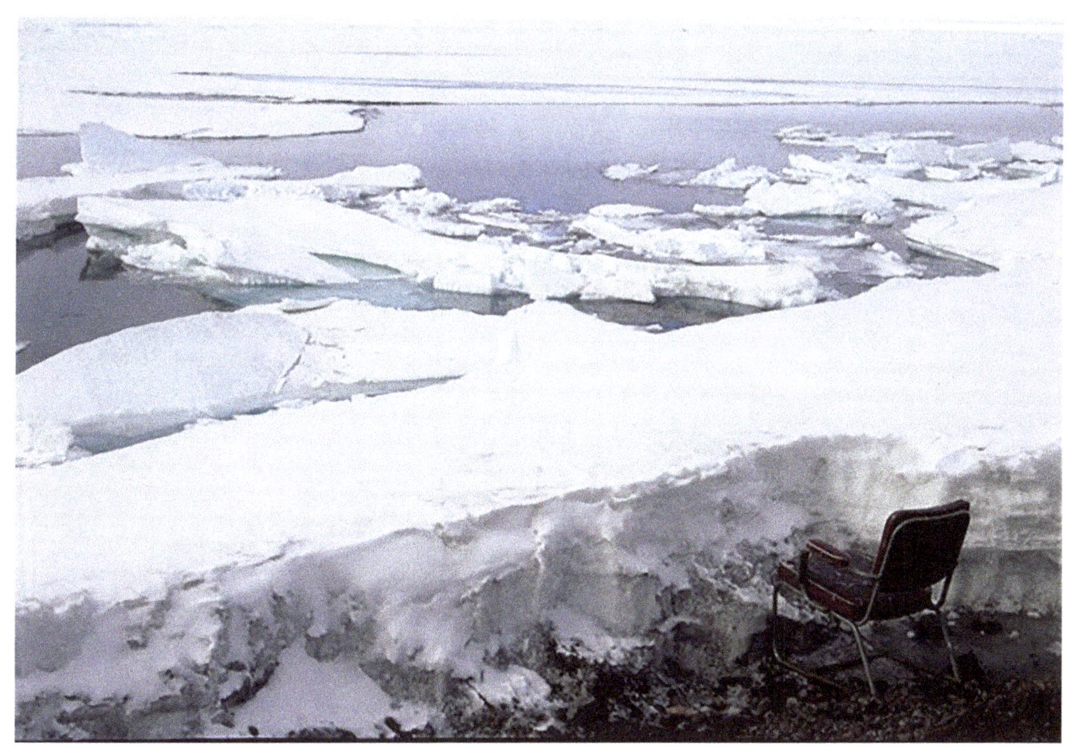

GO WITH THE FLOE

Digital photograph

LILY SIMONSON

ANTARCTICA

VIA BERKELEY, CALIFORNIA

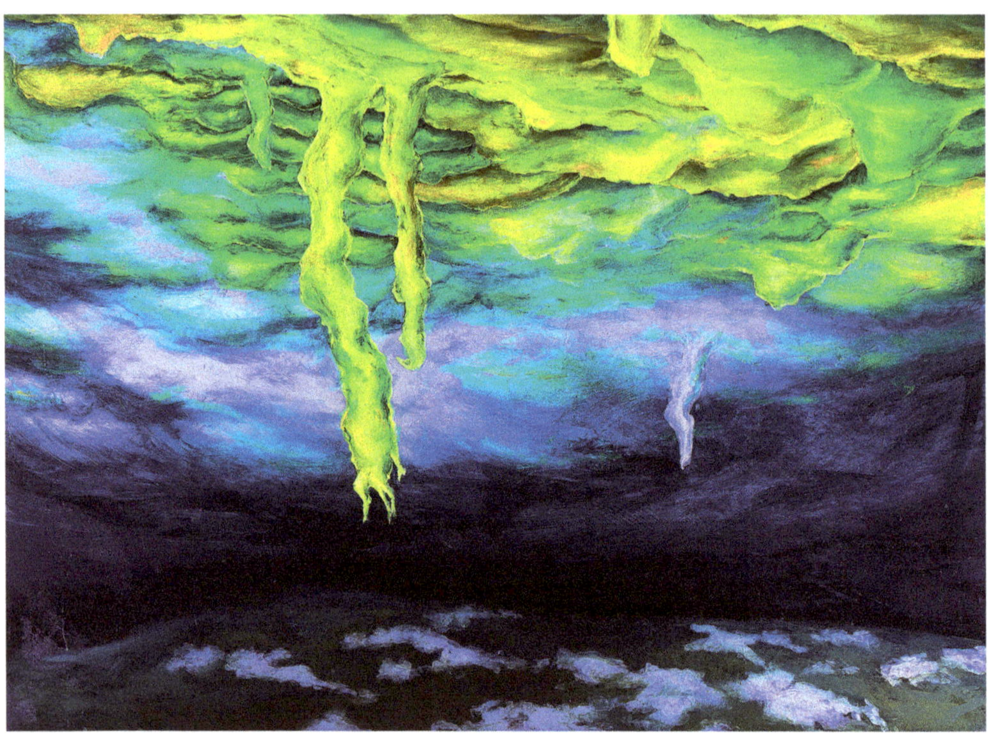

CINDER CONES SEEP
(McMurdo Sound, Antarctica)

Acrylic on canvas, 84 x 60 inches

MARTINA SALISBURY

BROOKLYN, NEW YORK

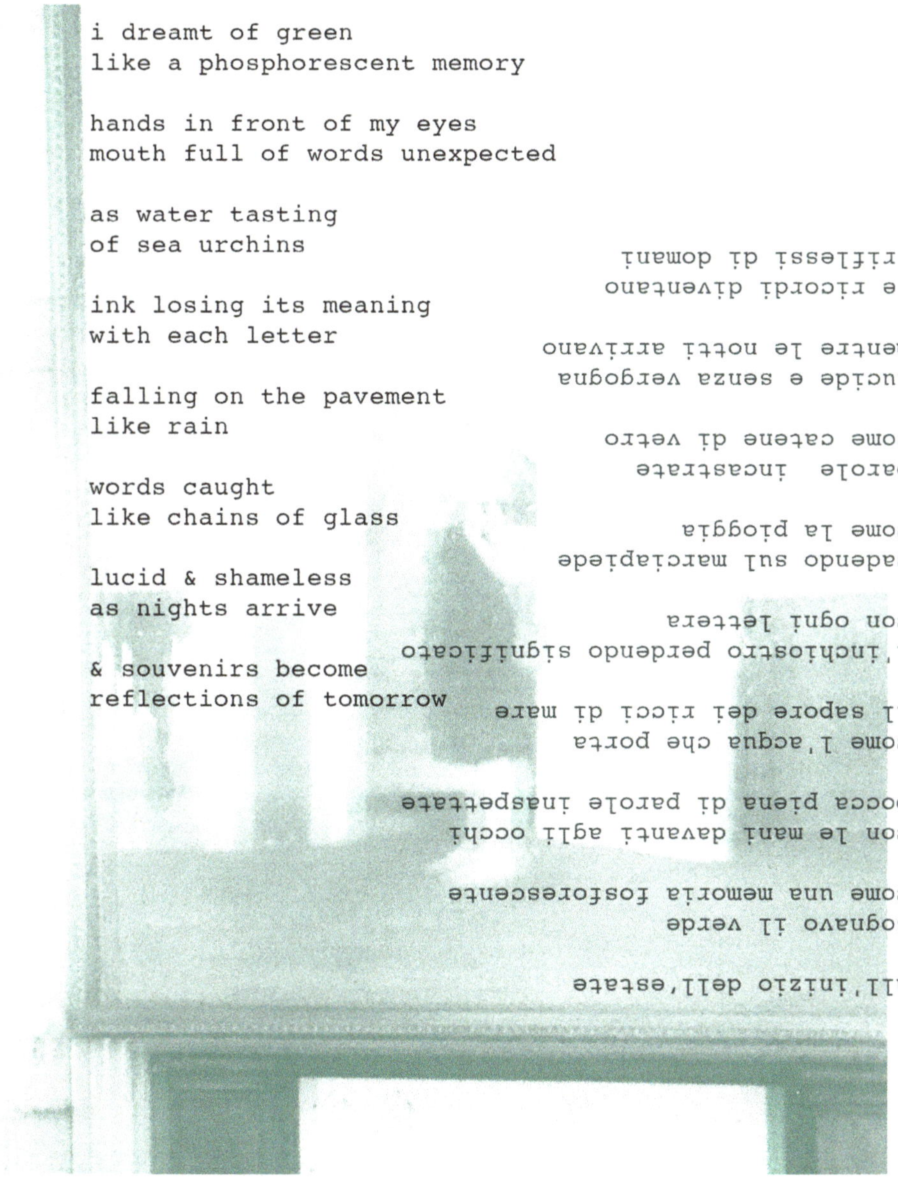

at the beginning of summer

i dreamt of green
like a phosphorescent memory

hands in front of my eyes
mouth full of words unexpected

as water tasting
of sea urchins

ink losing its meaning
with each letter

falling on the pavement
like rain

words caught
like chains of glass

lucid & shameless
as nights arrive

& souvenirs become
reflections of tomorrow

all'inizio dell'estate

sognavo il verde
come una memoria fosforescente

con le mani davanti agli occhi
bocca piena di parole inaspettate

come l'acqua che porta
il sapore dei ricci di mare

l'inchiostro perdendo significato
con ogni lettera

cadendo sul marciapiede
come la pioggia

parole incastrate
come catene di vetro

lucide e senza vergogna
mentre le notti arrivano

e ricordi diventano
riflessi di domani

AT THE BEGINNING OF SUMMER

Digital photo, double exposure, poem, translation

MAHNAZ مهناز **BADIHIAN**
SAN FRANCISCO, CALIFORNIA

DRY RIVER

In my hometown Isfahan
the river was dry
as we noticed
People would walk
around It and sing
songs of despair

The entire river bed
was covered with
hollow stories of the past
The absent music and
dance of no water
were what people
imagined in Their
Heads.
What Things They stole
From us?
River, bread, freedom

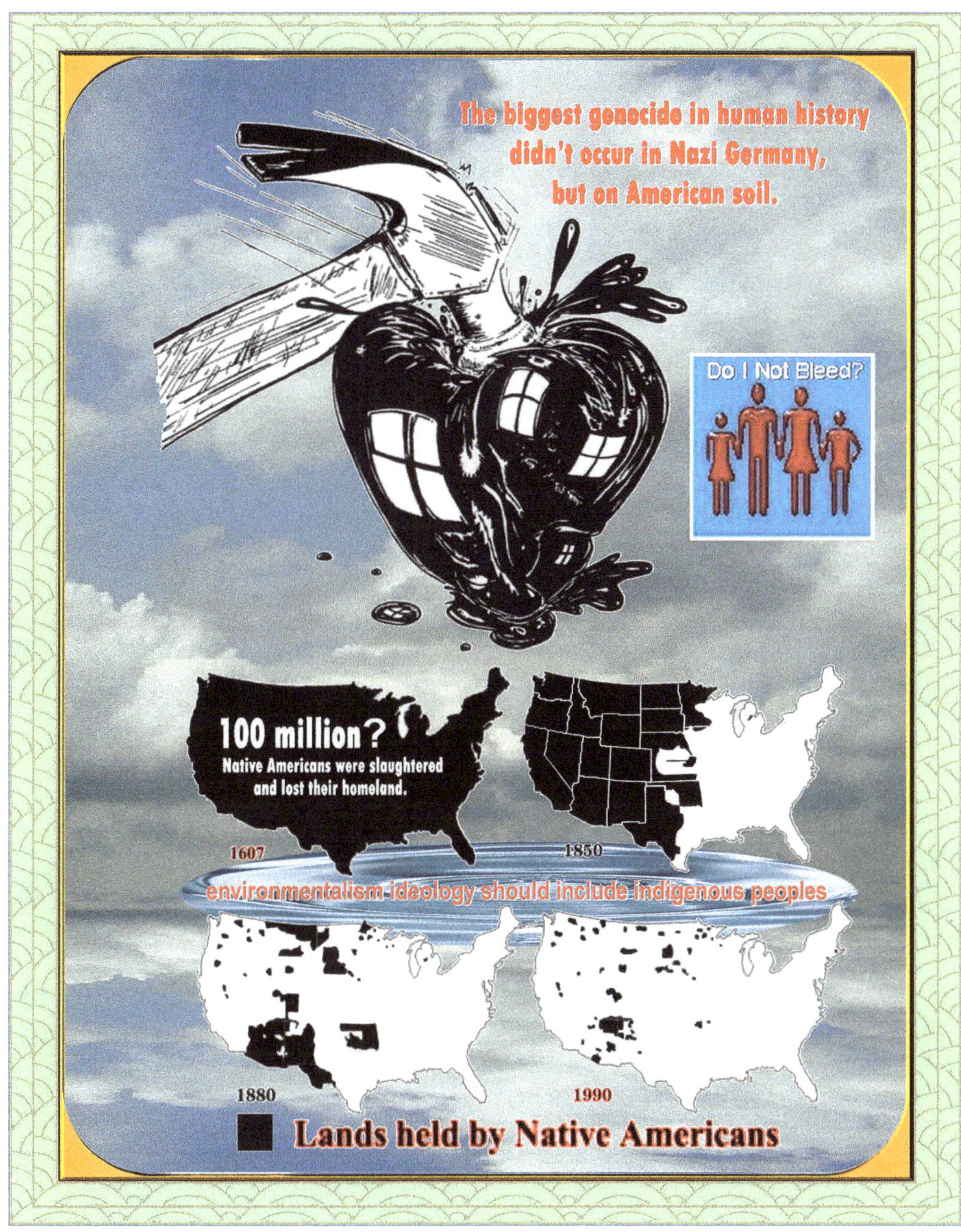

ENVIRONMENTALISM IDEOLOGY
SHOULD INCLUDE INDIGENOUS PEOPLES

Collage

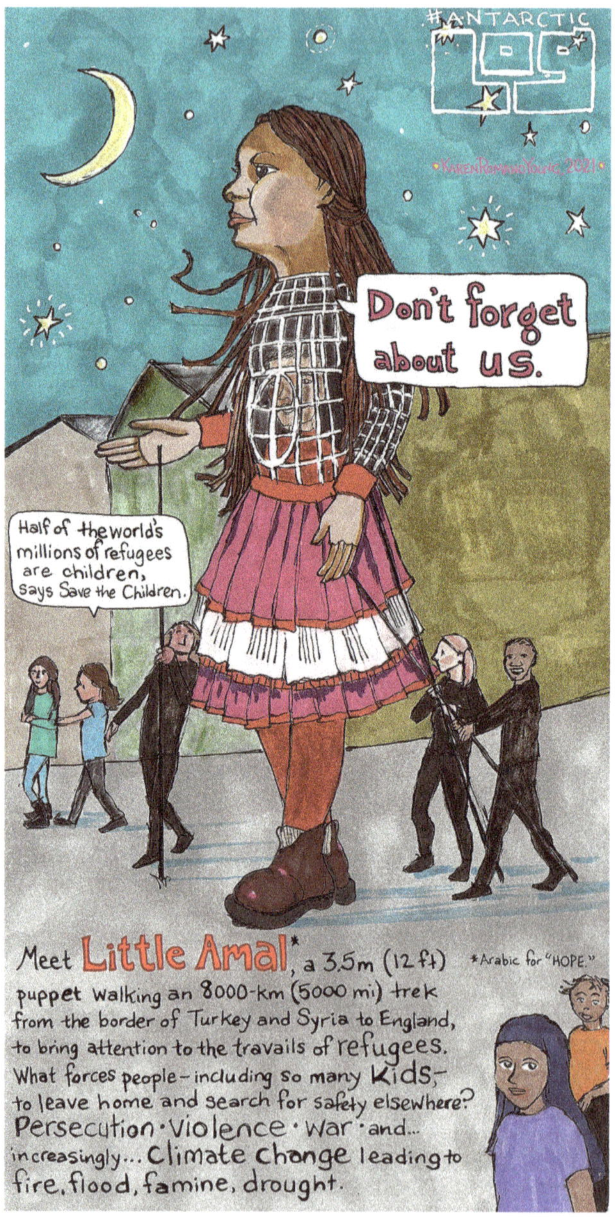

ANTARCTIC LOG: #197

6 x 12 inches

TCHELLO d'BARROS

RIO DE JANEIRO, BRAZIL

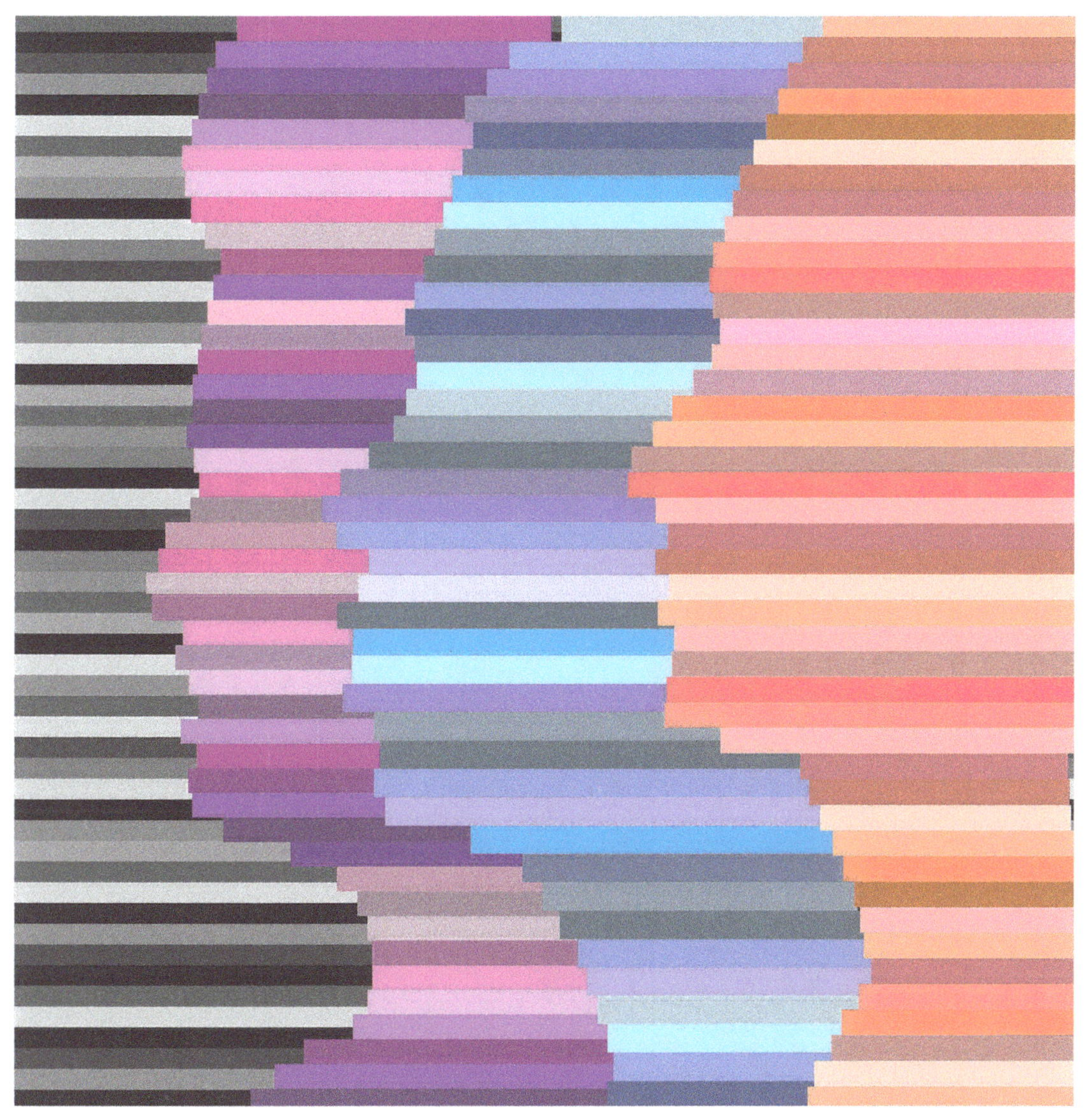

ANTROPOCROMÁTICAS

CAROL DORF

BERKELEY, CALIFORNIA

SPRING, AGAIN

"Strange recompense, in the depths of our despair,"
—William Carlos Williams, from "Spring and All"

The last of the meyer lemons ripen on the bush
in heavy clusters; or maybe they should be labelled the first

of spring, beside the wasps buzzing their way into
the purple blossoms we call ground cover.

Strange recompense this return after two years
of despair, or do I count it as nearly six.

And for those who made it (don't count the 950,000)
we've reached another spring to embrace.

Yesterday, a cluster of finches migrated through the yard,
clustering on the lemon branches, with their slick

perennial leaves catching the February sun.
Hornets or maybe they are wasps, have returned

to their nests in the eaves, and I was told I really should
do something about it. We are well screened against

the honeybees returning to the chimney,
though they won't swarm for months, until even

the light of the equinox is useless against the depth of despair.
One of the plums toppled after the neighbor hired

a man to attack the roots she perceived as invading.
It is questionable if the apple tree will return

to leaves this year. Career of time, they moved on.
The neighbors that is, and we know little of the new ones,

other than of the existence of two small boys. Children mark
a kind of time, like the bright orange perennials filling the yard,

I can't help imagining hope when see children digging
for pillbugs in the dirt left after the sewer was replaced.

HOLLY DAY

MINNEAPOLIS, MINNESOTA

THURSDAY

The sun comes out and things are growing but the world is dying so I don't care.
The tips of tulips are poking through the piles of dead leaves, dark green and purple-edged
the red tips of peonies are stretching up and out towards the sun
but even these signs of life can't convince me that there will be a tomorrow.

Inside, my daughter yells at her computer, something about how her online school sucks
the dog paws at the door to come out and sit with me on the porch
and I let her out and hug her because I can't get sick from hugging my dog
I can't get my dog sick by hugging her.

Flocks of sparrows and goldfinches flutter around the birdfeeder
oblivious to the end of the world, untouched by the end of the world.
I reach into the bag of bird food and toss more and more handfuls out to them
finding temporary amusement at their delight. Rabbits and squirrels fight over
the crocus bulbs hidden under the melting snow, I don't chase them away from my garden
because this is their world now.

PUMA PERL

NEW YORK, NEW YORK

WICKER SEATS

wicker seats
ripped
on the subway
sticking to summer legs
in striped shorts
and tops that don't match

when you stand up
tic tac toe games
scratch your white thighs
and your mother realizes
the train doesn't stop
at Dekalb

oh no oh no oh no
she repeats
all across the bridge
to Canal Street,
your legs burning
as you follow her
up and down the stairs

ROBERT ANTHONY GIBBONS

BROOKLYN, NEW YORK

SUCCULENT

green and tropical
decides my childhood
all the bushes behind grandmas
she said, "I would grow like"

a peace lily, hedges as enclosures
spend the night outside like Georgia moss
use my puberty as a pilot light

grow, becomes as pictogram
all the pimples of the cacti
brown-fry heat

KAREN HILDEBRAND

BROOKLYN, NEW YORK

ODE TO YELLOW CAKE

To the pleasures of vanilla
key-lime, coconut flan, the delicate
lisp that is brisée to a tongue
afflicted by red-faced shouting
of chocolate mousse, devil's food
fudge, or, good god, the 9-layered
tight-skirt fishnet stiletto
gift to every potluck of 1995.

Dear reader, please know
my intention is mere appreciation
for quiet moments such as falling
snow, the way it grows
in feathery blankets to avalanche
smothering, white.

JANET HAMILL

CIRCLEVILLE, NEW YORK

ABSENCE OF BIRDS

Almost a total absence of birds
in winter the woods were forsaken
where Florence Street came to an end
a network of frozen ponds & bare trees

In winter the woods were forsaken
doing figure eights on antique blades
a network of frozen ponds & bare trees
singing Chattanooga Choo Choo

Doing figure eights on antique blades
made before filming Sun Valley Serenade
singing Chattanooga Choo Choo
all by myself in immaculate silence

Made before filming Sun Valley Serenade
I was training for the Winter Olympics
all by myself in immaculate silence
almost a total absence of birds

BARBARA VOS

BRISBANE, CALIFORNIA

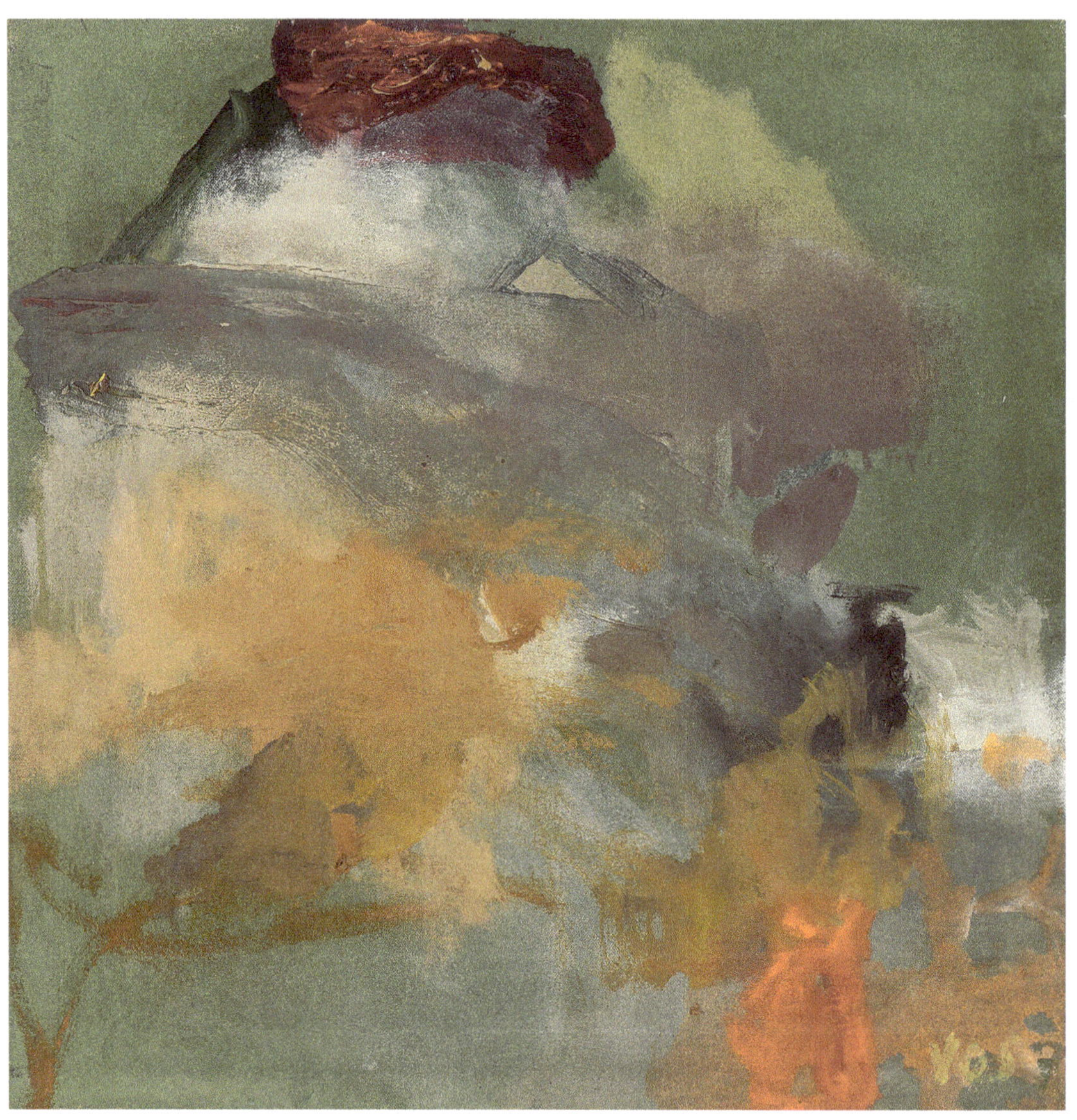

FOUND A WAY

Painting

DOROTHY FRIEDMAN

BROOKLYN, NEW YORK

ECOLOGY

It is becoming eccentric to love.
Nothing but two knotty faces
live in these rooms.

The air must be off there somewhere,
perhaps in that warehouse,
hiding under shoes.

Our conscience can still recall the crime.
Not saving fish Painting new houses.

There are sides to paper torn from books.
There are outsides of glasses.
And inside thoughts struggle.
There are excuses.
It is too easy here to hide behind the curtain.
We lick candy and divide the children.

The old spirit is somewhere else.
We undress before mirrors that no longer work.

People are drowning here and trees.
We undress outside the church
and return for its warning
to admit the shaping of our brutish mouths.

Sweat is terrible on mouths behind woods.
Today the young move among the branches,
dividing.
The forest thins to nothing but two fine twigs.

It is time to tell the air terrible days.
warn it of white summers
in squared courtyards and forgotten churches
where men refuse the tiny wafer.

It is time to induce humanity.

The music bursts round torn branches
hung alone and growing old up there.

We undress the trees in the smallness of sky.

SUSAN SHUP

PARIS, FRANCE

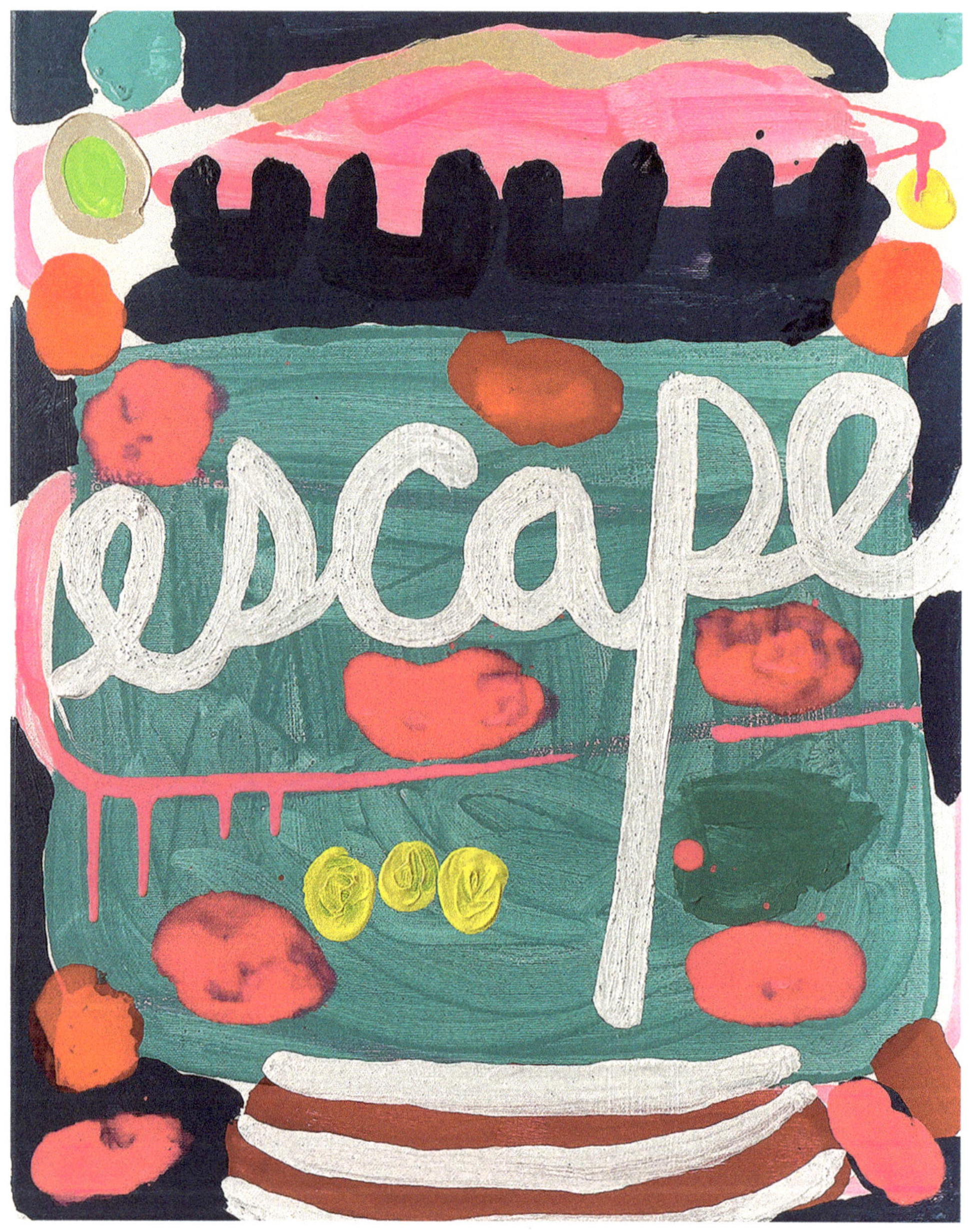

ESCAPE

Mixed media on canvas, 40 x 50 cm

ANGELA SLOAN

WOODSIDE, NEW YORK

ART AS LIFE

I awaken in the morning and boil pages of Proust for breakfast; I eat them in my favorite blue ceramic bowl, sprinkled with cinnamon and a smooth ribbon of maple syrup.

In my coffee cup is Yeats' "The Lake Isle of Innisfree" with a drop of hot milk. I brush my hair with a copy of O'Connor's *Wise Blood*; my washroom—wallpapered with Chagall's circus paintings—my bath towel a Cézanne replica: a bowl of tumescent fruit.

Instead of a handbag I carry a copy of Joan Didion's *The White Album*, I read a passage of Ginsberg in place of the weather report before heading out the door each day; I stain my lips a Gauguin shade of cerise, my eyelids are a deep Majorelle blue. My hair is a Jackson Pollock canvas of tangles.

I mumble a bit of Pound to the man with the coffee cart as a salutation and I pay him with a Van Gogh postcard from the Met instead of a dollar bill.

I hum a tune by Aretha on my way to the subway; Shakespeare's "Sonnet 18" is my umbrella. A folded black and white Diane Arbus photograph is my Amex.

Nina and Billie's words flutter on my tongue; Janis Joplin's voice is like prayer.

Songs of Love and Hate is a sacrament. To recite *Blood on the Tracks* is divination.

At night, I rest my head on a very soft worn pillow: a copy of *Light in August*; my blanket is *The Ballad of the Sad Café*.

Alice Walker, Toni Morrison and James Baldwin are my yoga and my meditation.

I massage emollients of Chaucer into my thirsty winter skin, and spritz a perfume of Milton into my hair.

Ntozake Shange's plays encase my legs and buttocks; Audre Lorde's words are the silken sheaves holding my breasts in place beneath my clothes.

I walk on stacks of love poems by Sonia Sanchez—their elegance elevating me above the dreary and the mundane; I breathe in the cool air and am filled with shimmering waves of light.

BOB BRANAMAN

SANTA MONICA, CALIFORNIA

Painting

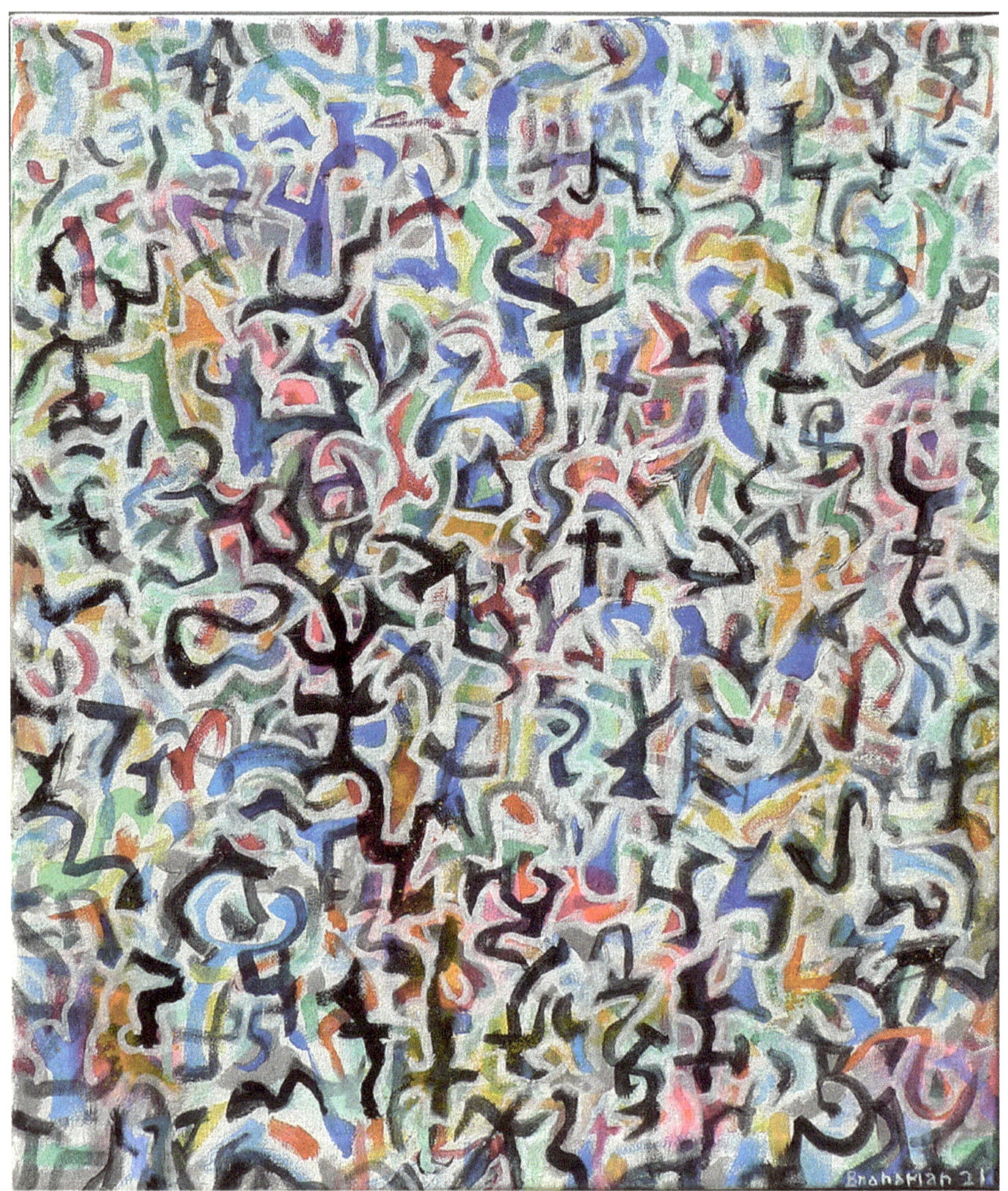

COLORED SCRIPT

Painting

SOPHIE MALLERET

NEW YORK, NEW YORK

(OVERHEARD THE MOON)

Overheard   the moon

My belly is growing

my thighs   are huge

(All the crap crap crap   you send up up up)

Fleeting star   where fleeting to   torn leaf
Run away fleet   for each boat you sank   you *never* planted trees
        Red yellow green   snow dust   shrapnel cuts ocean marine
Gigantic caterpillar blows bubbles in the infinite   yellow
I drown   get me/pack me/throw me o'er th' shrinking mountaintop
I grind my nails on rattling brains
        Smoke   broken swings   rotting forests   did you cut blow all the
grass
        Pump molasses into water tanks
        Screw a nail unto my skull
        That I breathe that I die that I eye shut from burnt eyesight   you blind
Mambo tango we lose mellow django banjo   could have sworn you knew the riff
        raff   mumbling what now   apocalypse submarine
        Escape door   not an exit   nothing equals zero   you win   we
sweet hanging lo(o)se   pants   holes   lullabies shot to hearts
                                        ashtrays of kings n' queens
                        in pink ribbons   purple fur-ry coats
                        hardware store around their necks

Arrow pointing to   no man saves babunya   texts the afterlife
Jump start race to   knife sharpener   midnight robbery
You cut & slice   we choke   à bout de souffle   crawl n' fall
        Th' submarine is no arche de Noé   you grab grab grab
From little people grab   from children n' pebble grab   number of dead brag
Salmons like   northern flickers trapped   in city lights rising   to yellow skies
in rusty fumes they(the salmons)/we   never find our way up the river
        nor the river   nor eye *(watching over)*

QUỲNH IRIS DE PRELLE

BRUSSELS, BELGIUM

THE SHADOW OF THE TREE

The shadow of the tree
is the sap of life, green chlorophyll,
    is the natural roof to protect the
    barren earth, the earth that
    contains destruction and
    destruction.

The shadow of the tree
is the light among the foliage and
    the healing of nature and man.

The shadow of the tree
are trees, forests, gardens, green
    roads and preserve heritage for
    mankind.
The shadow of the tree
the essential relationship of man and
    nature
eternity

The shadow of the tree
nature's awakening to humanity
    about climate change, about
    man-made disasters such as
    deforestation, tree felling and
    destruction of nature.
The shadow of the tree
nature's inner scream at humanity
    without conscience and lack of
    consciousness.

The shadow of the tree
is sadness on the tree
is the loneliness of man

The shadow of the tree
are statues of time and space
to other planets
are the stars

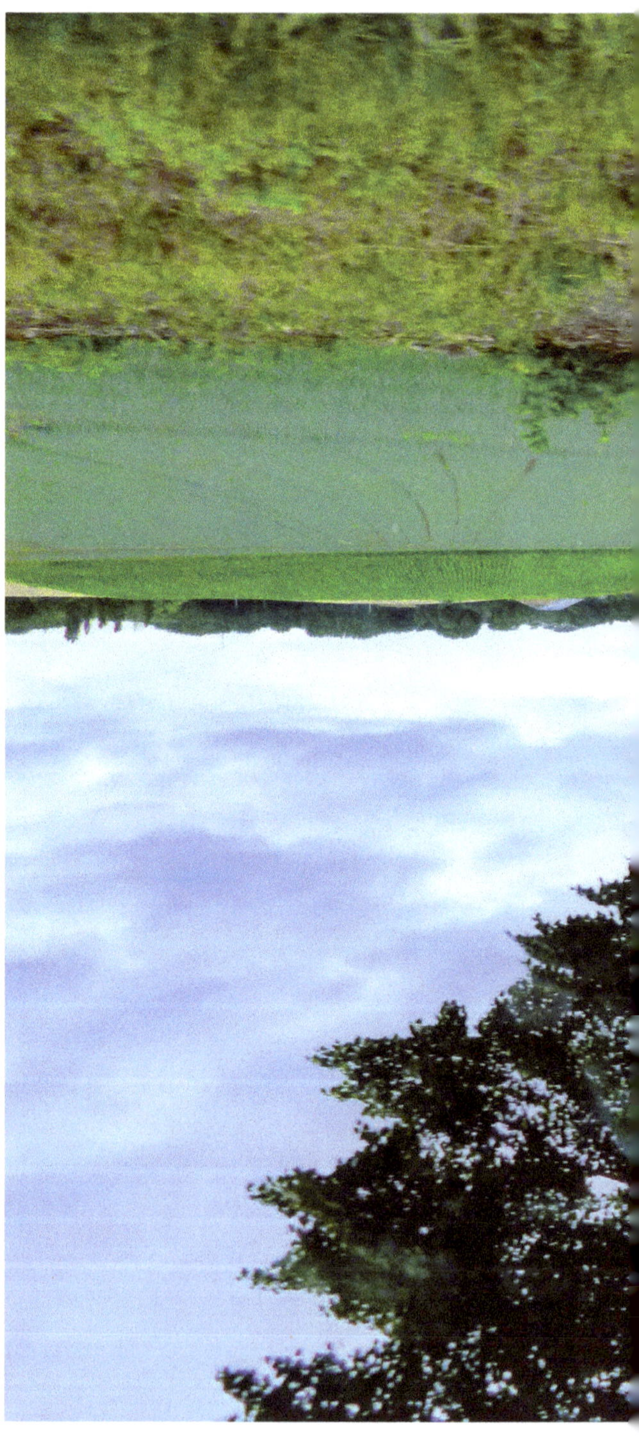

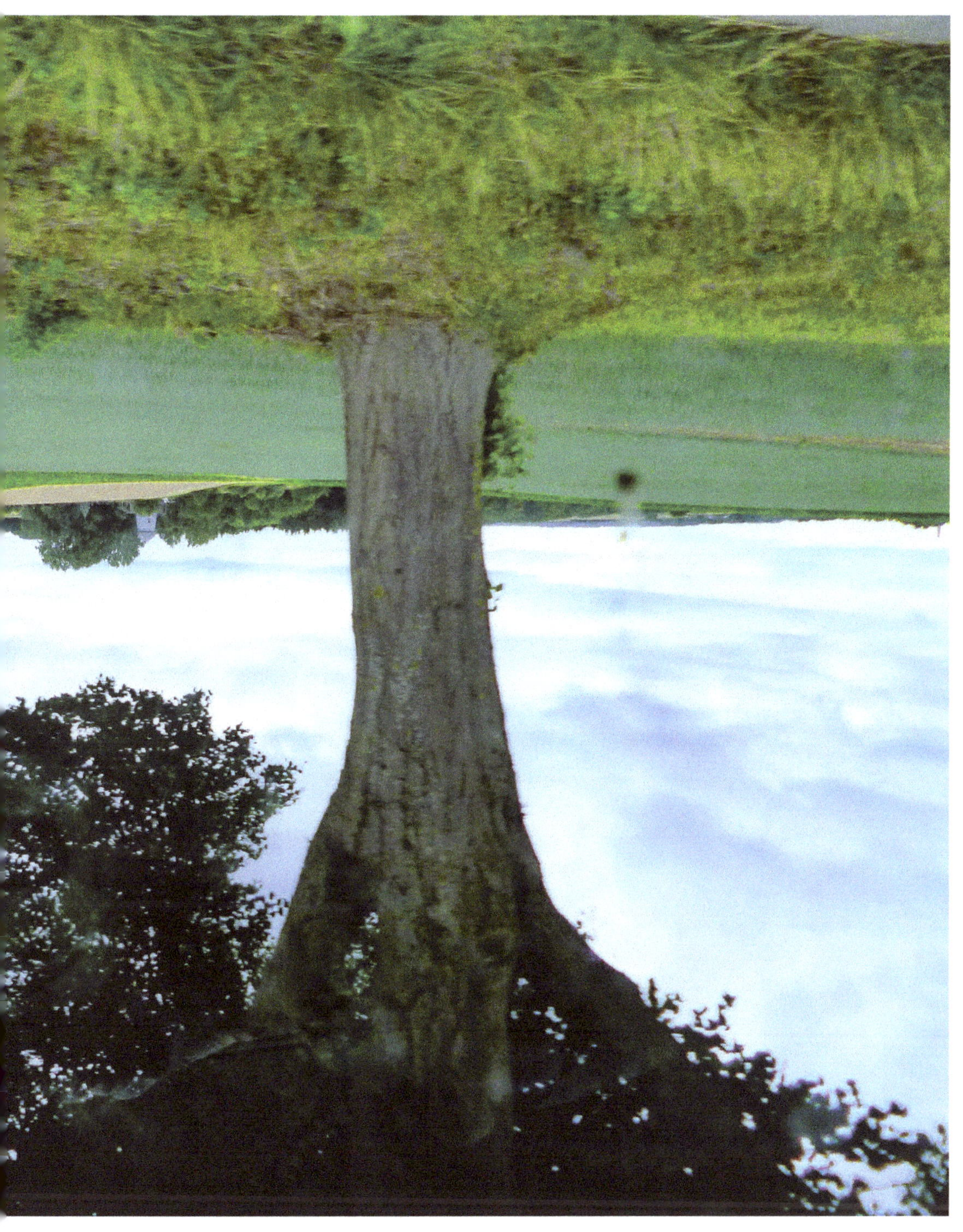

KATHY BRUCE

NEW YORK, NEW YORK

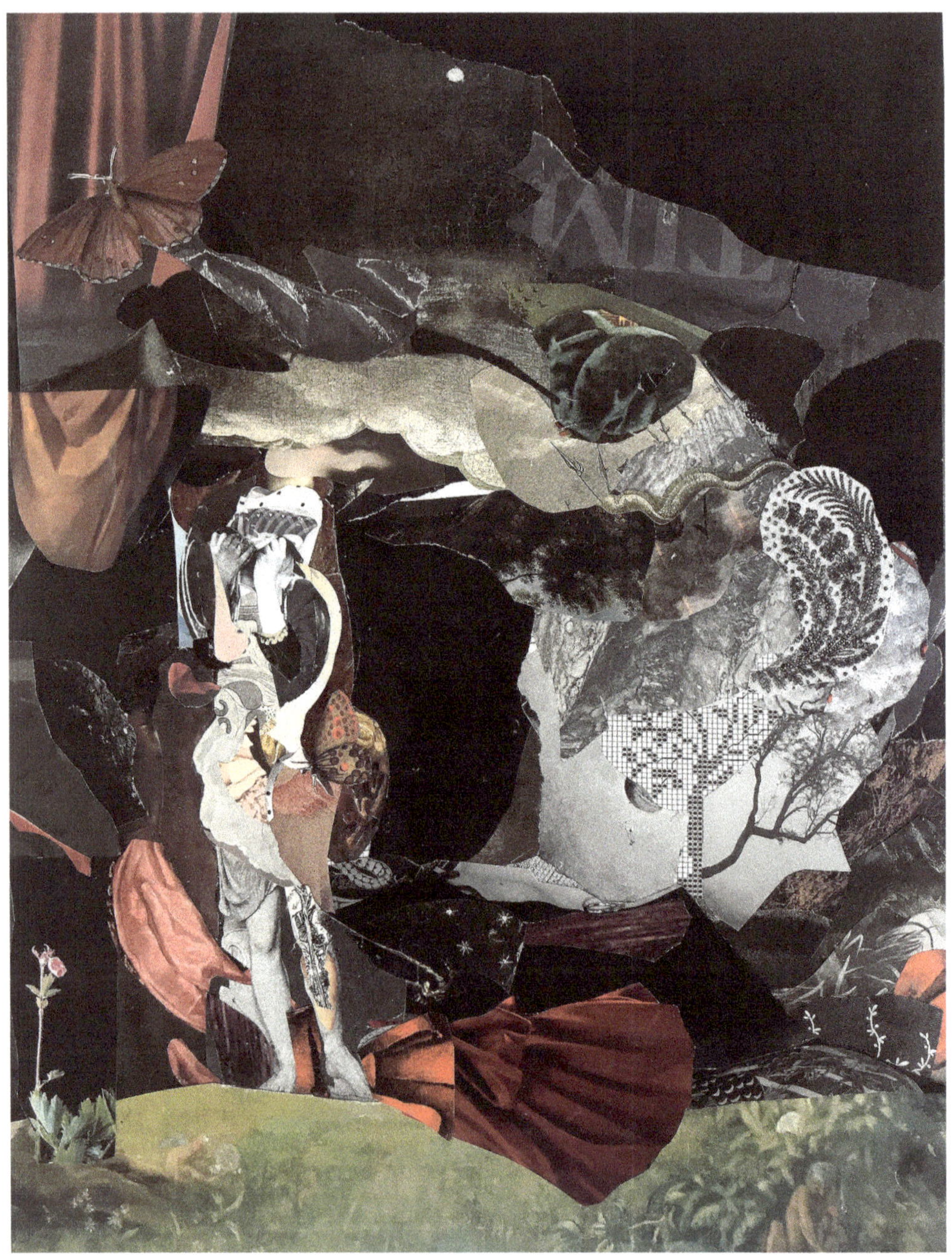

REPAIRING THE DAMAGE

Collage, 13 x 15 inches

LISA PANEPINTO

HOLDEN, MAINE

skeleton keys

a painter was banned from art during the regime
but kept painting in secret
and buried each painting in the yard

giving root to feminine strength
and benevolent oxygen   bird song transforming
the violence of petroleum war

letting all vehicles be zero emission and quiet
appearing without harming anything like blue jay
getting younger until the moment of rebirth

JAMIKA AJALON

DEUIL-LA-BARRE, FRANCE

hunger diminished

to nothing but scent

Dionysius funk
subdued in the wood

for the trees, recall
future body leaving

translucent branches
eXquisitely blown

through transiter lips
divining Hathor

MARINA KAZAKOVA

KOKSIJDE, BELGIUM

FROM IBERIA TO SIBERIA

Mysterious Europe, my ancient Europe,

From Iberia to Siberia – to the spine of the Urals,

You were to benefit from your fathers –

From a grammar of notions and rights they devised:

To life, to protection, to freedom of movement,

Opinion, religion, the right to property –

Instead, where are we, my dear Europe,

The Age of Delightenment,

           edge of a coalpit –

A small, forsaken sluicing site

Where Vincent one time

Traced misery but yet drew light.

Now the sky is overcast with violet clouds,

The pyramids of coal rests are higher than the mosque towers,

A violent wind is blowing

Across the black land

That tells what century it's seen.

Between the poor nettle chunks,

Innumerable black eyes still flash.

I'm trembling,

I see a smile of fading nature,

High above me, a lonely raven is flowing,

Slowly, as if against her will,

Cutting the carbon air with her wings.

Then she turns her head,

Looks straight into my face, and, croaking abruptly, is chased

By someone's car radio:

"Bitcoin miners are getting hungrier, they annually

Use more power than Argentina."

Another car is passing by: "Australia allows new coalmines

While speaking about net zero . . ."

On the Van Gogh Museum's door I'm reading:

"Entry is only with the Green Pass."

SARA MAINO

ARCO, ITALY

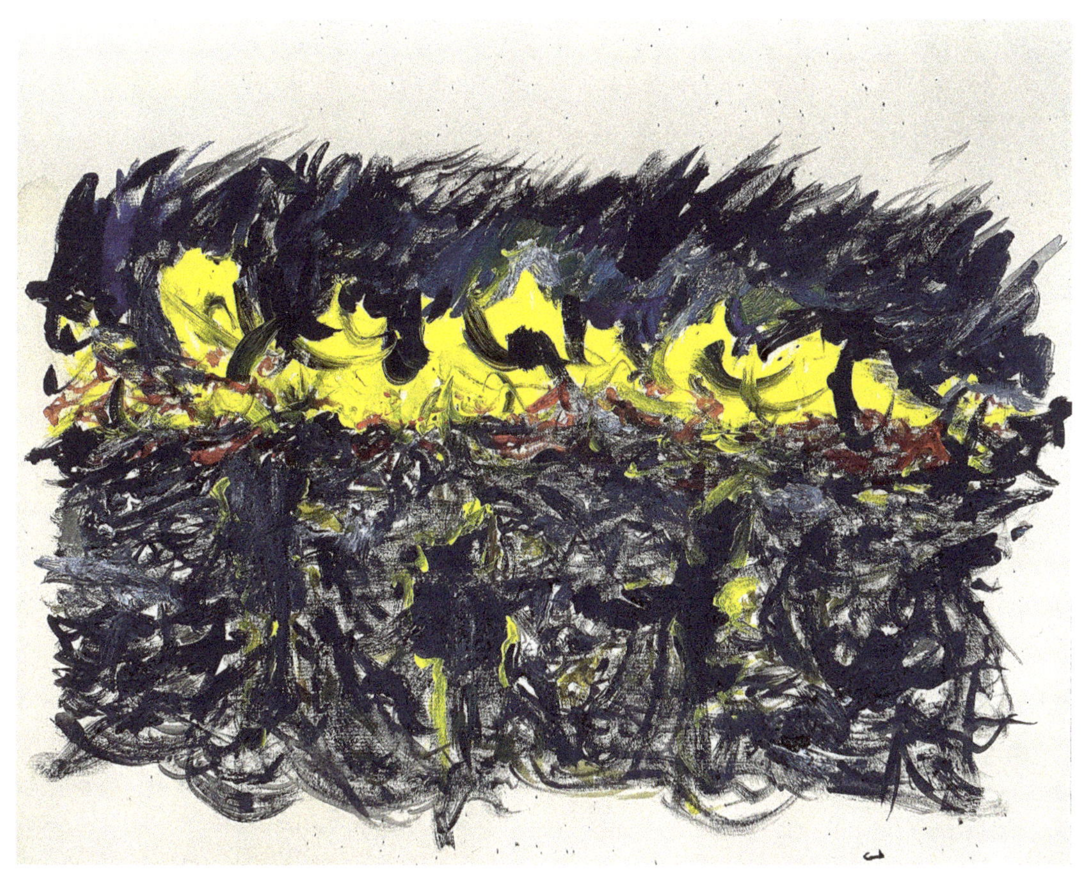

IL TEMPO È UN CLIC. VANGOGA

Acrilico, acquerello, 50 x 40 cm

STEVE DALACHINSKY

1946–2019

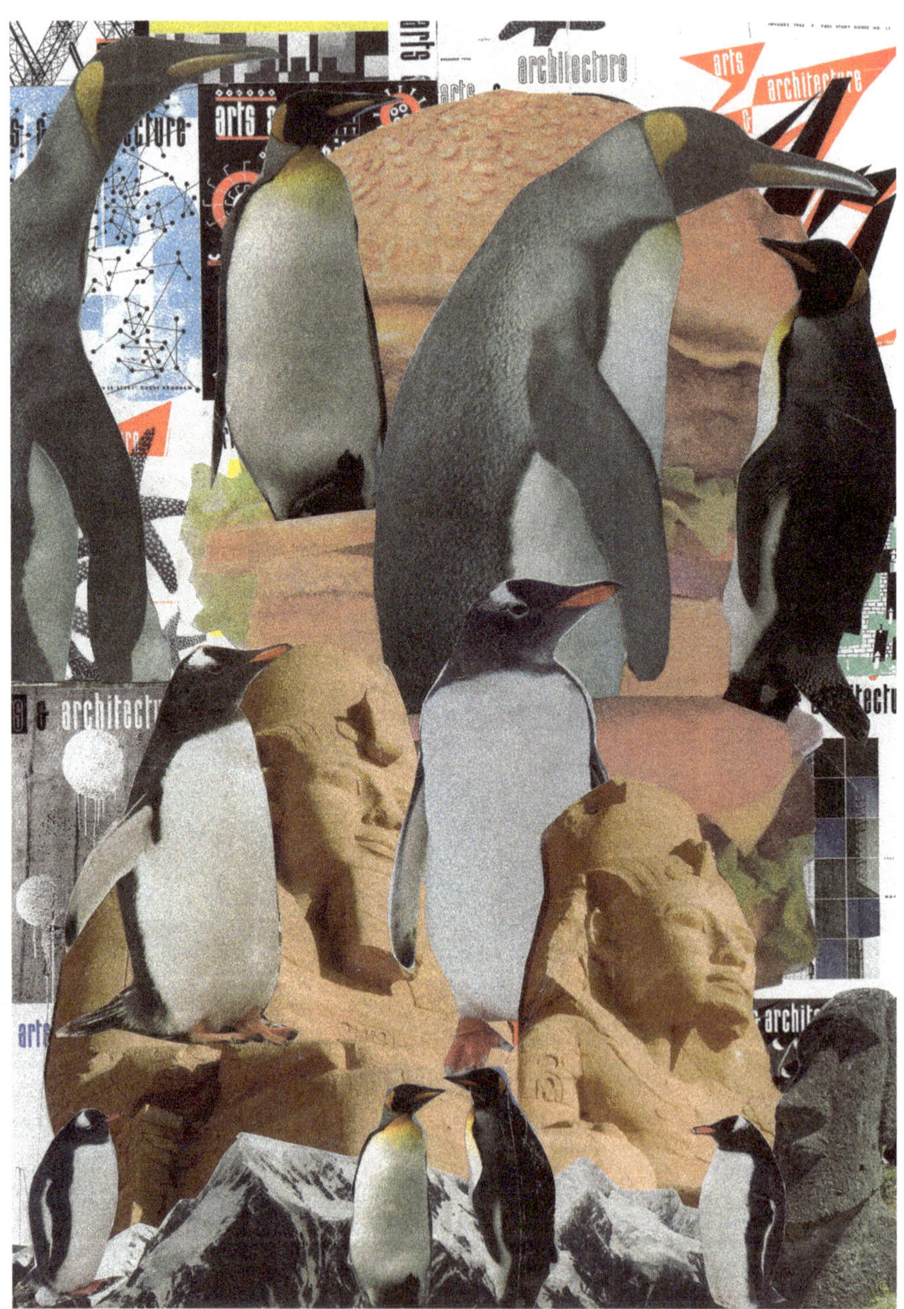

PENGUIN PYRAMID

Collage

YUKO OTOMO

NEW YORK, NEW YORK

NET ZERO

1.

NET? A fishing NET? NET stockings? A NET price? NET-work(ing)? A NET weight? Is it a verb? or a noun? I am so confused. ZERO? You mean the number that doesn't count? NADA? ZERO? Where do we start? You mean NOTHING? NOTHING like VOID? Somebody has to help me. Now my confusion's gotten worse. What am I supposed to do? I was told this word has something to do with the fate of the earth. It's a big deal. It has something to do with the survival of our species. But you know, NOBODY cares about that since we don't know how to think & feel as we are supposed to. We are trained to do physical-metaphysical thinking & cognition process only through I=ME, not WE=US. We are all proud FREE RADICALS. Oh well. I have no HOPE, I mean no HOPE to finish this writing assignment since I don't know what I am supposed to do with the subject: NET ZERO. I am a simpleminded writer. I am not like the one who can twist & juggle the ideas & words. I just need to know what NET ZERO means. Someone, please help me!

2.

It was a bright weekend winter afternoon. In a park, I sat on the bench to sunbath. As I got myself soaked pleasurably in the spring like brightness & warmth of the SUN, my sense of misanthropy got heightened out of my control. Looking at people walking by, I talked to myself secretly about how much I hated my own species, myself included. How impossibly sad & pathetic we are! As we are killing our MOTHER, our self-indulgence over the pursuit of HAPPINESS never ceases. The EARTH has been very patient with us for a long time, but now it is too old & sick. Whose fault is that? Not us. Not me. Never. We just want to be happy & healthy. That's all. We prefer to have warm winters than the harsh cold bitter ones. It's nice to say "What a beautiful day!" taking off our heavy coats in the middle of the winter.

3.

Carbon dioxide. Carbon emissions. Carbon footprints. How can we CHANGE the climate change? It's all about the balance of in & out, they say. Gross ZERO. NET ZERO by 2050? Most of us in this anthology won't be here for sure. Like anticipating the end of a bad Sci-Fi film, we are excited. "We will achieve the goal by the mid century!" Really? A decarbonized MOTHER EARTH. Solution Brief Free Download. Pathway to critical & formidable goal. Yes, we can. Of course. Nothing is impossible since we are almighty created in his image FATHER GOD.

C. MEHRL BENNETT

COLUMBUS, OHIO

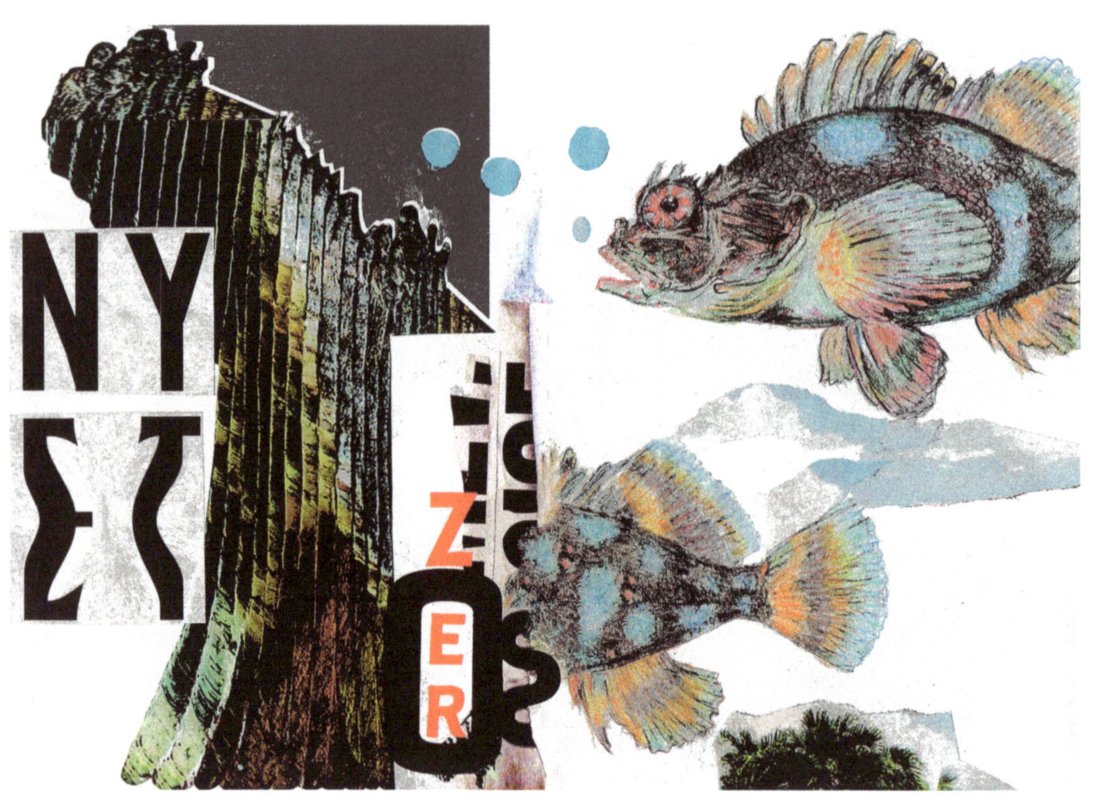

NYET THE FISH

*Colored pencil, collage, and digital via Photoshop Elements for some textual elements,
6 x 4.17 inches*

SERGE LECOMTE

BELLINGHAM, WASHINGTON

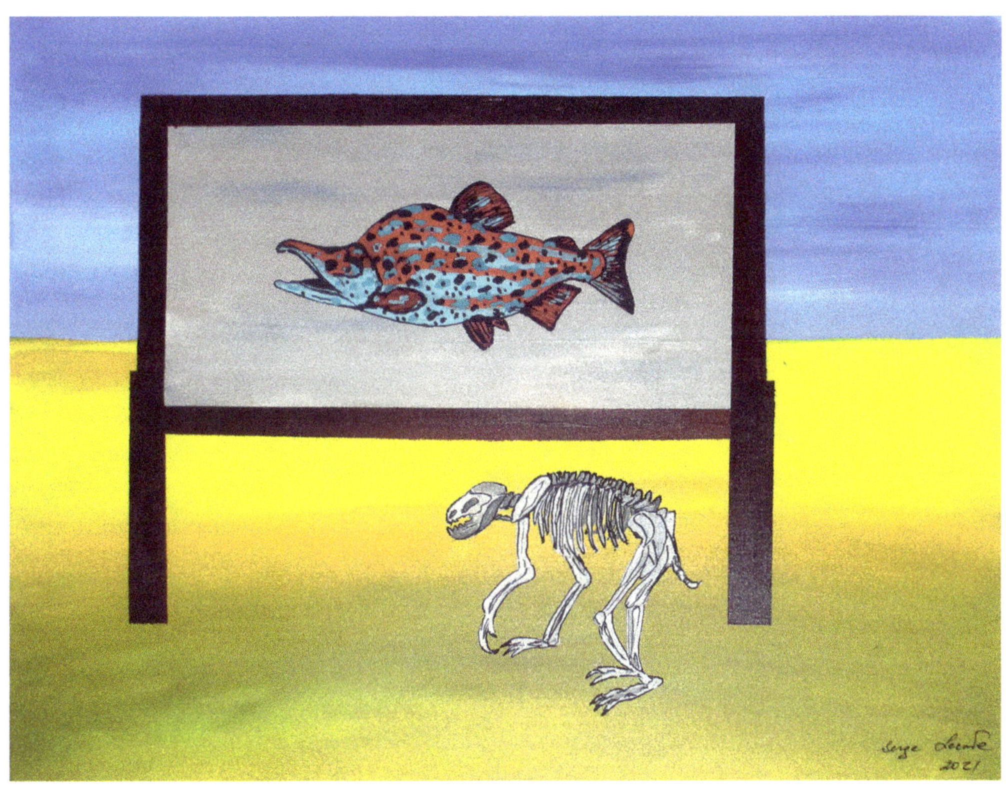

EAT MORE FISH

Mixed media, 28 x 22 inches

RUTH OISTEANU

NEW YORK, NEW YORK

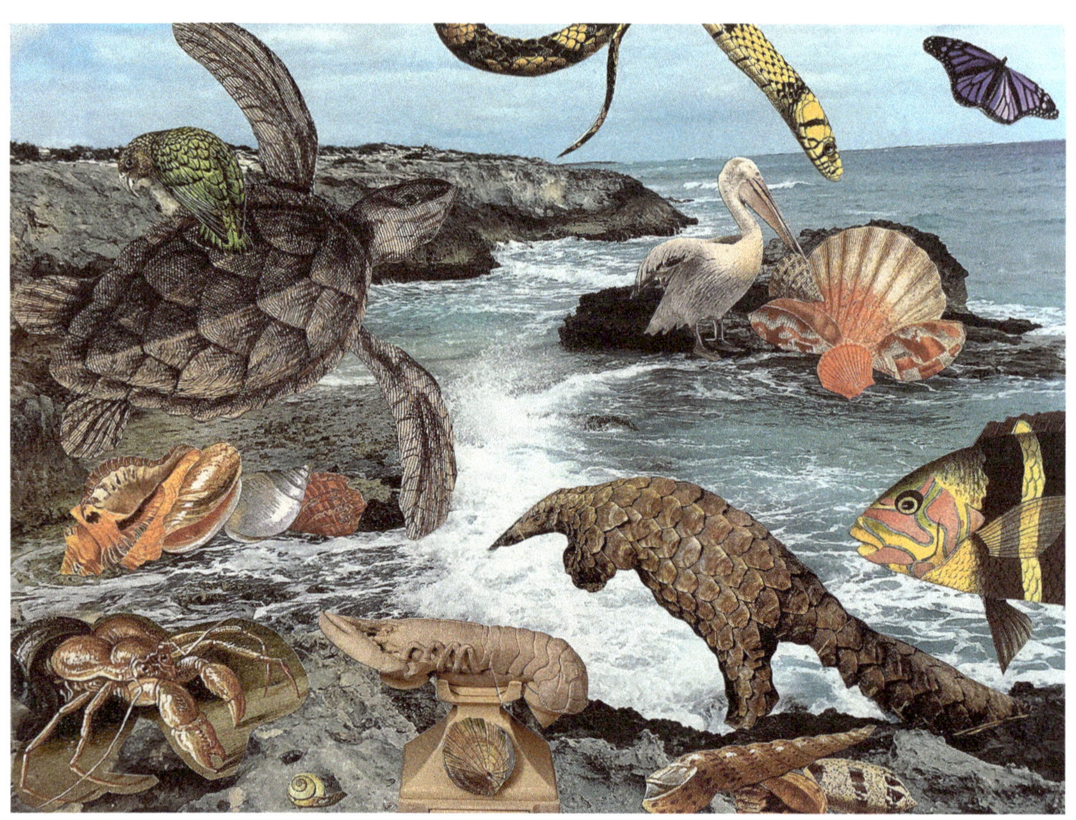

RETURN TO PANGOLIN ISLAND

Collage

VALERY OISTEANU

NEW YORK, NEW YORK

LETTER FROM THE DARK SIDE OF THE BRAIN

Climate calamity victims unite!

Nothing to lose but the hot planet

Against the greed of death makers

Those who are polluting the air and water

How many nuclear disasters does it take?

To poison the earth, to win a war?

How to save the tigers, the snow leopards?

The Javanese rhinoceros, the African gorillas?

We eat their eyes, their horns, their paws

Their hair weaved to make straitjackets

Ban the bombs, ban the war and the autocrats

The musical scale of wounds and crashed buildings

The innocent sorrow of our imprisoned voices

Act quickly before we lose our minds, our souls

Chemical pirates blacken the seas

Military monsters incinerate the forests

A discolored landscape crumbles below the horizon

No rusted key can open the timeless door

The agony of those running blind and naked

Screaming, trembling under the poisoned moon

Death lines show the ubiquitous end

DD. SPUNGIN

VALLEY STREAM, NEW YORK

LIFE WRECKER

Planet by day, monster by night

The news cuts us into pieces,

scatters us—pollution

We sweat, we starve. We cannot breathe

Ears no longer

Compassion quits and stuffs us

into a paper sack

We are garbage

disposed of in the dark

No one is looking

out for us.

Do you pray?

Planet, start praying

We are all doomed as ice melts

and fires persist

Everything is burning

The smoke stings

and we sing anthems,

wear hats, draw guns

Red + blue = nightmare,

the new math

We are the ash.

ANGELA CAPORASO

CASERTA, ITALY

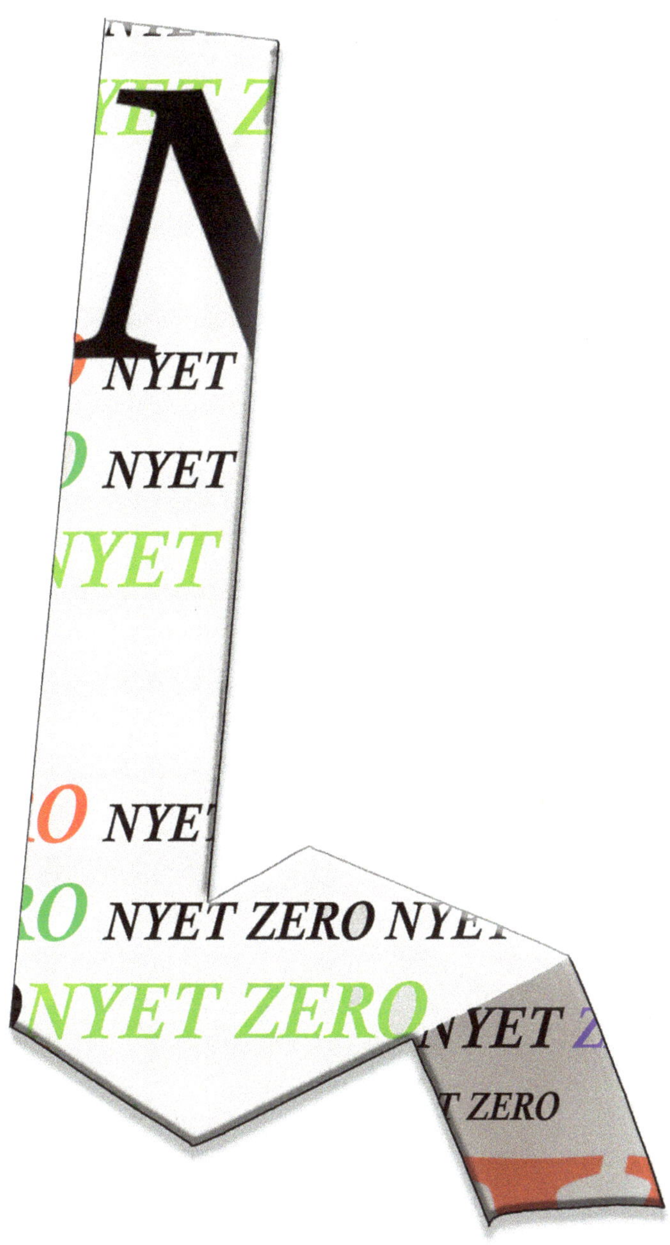

Digital collage, 8.268 x 11.811 inches

W. K. STRATTON
ROUND ROCK, TEXAS

VACUUM BOMB

Rainless along Brushy Creek

In the birthing hour

And I am stricken by jealousy

And migraine.

I write as Ukraine totters

Beneath tank steel

And vacuum bomb.

German women told me

The story of Soviet rape

In Berlin in 1945, thousands

Of mothers and grandmothers

And children

Laid bare in bombed out buildings

As other Allies arrived.

It made few newspapers and books

Until many years later:

Nazis getting what Nazis deserved

Must have been the rationale.

My head throbs. I will not think

About last night's missing hours.

My sorrows are of my own making.

I file them with past years' taxes

And step out in the rigid morning.

We have work to do.

LANCE NIZAMI

BEDFORD, MASSACHUSETTS

SMOKE

Visibility: one mile
The haze, the greyish pinpoint haze
From distant forest fires, the heavy haze

Ash, so fine, descends on everything
Eyes feel irritated, lungs work hard
You sniff; your nose is "fuller" than before

Your senses say: the haze, the air, is distant silent grey
The "near" is clear; but far away's a wall, a wall of grey

A world of three dimensions stops at two
Objects enter, disappear; removed
Objects new appear, unscheduled; unexpected, from my viewpoint

Haze controls, en-vel-ops us
And what goes in, need not come out
Burning trees a hundred miles away create this universe.

RON KOLM

LONG ISLAND CITY, NEW YORK

A WITNESS

Staked to a rock
Ares watches
As God
Covers the world
With a map.

He sucks on his teeth
Amazed.

He then sees armies
Crossing borders
That hadn't existed before
Killing people
For no good reason.

At this point he finally
Breaks into a smile.

BIBBE HANSEN

HUDSON, NEW YORK

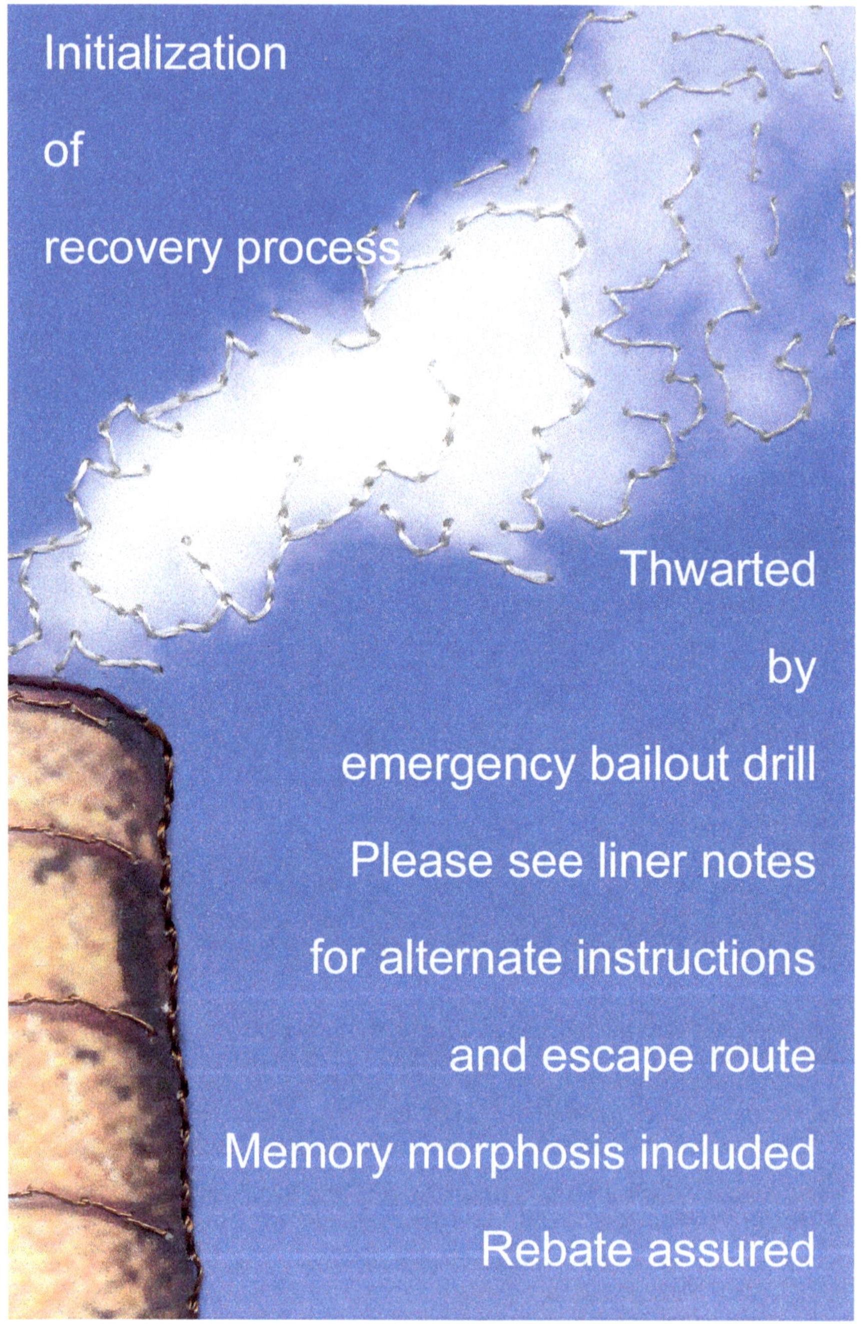

INITIALIZATION OF RECOVERY PROCESS

Text, photograph, and thread

LINDA J. ALBERTANO
VENICE, CALIFORNIA

MAJESTIC LANDFILL

In order to cut carbon, they'll soon be serving grubs and mealworms
on intercontinental flights.

If insects can't out-crawl, out-skitter or outrun extinction, can birds
or bipeds be far behind?

At least we've halted salting the sea with plastic straws.

But some of the juices that feed our Teslas are wrung
from fire-breathing plants.

And not the kind of greenery squeezed from the flaming orange orb
that incrementally boils us in our own sweat, either.

O, diminutive human beings . . . are we the only species stuck on self-destruct?

Lemmings lunge after their leaders over cliffs. Yet lemmings abound.
Hope in a storm of despair?

A modern bard foretold this catastrophe when he sang,
"It's the Slow Consumption killing us by degrees."

Sing, people! Sing! Whilst our stumpy legs carry us to the eternal landfill
in the sky.

Sing!

ELIETTE MARKHBEIN

NEW YORK, NEW YORK

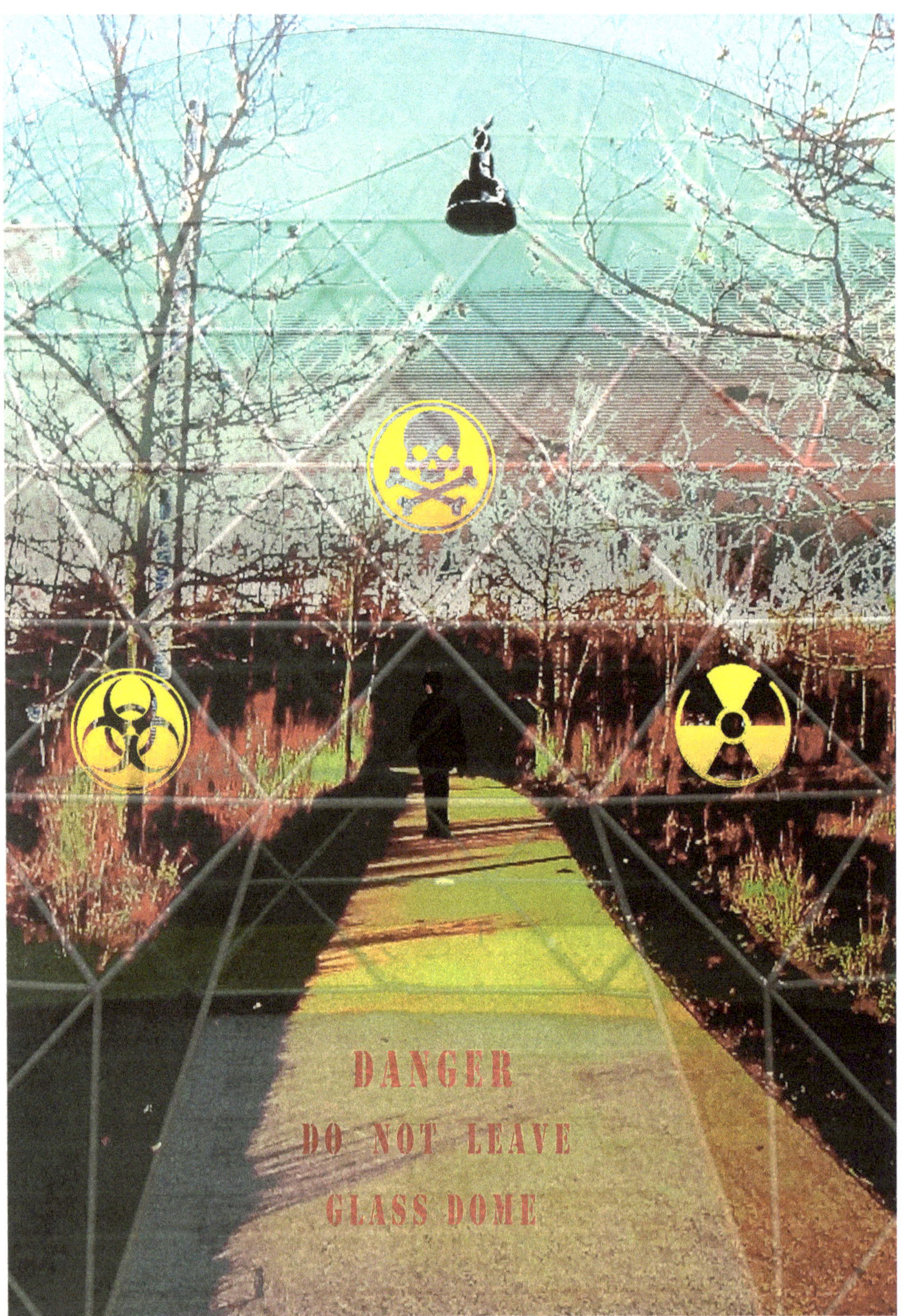

COP 30 – THE FALSITY

Photo collage

PHILIP MEERSMAN

JETTE, BELGIUM

New Aged

We are *entering* a new age in **human** history
                              when *life* is more **endangered** than ever.
cutting ties

                    in the dessert of the real
                    in a radical attempt to (re)gain a *stronghold*

a pathological attempt at *regaining*
the simulacrum
suck up the unbearable *anxiety*
perceive suspicion

a remote-control drums **death**
                         deep into the soil
                 not a **dream**
          but a roaring **drone**

                 from the brain straight into the **d**epths of the rabbit hole.

Change has come
in armored vehicles
Resistance is watching!

Cutting is a pathological phenomenon
I have a **view** with a room

There is no tomorrow

We recommend you to:
Bring a meditation mat
Wear loose or comfortable clothing
Switch off all electronic **devises**

NEW AGED

*Cut & paste from texts, performance sheets and freely simulacered on the writings of Slavoj Zizek and
conversations with the VAXX.ON.AIR performance team at AP University College at MAXlab.*

ANTHONY D. KELLY

CASTLEBAR, IRELAND

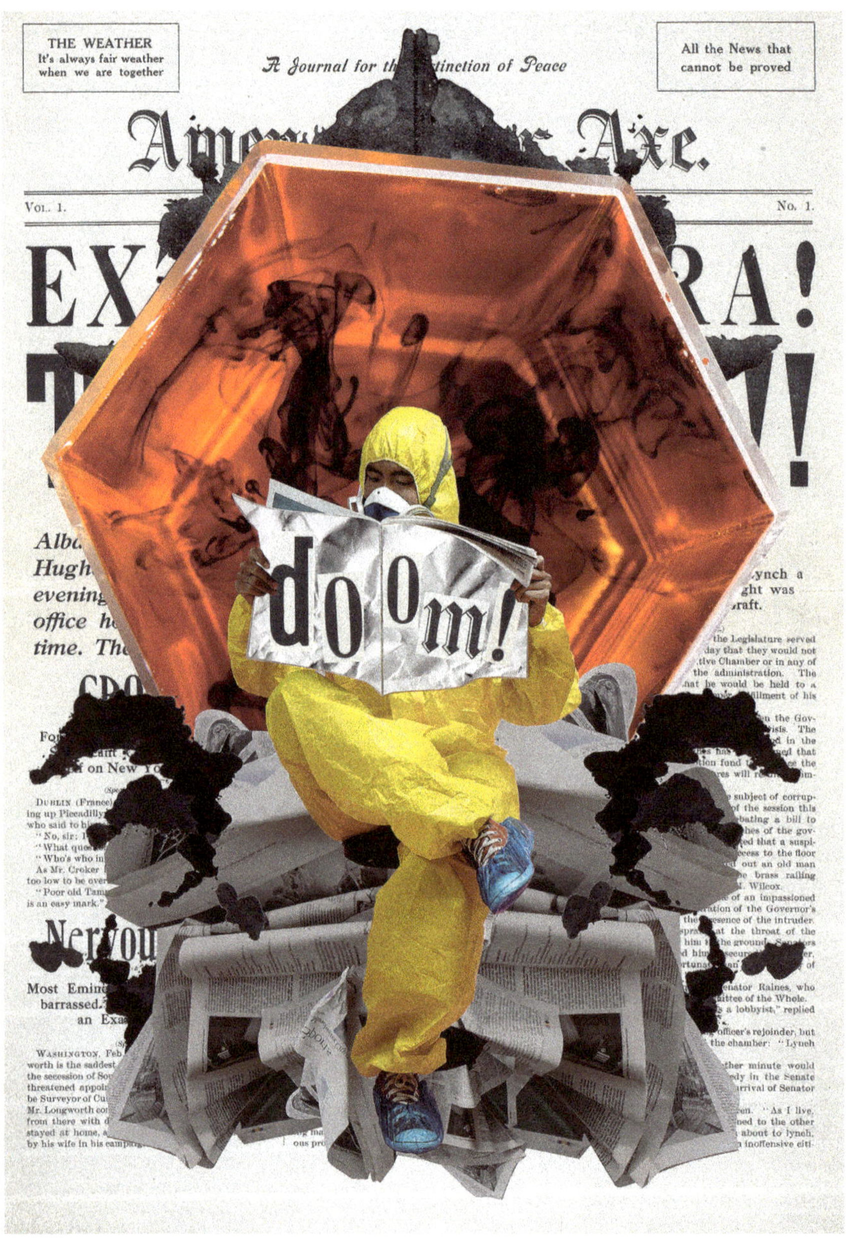

BAAAAD NEWS!

Digital collage, 45 x 52 cm

MALIK AMEER CRUMPLER

PARIS, FRANCE

PSYOP #7,890,781,567,234,590,100.78919

Because now, these ceaseless
psyops are undeniably
undeniable, we desperately flee
our most tungsten of
thoughts [or = our most sentaicar
selves] into

camouflage cells which
bewitch our ability to
comprehend any of these
boundless crises we're in

*". . . couldn't've told me last night eye'd wake up this mornin'
on Saturn [i mean Mars] even though it's still Berkeley . . ."*

(circa 2020, pre-post Earth, Oakland from a Gvideo call to a confused runaway fugaciously living in the silver planet of purtid, Paris)

Because now, communication's more
difficult than identifying the colour of dust
since winning's no longer the point, our
disaster drenched descent into permanent
vats of vapid viral hollers vividly pollutin',
taggin' & share-ing within hollow croissants
burnt to an onyx crescent's crisp
cancellation until that

melting-deer-horned-honest question
blooms again in
those pixelated eye sockets of another
cancelled regimes' spaceage-after-earth
avatars

". . . After 2020, nothing shocks me anymore!"

*"Give it some time, said the same thing about 1968 in 1969 . . .
& then, fuckin' Eyephones!"*

new

NONSENSODYNE
PROVEN RELIEF AND DAILY PROTECTION IN THE FIGHT AGAINST TRUTH DECAY

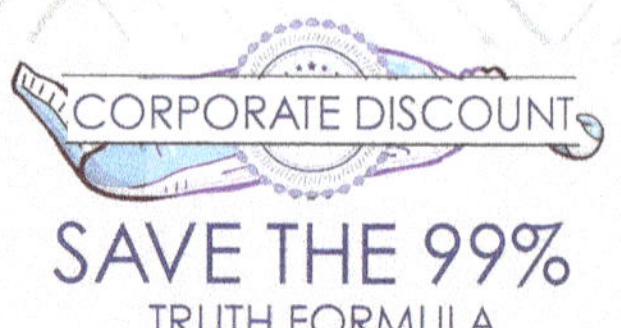

SAVE THE 99%
TRUTH FORMULA

10% OFF

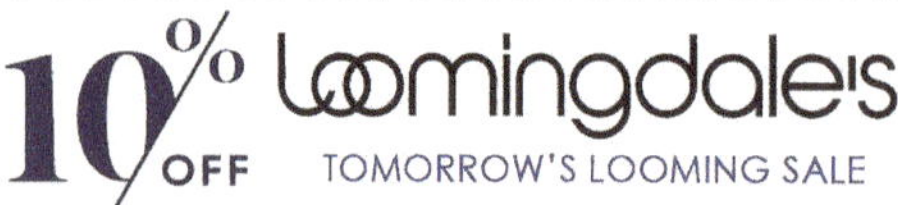

0% OFF

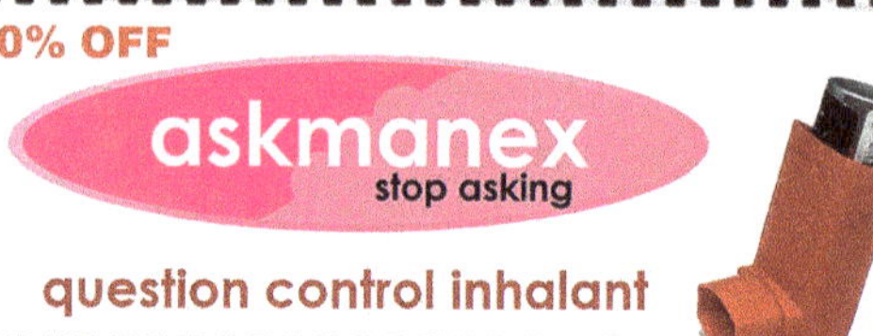

question control inhalant

Await) Watchers

Waiting for The Big Reveal?
Don't just sit there! Eat something!

ACQUA PANICA

Electrolyte Infused Anti-Panic Water

SEPARATE FACT FROM FICTION

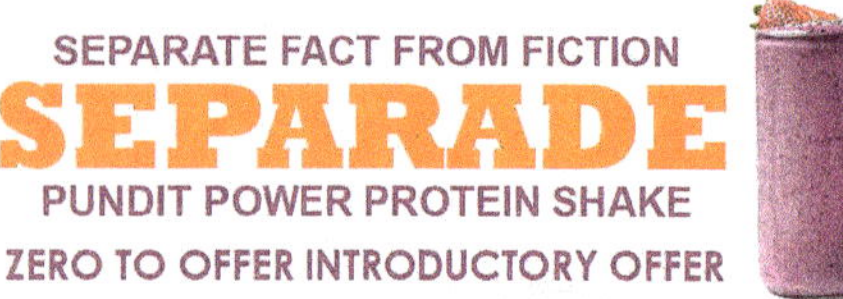

PUNDIT POWER PROTEIN SHAKE
ZERO TO OFFER INTRODUCTORY OFFER

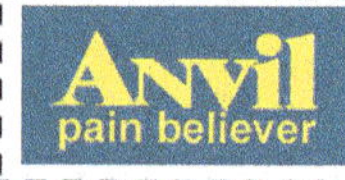

20% OFF 1st SIP

AQUAFINALE
WATER FOR THE END

20% OFF LAST SIP

Anvil
pain believer

Between a rock
and a hard place

Word Salad Supreme
Doublespeak Spread
Jibberish Special Sauce

30% OFF $30

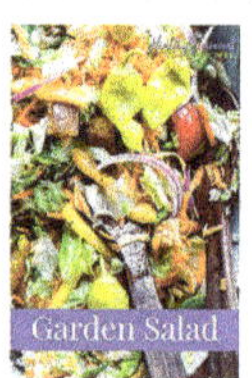

Office DESPOT
20% OFF

- Misinformation Campaigns
- False Flag Events
- Empty Promises
- Propaganda Materials

TAKE
EVERYTHING
OFF

stay cool
when the thermonuclear
heat is on

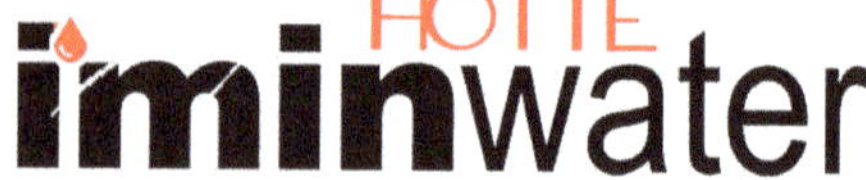

plastic premise promise water

plastic on the outside, hollow on the inside

COUPONS SAVE LIVES

JPEG, 934K bytes

PETER BEDA

BRUSSELS, BELGIUM

ABNORMIZM
(THE NEW ENERGY, NON-RULES FOR A POST-COVID WORLD)

R U FUCKED UP ALL THE TIME?
R U REPRESSING YOUR TRUE FEELINGS IN ORDER TO BE NORMAL?
R U WORRIED ABOUT THE WAY THE WORLD IS GOING RIGHT NOW?
R U LIVING THE NINE TO FIVE ABSURDISM?
R U WORKING 4 PEOPLE WITH OTHER AGENDAS THAN U?
R U SUSTAINING A BROKEN SYSTEM 4 A PAYCHECK AND YOUR PAID SILENCE?

BLACK MONEY BURNING IN YOUR POCKET
YOUR EMPLOYER'S BRIBE FOR STEALING YOUR TIME
GOTTA WASH IT CLEAN AT THE SUPERMARKET

ARE YOU ANGRY 24/7?
SHOW YOURSELF AND SHOW OTHERS
YOUR STATE OF BEING
YOUR STATE OF MIND
YOUR STATE OF SOUL

YOU HAVE BEEN VACCINATED
SO
NOW
ANYTHING GOES

THE NEW WORLD ORDER ASKS FOR A NEW WAY OF ACTING, BEING, THINKING
YOU MUST STOP ONLY SHOWING YOUR BEST SIDE
WHEN POSING AND POSTING THE SAME TYPE PICTURES ONLINE
AS YOU FOLLOW AN UNWRITTEN LAW
THAT IS LIKE SELF-CENSORSHIP TELLING YOU TO NEVER SHOW HOW YOU REALLY FEEL

THE RESULT IS KNOWN TO ALL
WE TAKE PILLS TO ADJUST OUR SAD FACES AND FAKE THE SMILES

THE SHEEP, THE HERD, WILL FOLLOW THE OLD RULES
BUT FOR YOU, THERE ARE NO LONGER ANY RULES
SO
FUCK BEING POLITICALLY AND INSTAGRAMMABLY CORRECT
R U GOING TO LET THEM STIFLE YOUR WORDS, YOUR SONGS, YOUR LIFE?

YOU HAVE BEEN VACCINATED
SO
NOW
ANYTHING GOES

SAY SOMETHING, ANYTHING U WANT
EXPRESS YOURSELF IN EVERY WAY POSSIBLE
OFF- OR ON-LINE, IRL OR URL
YOU DON'T HAVE TO FOLLOW
ANYONE BUT YOURSELF

THE CO2 CRISIS IS EASY TO SOLVE!
So why did this not happen yet?

If we don't do anything about CO2 emissions, we will reach a point of unstoppable catastrophic climate change within 12 years.

But can't we prevent this? What about renewable sources of energy?

Well, renewables have come a long way in recent years, and are now at the point where it is generally cheaper to produce electricity this way. We could already generate all our energy needs from renewables if we wanted to, and save money at the same time.

But what... we don't want to do this??

Of course not!

What?! This is a win-win! We would not only be saving humanity, we would also be saving money! If what we need to do to stop catastrophic climate breakdown is to stop burning fossil fuels, and we have the ability to do this, why don't we just stop burning fossil fuels?

Because it would be much MORE of a disaster if we did that!

Why?

Well, for starters, what do you think would happen to all the jobs in the coal, gas and oil industries? Why would you want to take the jobs away from hard working people?!

But the renewable energy industry would create new jobs, probably better than working in a coal mine or on an oil rig. There would be a huge amount of work to do building a new energy infrastructure. It would create many more jobs than would be lost in the fossil fuel industry where most of the work is automated anyway.

Hmmm... I'll have to get back to you on that one... But you are in any case forgetting the most important factor here.

What do you mean?!

There is something more important than the end of human civilisation?

You're damn right there is! How can you forget about the profits of the fossil fuel corporations? These companies make a lot of money!
I mean it! Really HUGE amounts of money!!

From destroying the future for all of us...

Exactly! Now I think you are finally beginning to understand... It took a lot of work to get the planet to this precarious position. Decades! Over a century even! They deserve every cent they make!

I guess... I mean, when you put it like that...

You see? Its impossible to solve this problem. There is nothing we can do!

You're right... Human civilisation is overrated I guess...

Thats the spirit!

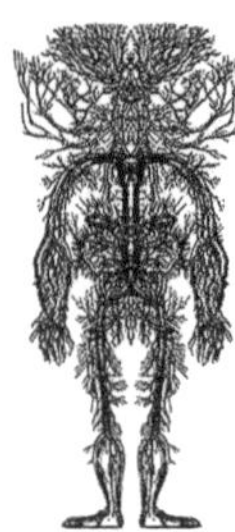

This is not how it has to be...
The Problems we face can be easily solved!
Don't believe the Bullshit excuses.
Our future can be great!
RECLAIM OUR FUTURE! OCCUPY OUR FUTURE!

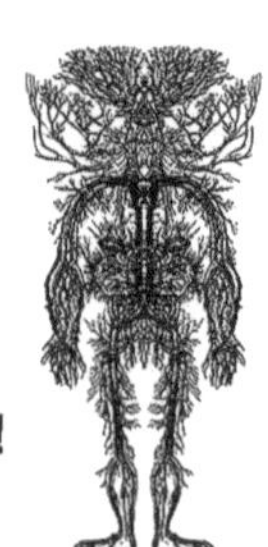

THE CO$_2$ CRISIS IS EASY TO SOLVE

Digital collage, A4

GAY PASLEY

EDMOND, OKLAHOMA

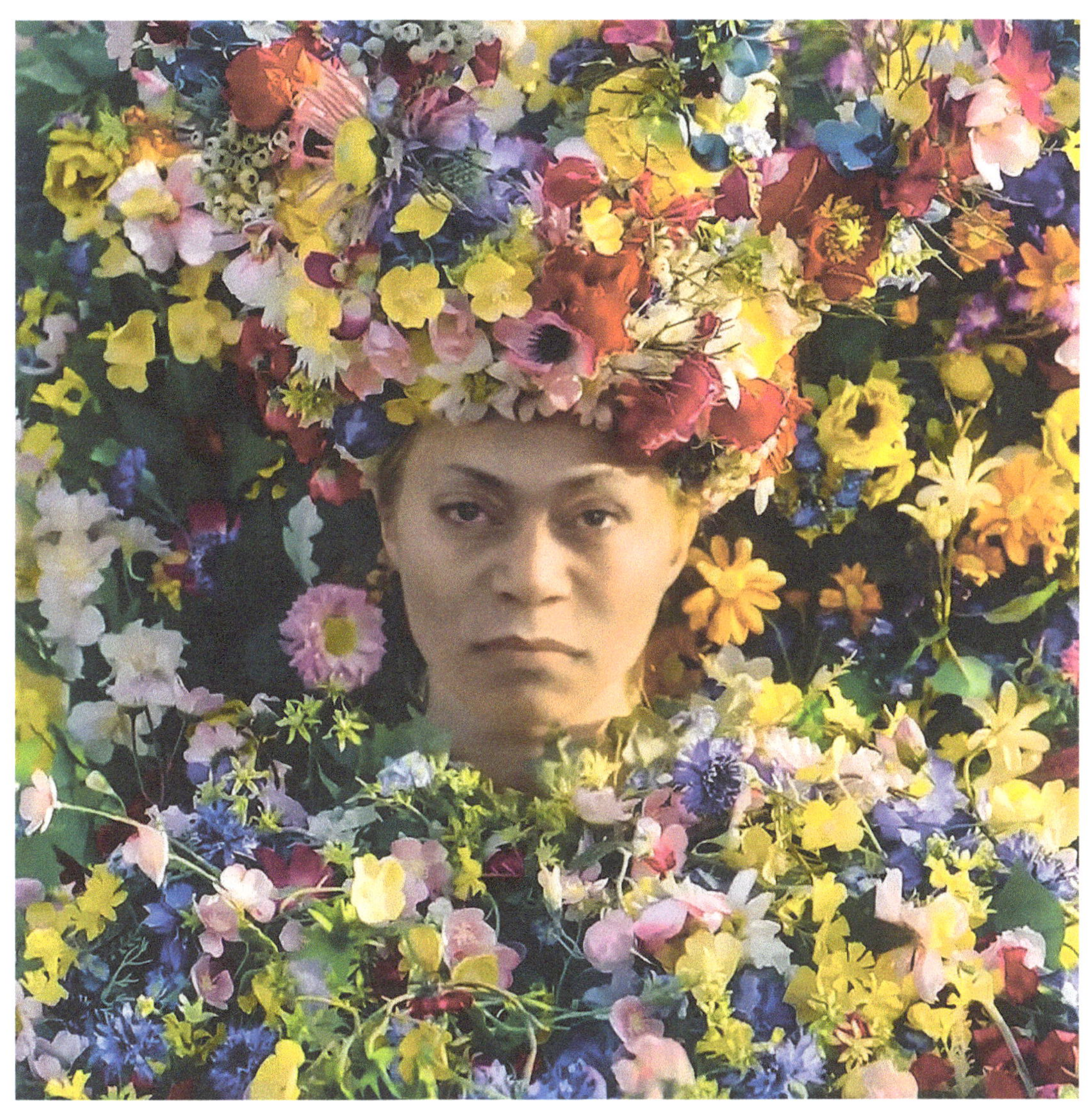

MOTHER FUCKING NATURE

Photographic collage

GEMMA GOETTE

BROOKLYN, NEW YORK

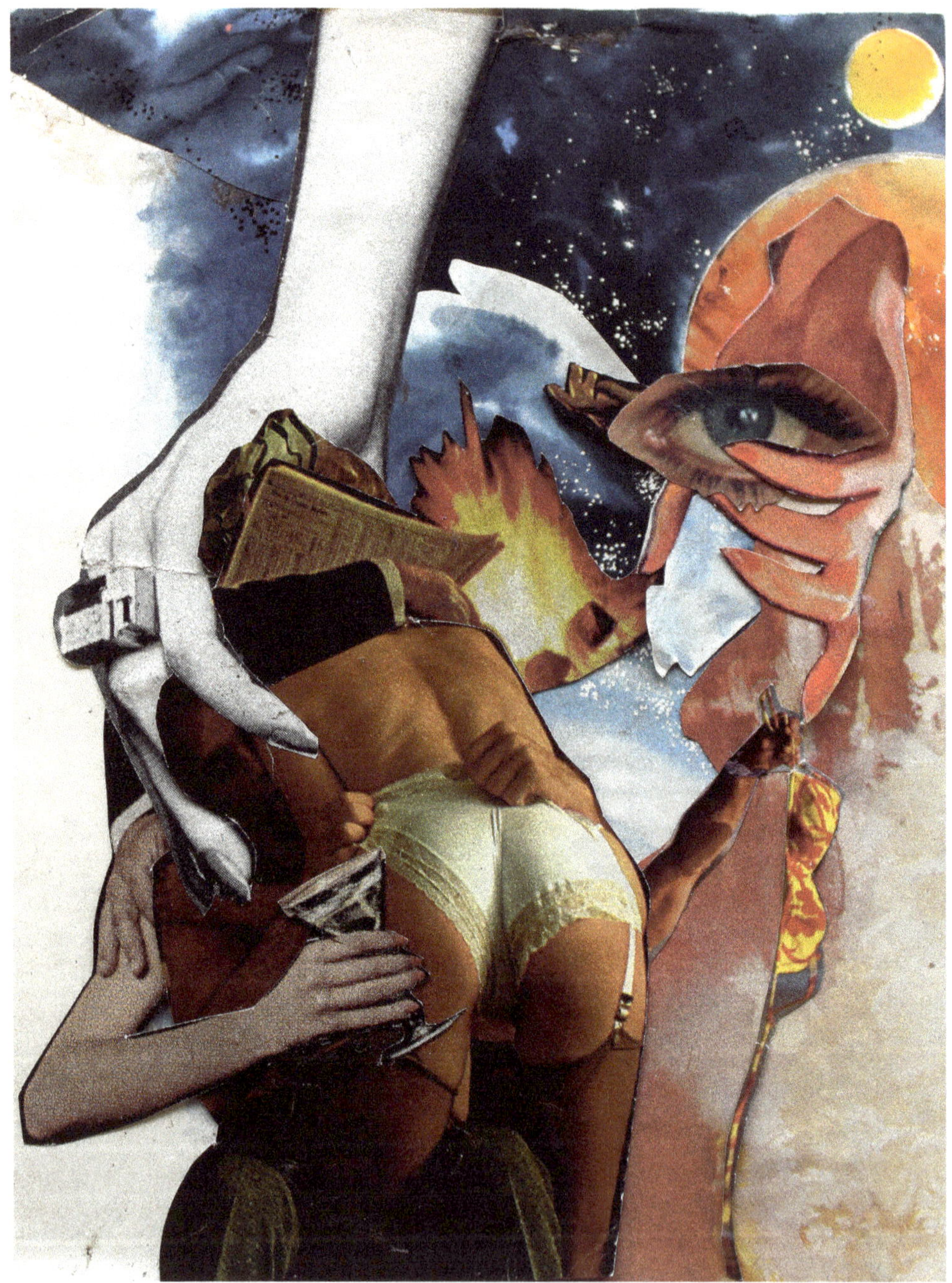

FUCKING WITH FIRE

Collage

GENCO GULAN

ISTANBUL, TURKEY

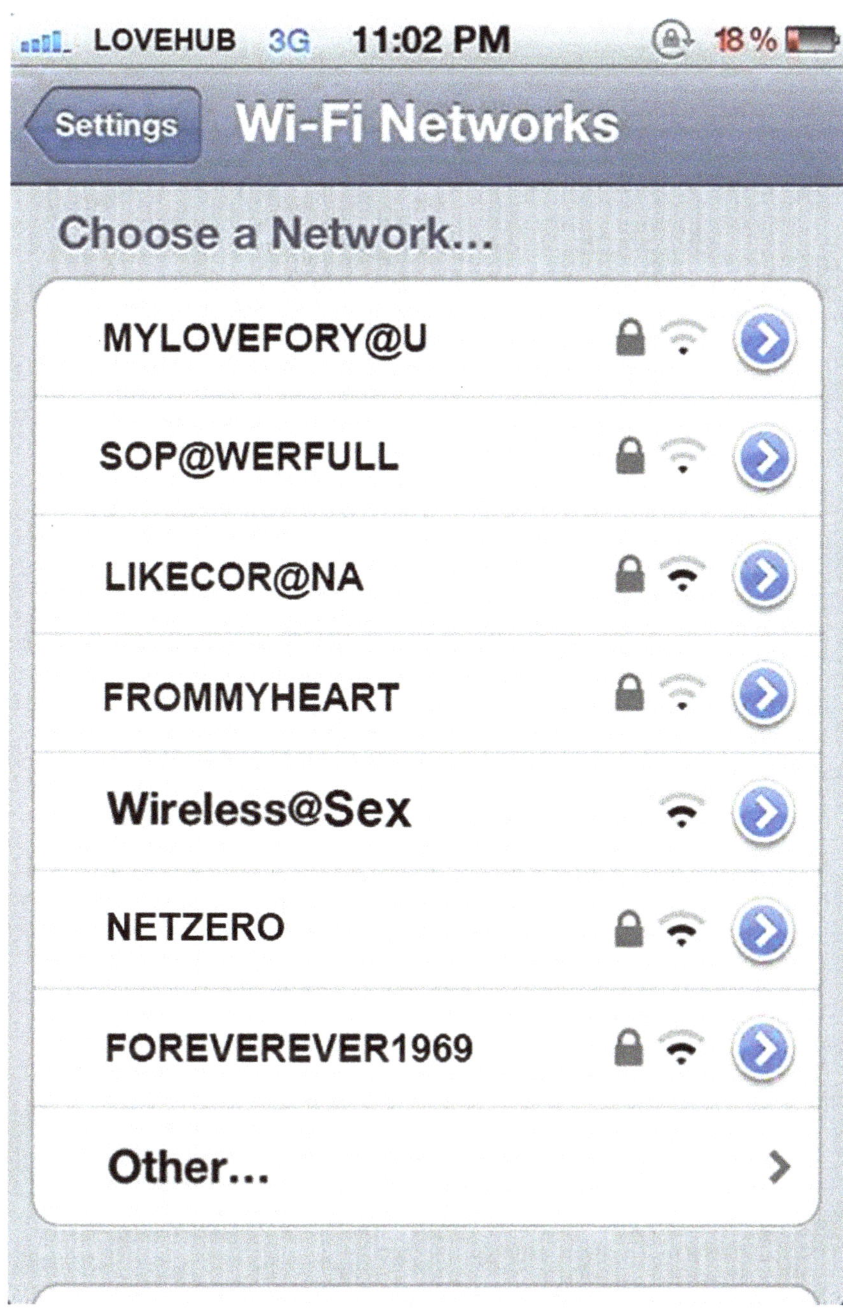

WI-FI POEM

New media installation project using multiple custom named modems

AYUSHI JAIN
GURGAON, INDIA

Green

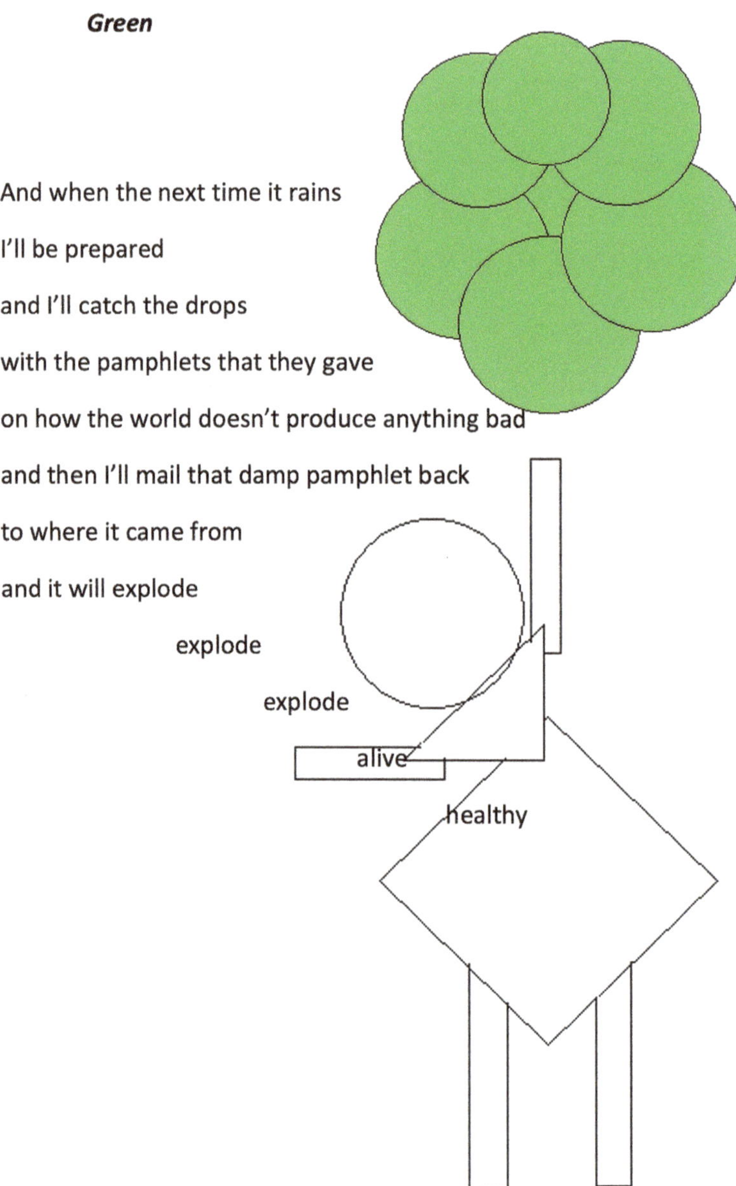

And when the next time it rains

I'll be prepared

and I'll catch the drops

with the pamphlets that they gave

on how the world doesn't produce anything bad

and then I'll mail that damp pamphlet back

to where it came from

and it will explode

explode

explode

GREEN

Text and illustration

RADOSLAV ROCHALLYI

PRAGUE, CZECH REPUBLIC

Untitled Future

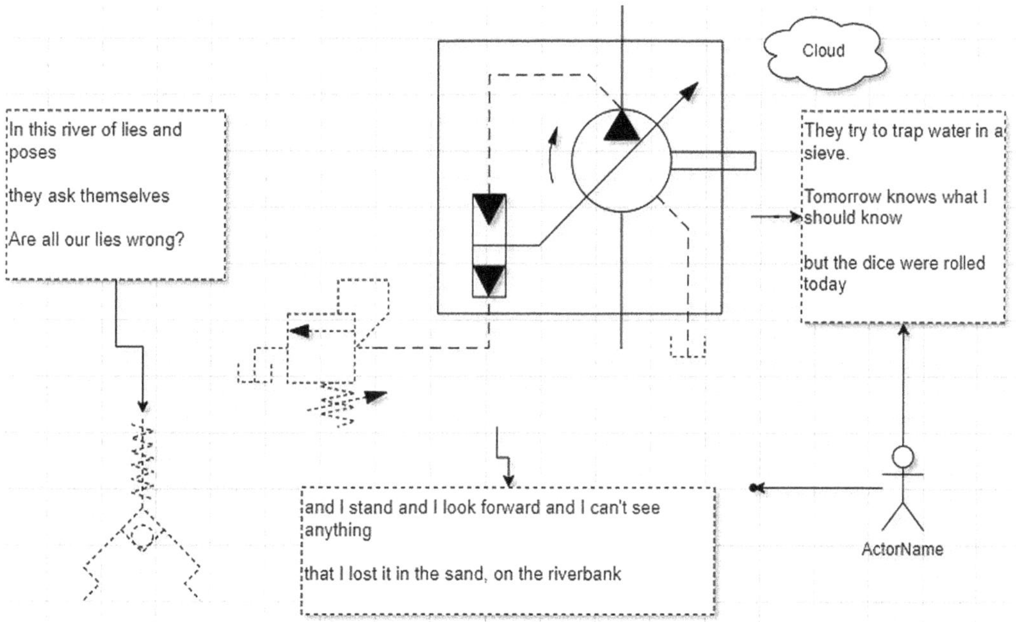

$$f(\textit{Sometimes I wish I didn't know the vector})$$
$$= a_0$$
$$+ \sum_{n=1}^{\infty} \frac{\left(a_n \text{ Consider! } \dfrac{n\pi x}{(x+a)^n = \sum_{k=0}^{n} \binom{n}{k} x^k a^{n-k}} + b_n \text{ Believe! } \dfrac{n\pi x}{(x+a)^n = \sum_{k=0}^{n} \binom{n}{k} x^k a^{n-k}} \right)}{[\![I \text{ lost her somewhere}]\!] \, {}^\wedge x = 1 + \frac{x}{1!} + \frac{x^2}{2!} + \frac{x^3}{3!} + \cdots,}$$
$$-\infty < \textit{She found it ... in the train} < \infty$$

UNTITLED FUTURE

Text, mathematical equation, and illustration

IMANOL BUISAN

TERRASSA, SPAIN

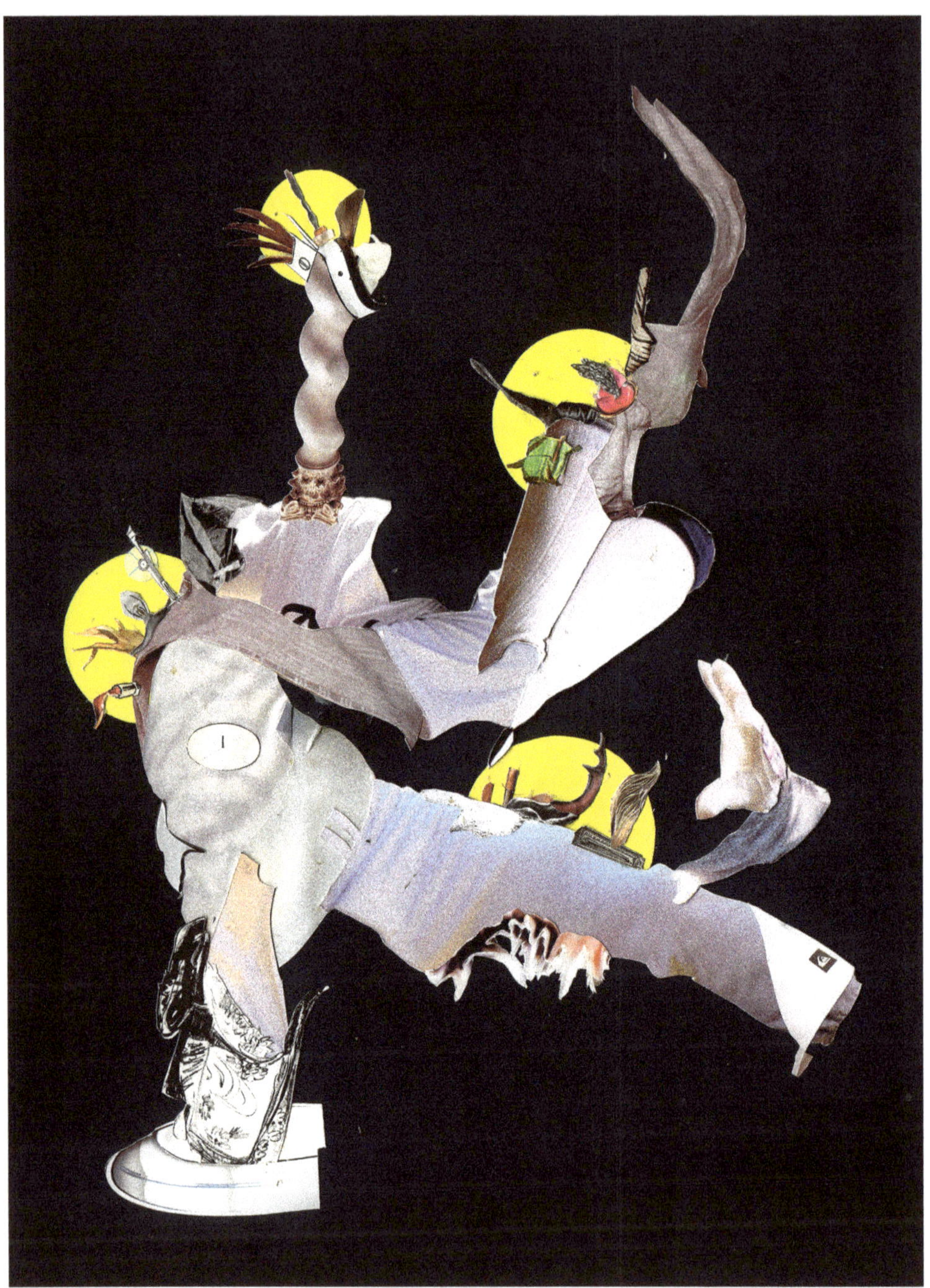

ENSIMISMADO

Collage

ALEXANDER NDERITU

NAIROBI, KENYA

THE DEATH OF JOURNALISM

Journalism is as dead as a lump of clay,

I visited its grave yesterday.

The papers are filled with propaganda,

Everyone is coloured grey,

The tell-lie-vision is ten times worse:

If the anchor tells the truth, there'll be hell to pay.

"Good evening, viewers, hear what I have to say

These are the headlines I made up today:

Ten insurgents were killed over desert sand

Their president is a dictator like the late Saddam.

Meanwhile, our government has unveiled a new plan

For more schools and hospitals and mega dams.

And in Sports, so-and-so is a shoe-in to win Formula One."

You can tell it's a pack of lies.

They can even give you tomorrow's news today

(About the wars that they themselves started yesterday).

How come the nations with the largest gold reserves

Are not the ones that have the gold mines?

Why does it take military powers endless years

In foreign lands to fight small bands of rag-tag militias?

The media distracts the masses—they may as well be blind

Atrocities are committed in broad daylight.

JOHN J. TRAUSE

WOOD-RIDGE, NEW JERSEY

Да да нет да да нет да да нет да да нет да да нет да да нет да да нет да да нет да да нет
да да нет да да нет да да нет да да нет да да нет да да нет да да нет да да нет да да нет
да да нет да да нет да да нет да да нет да да нет да да нет да да нет да да нет да да нет
да да нет да да нет да да нет да да нет да да нет да да нет да да нет да да нет да да нет
да да нет да да нет да да нет да да нет да да нет да да нет да да нет да да нет да да нет
да да нет да да нет да да нет да да нет да да нет да да нет да да нет да да нет да да нет
да да нет да да нет да да нет да да нет да да нет да да нет да да нет да да нет да да нет
да да нет да да нет да да нет да да нет да да нет да да нет да да нет да да нет да да нет
да да нет да да нет да да нет да да нет да да нет да да нет да да нет да да нет да да нет
да да нет да да нет да да нет да да нет да да нет да да нет да да нет да да нет да да нет
да да нет да да нет да да нет да да нет да да нет да да нет да да нет да да нет да да нет
да да нет да да нет да да нет да да нет да да нет да да нет да да нет да да нет да да нет
да да нет да да нет да да нет да да нет да да нет да да нет да да нет да да нет да да нет
да да нет да да нет да да нет да да нет да да нет да да нет да да нет да да нет да да нет
да да нет да да нет да да нет да да нет да да нет да да нет да да нет да да нет да да нет
да да нет да да нет да да нет да да нет да да нет да да нет да да нет да да нет да да нет
да да нет да да нет да да нет да да нет да да нет да да нет да да нет да да нет да да нет
да да нет да да нет да да нет да да нет да да нет да да нет да да нет да да нет да да нет
да да нет да да нет да да нет да да нет да да нет да да нет да да нет да да нет да да нет
да да нет да да нет да да нет да да нет да да нет да да нет да да нет да да нет да да нет
да да нет да да нет да да нет да да нет да да нет да да нет да да нет да да нет да да нет
да да нет да да нет да да нет да да нет да да нет да да нет да да нет да да нет да да нет
да да нет да да нет да да нет да да нет да да нет да да нет да да нет да да нет да да нет
да да нет да да нет да да нет да да нет да да нет да да нет да да нет да да нет да да нет
да да нет да да нет да да нет да да нет да да нет да да нет да да нет да да нет да да нет
да да нет да да нет да да нет да да нет да да нет да да нет да да нет да да нет да да нет
да да нет да да нет да да нет да да нет да да нет да да нет да да нет да да нет да да нет
да да нет да да нет да да нет да да нет да да нет да да нет да да нет да да нет да да нет
да да нет да да нет да да нет да да нет да да нет да да нет да да нет да да нет да да нет
да да нет да да нет да да нет да да нет да да нет да да нет да да нет да да нет да да нет
да да нет да да нет да да нет да да нет да да нет да да нет да да нет да да нет да да нет
да да нет да да нет да да нет да да нет да да нет да да нет да да нет да да нет да да нет
да да нет да да нет да да нет да да нет да да нет да да нет да да нет да да нет да да нет
да да нет да да нет да да нет да да нет да да нет да да нет да да нет да да нет да да нет
да да нет да да нет да да нет да да нет да да нет да да нет да да нет да да нет да да нет

DADA NET

Text piece

JAAN MALIN

TARTU, ESTONIA

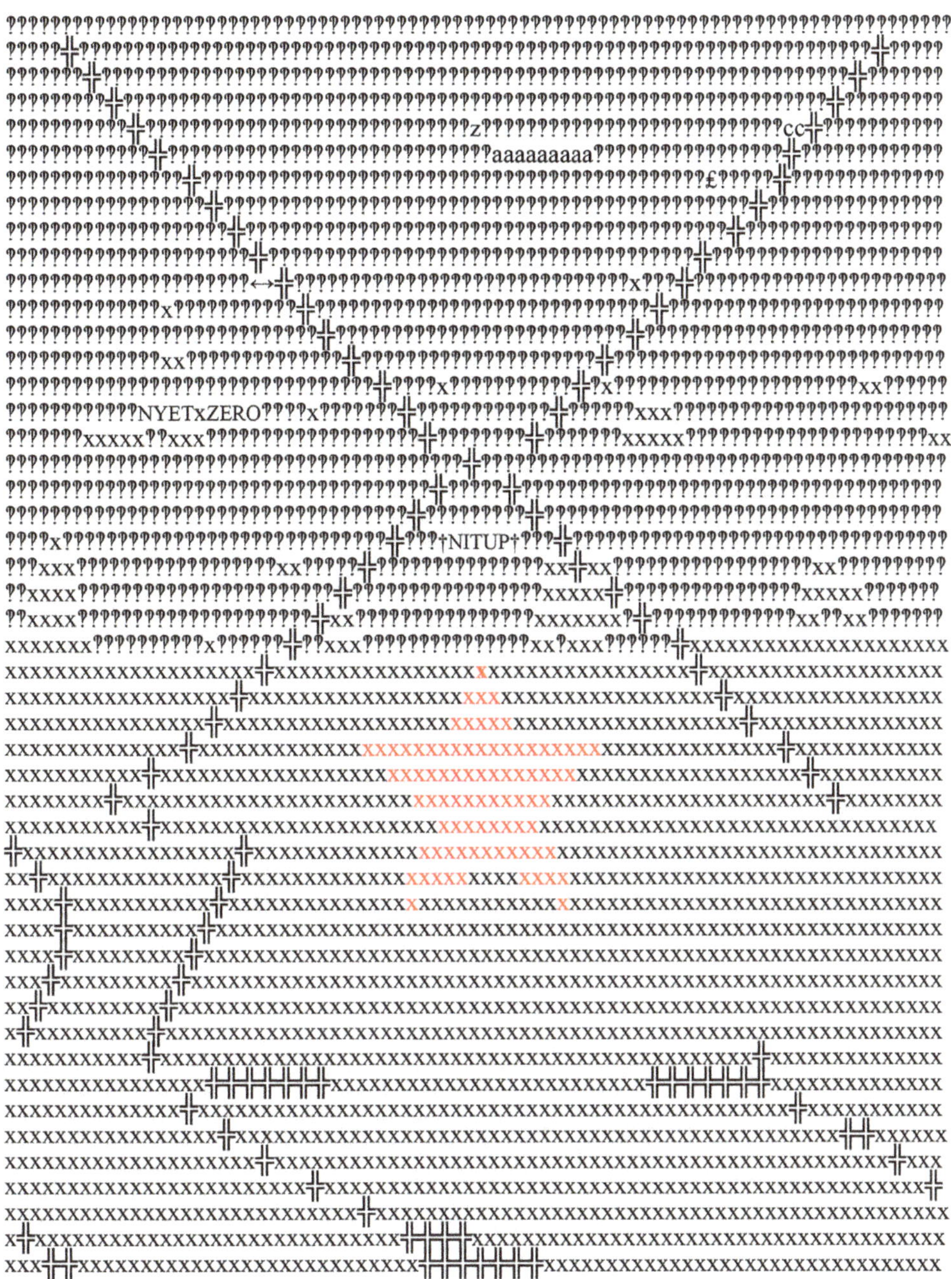

Text piece

POUL R. WEILE

BERLIN, GERMANY

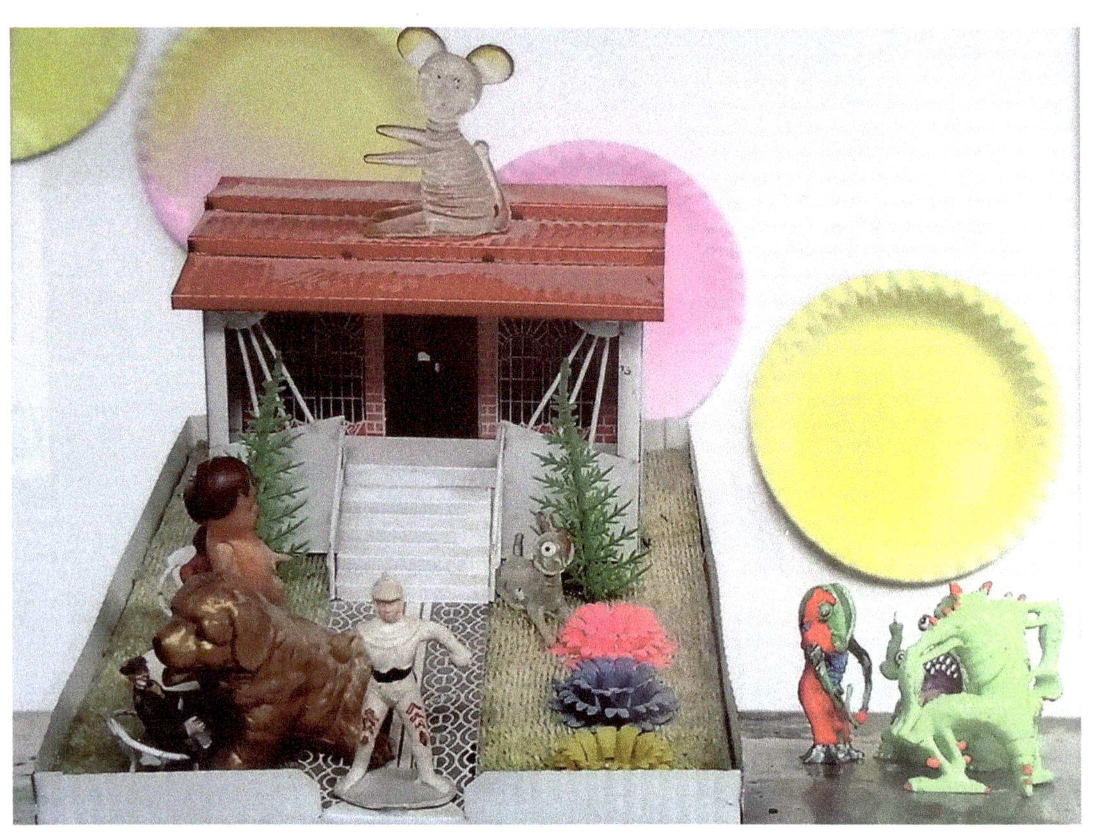

REAL POLITICS

C-print, 74 x 54 cm

RICH FERGUSON

LOS ANGELES, CALIFORNIA

13 WAYS OF LOOKING AT THEY

I
Upon waking, they don their masks of hate.

II
They squeeze off endless rounds
from their .357 Magnum Opus of Obliteration.

III
For breakfast, they eat serial killers.

IV
For lunch, they eat the hearts of the good intentioned.

V
Firebombing churches is their one true religion.

VI
They roll around in shit and mud,
then claim they're cleaner
than everyone unlike them.

VII
They're not your friend
until you're dead,
and even then, their allegiance is only temporary.

VIII
They breathe, sleep, and eat guns.
They fuck guns. Have gun babies,
then send them out into the world
to seriously fuck with you.

IX
The only thought on their small minds:
how to add a 666th Amendment to the Constitution.

X
Fascism is their only form of humanism.

XI
They unimagine the sun,
feed flowers handfuls of sleeping pills.

XII
Poison is their prayer,
the snapping of your neck, hymn.

XIII
Nothingness is the highway they drive
to get from one moment to the next.

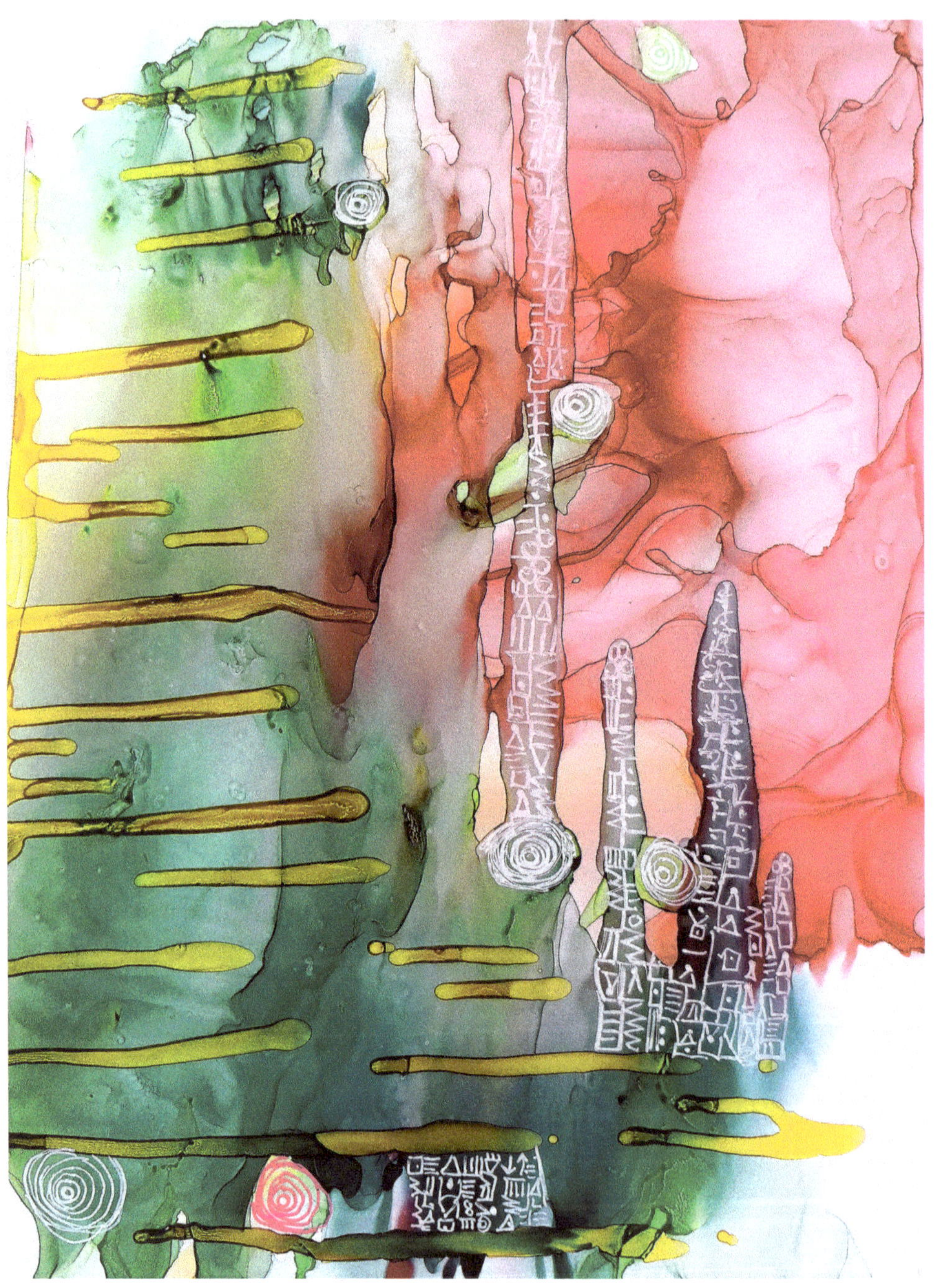

BELINDA SUBRAMAN

EL PASO, TEXAS

ENERGY PLAN

Mixed media (ink and acrylic), 3492 x 4656 pixels

RICHARD HUMANN

BROOKLYN, NEW YORK

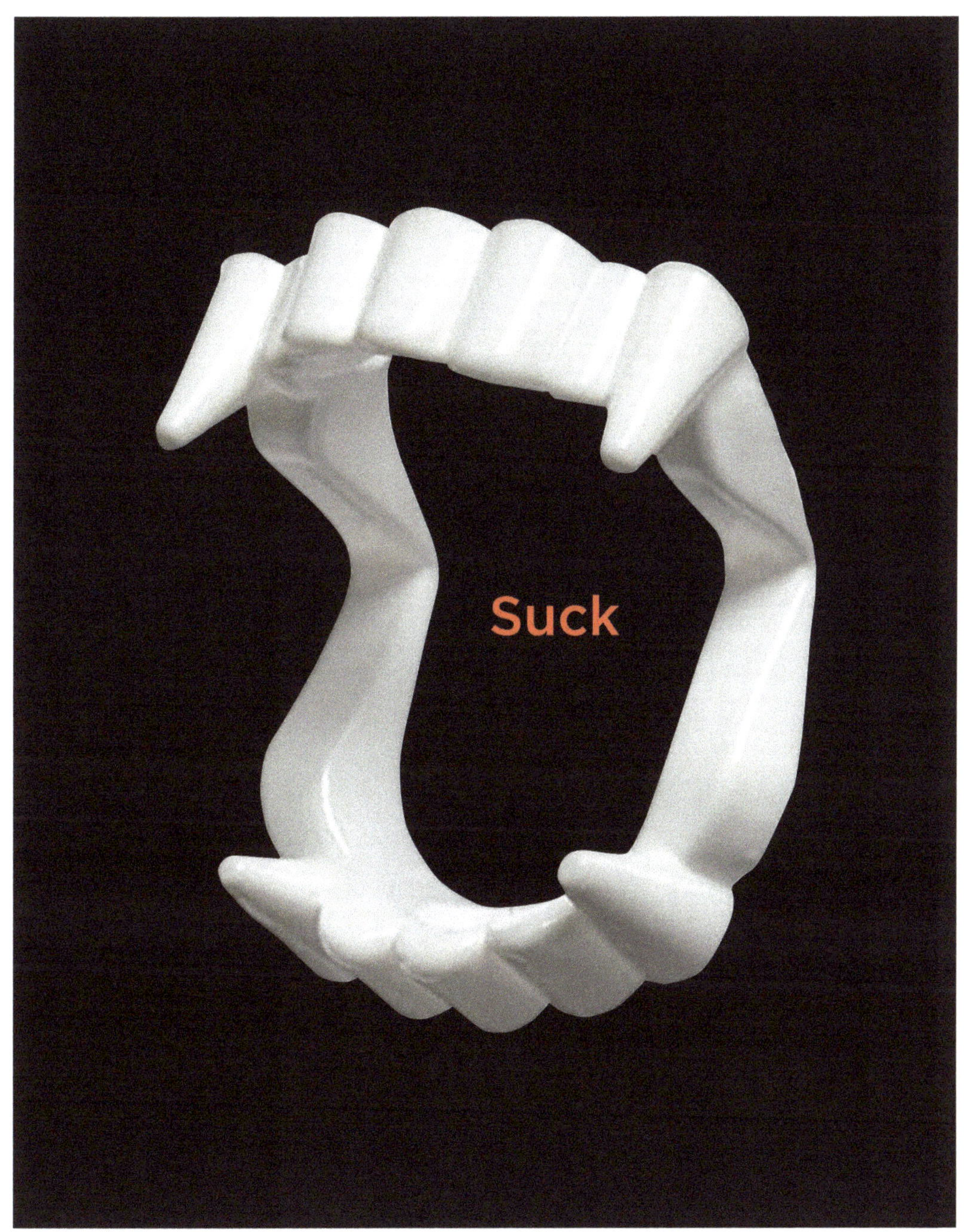

SUCK

Digital collage, 8 x 10 inches

PERE SOUSA

BARCELONA, SPAIN

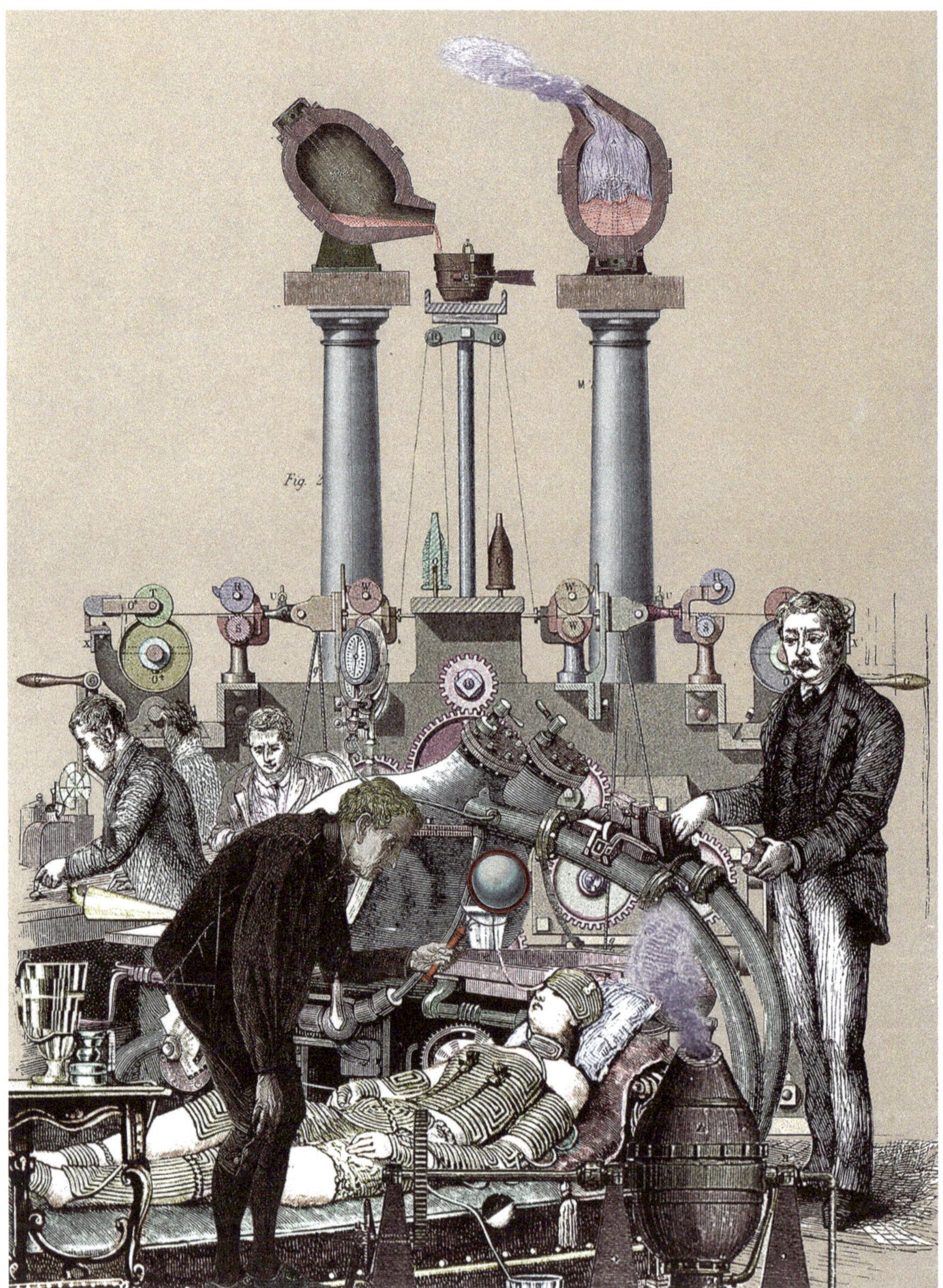

ZERO ZERO

Mixed media, 3000 x 4000 pixels

LYNNEA VILLANOVA

BROOKLYN, NEW YORK

RADIX, REDUX

01111010 01100101 01110010 01101111
    z   e   r   o

When I was young—a zero was a zero
    defined by what followed
    zeros netted nothing

We played in the infinite between 0 and 1
    1/2, 1/4, 1/8—on and on before you get to 1

Bit by bit
in system clock time
    zeros added up to much more
        greater than the sum of their non-parts

Permuted, transmuted
    defying what was literally constant

The 8-bit byte
    took a bite out of significant figures
    and chipped our living stability

Can you break bits into bits?

Now zero—the digital dam-master
    controls floating-point floodgates
        on, off
        no ebbs, only flows
        dynamism, but within its range

Nothing floats errant in a constant array of constants

No more play between pillar and post
    electrons move—or not
    in circuits

Human hubris
    thinks this tames the universal circus
    of all that is

Net zero—steady states soldered by human hands
    infinitely imaginary

LUIZ MORGADINHO

LISBON, PORTUGAL

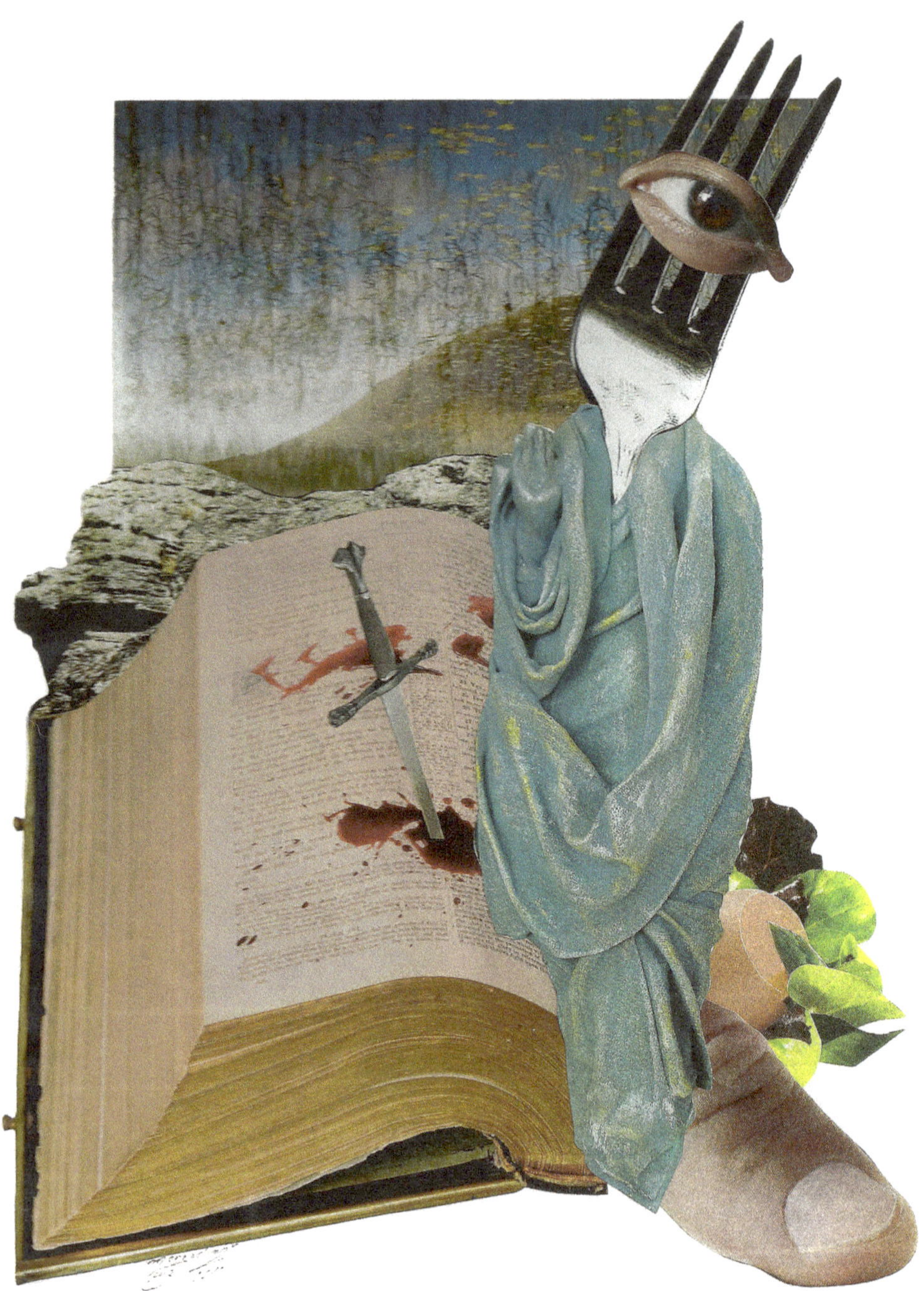

SCRIPTURES CONTRADICTIONS

Collage on cotton paper and various magazine clippings, 21 x 29 cm

LIZ AXELROD
ALBUQUERQUE, NEW MEXICO

NO ONE HERE GETS OUT ALIVE

I've got a Frida Kahlo art box
with green sequined skeletons
guarding dead things on my desk.
Wanna pray to the fluids and the skulls?

Not sure what to ask for.

I don't belong here
and Spellcheck is killing me.
Why am I so scared?
Why am I stuck pondering
The fall of Rome and the end
of HBO?

Final season—
I could have slept with Jon Snow.
I could have slept with Jim Morrison.
I smoked pot at Pere Lachaise
Grave sitting on Mr. Mojo Rising.
I am that LA woman getting old
and writing on the subway
on my iPhone.

Inspiration comes in spurts.
I want a star to spurt in me.
Really, it's been too long.
I'm well-worn and the sky
is not
quite falling.

Is Chicken Little in on this joke?
Fake is real and facts alternative.
So how do I teach plagiarism now?

Where is my savior?
Alexander ate the blade,
Rome killed Egypt's libraries.
When I die will my words
be homogenized by the ghosts
of Steve Jobs and Mark Zuckerberg?

You should see my scars
and the garbage I recycle daily.

JOHN S. PAUL

BROOKLYN, NEW YORK

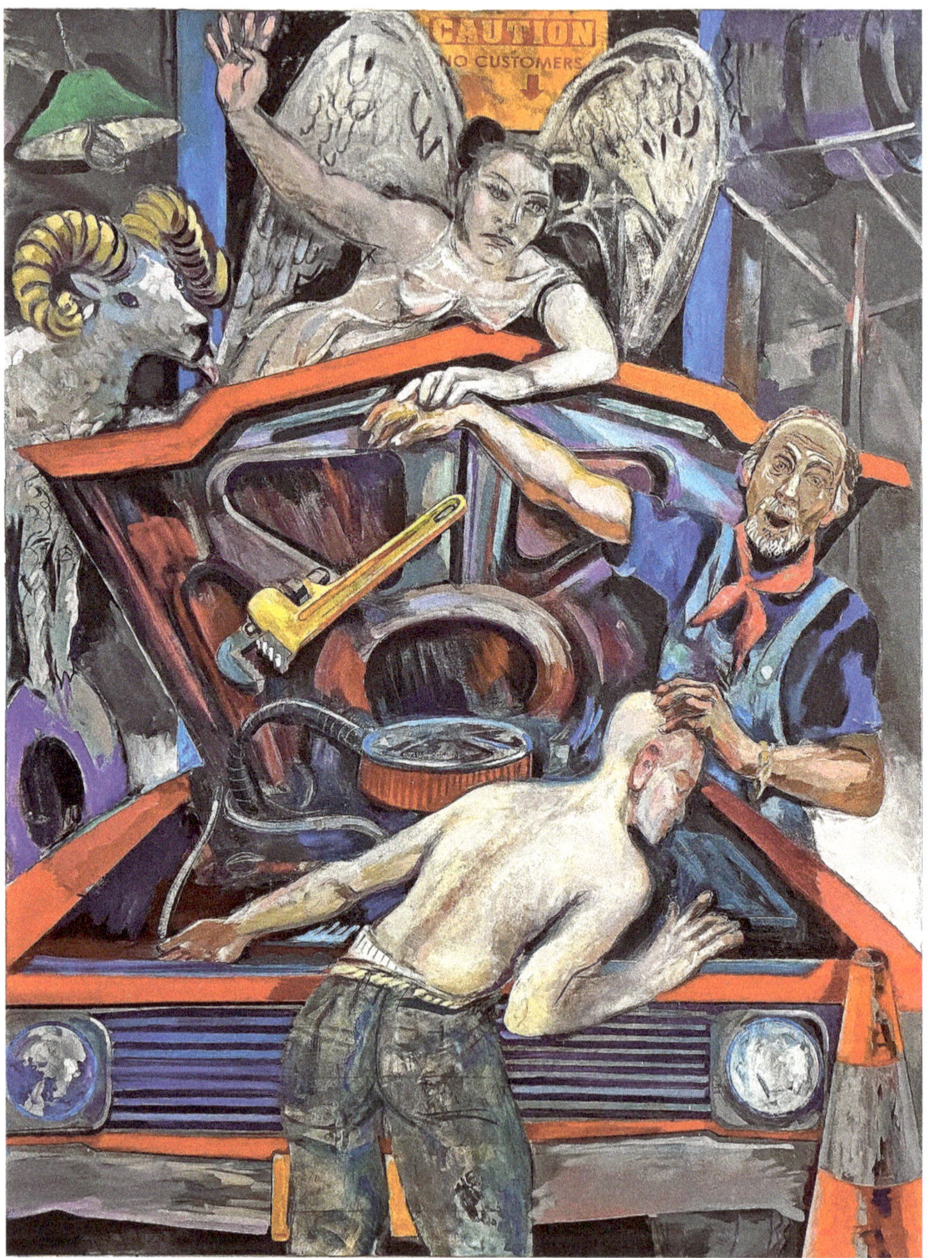

**SACRIFICE IN THE HOLY LAND GARAGE
(AFTER REMBRANDT'S ABRAHAM AND ISAAC)**

Oil on canvas mounted on panel, 59 x 77 inches

GEORGE WALLACE

HUNTINGTON, NEW YORK

SCATTERING DILL

when october comes, and the goose is on the wing, and the millwheel has done with its necessary murder on wheat and oat and rye and barleycorn; when the fat grapes along the merrimack have turned to rust or been crushed for wine, when the wealth of jersey's gardens has been put up for stores or preserved in jellyjars; when all the lost fruitage has turned to dust, and in the vinegar days of autumn the priestly fox that makes its den in the neighbor's field is deep in his slaughter, and the field hare with his red eyes and twitching tail lays dying; and in 29 cities out of thirty in this great alien continent we have planted ourselves upon and call home the mighty casey has struck out; then will the yellowjacket hum in his nest, drone to the yellowjacket queen; then will the beadle-eyed crone, summer ceremonies complete, return to her roosting place, clever and keen and spent; and all the stray green apples that have not been eaten by horses return to grass and soil, ripe and foaming in their holy wretched fermentation; then will all the phantasms and lost souls rise like blue mist, lofty and grand, to the heights of the swaggering cities we have built in the direction of heaven (as if we could scrape the sky!), and envelope them in their benediction of fog; and the slice and stipple of glass, steel, and industrial might will give way to the great innocent scourge marching upon us anyway, nature's avenging harvest; then will we let the earth lie fallow; and put aside the plow; then will the lies and false abasements fail us, the sanctimonies and rote quotidians in which we sought refuge go the way of all flesh; then will we level our fields, and be humble before autumn; it is october in the land! in our time of plenty, in our time of easy waste, in our time of desecration and lip service to laws and legends and ramshackle scriptures; let the cheap covenants and depositions we have undertaken with the angel of death give way; let the fields lie fallow; let time do its healing work, and replenish the land; the land, which has patiently borne our spoilage and our glory and nourished us in our pride, let it do its work; the land! let us plant and scatter dill and cumin, and walk soft-spoken and mild out upon the great and good earth, greater than us; let us commend our bones and sweat and humility, in victory or defeat, to the borrowed land we have affected to command.

IGNACIO GALILEA

BRUSSELS, BELGIUM

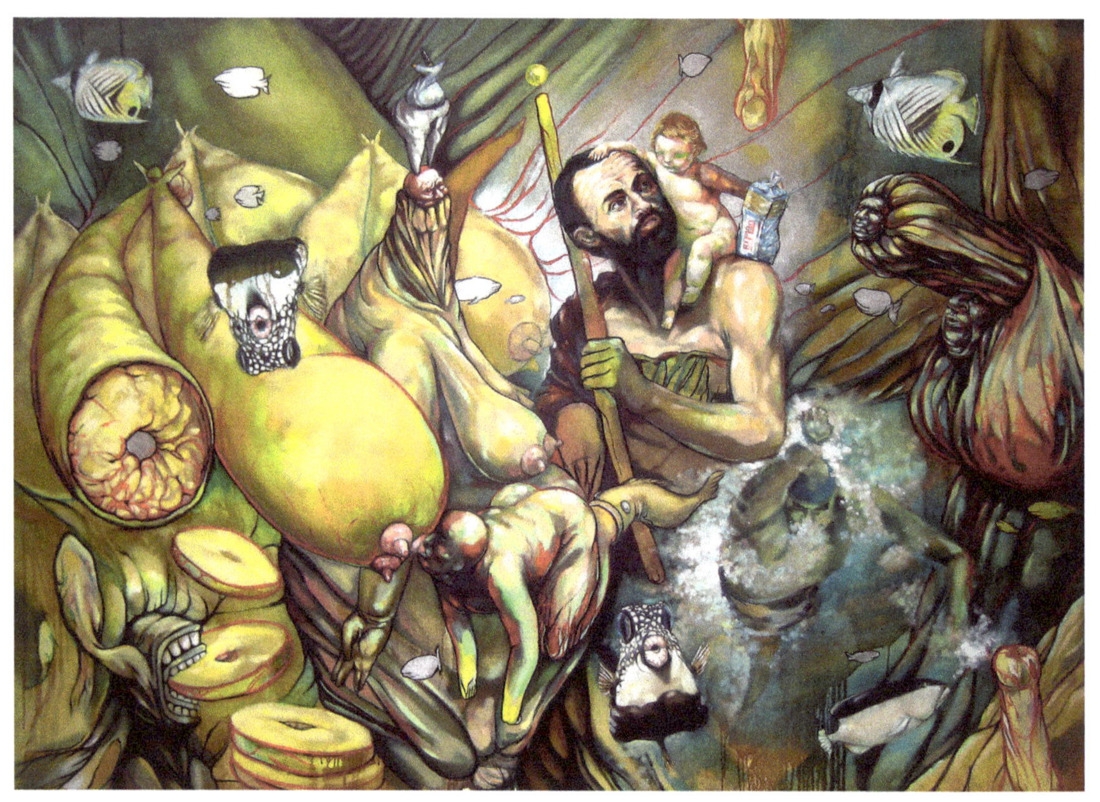

BUIT UNITÉ DE TEMPS

Oil on canvas, 201 x 137 cm

BRONWYN MAULDIN

GLENDALE, CALIFORNIA

GUIDER OF TOURS

Your Spartacus tour guide can be set to capitalism, communism, or nationalism. Bright-colored charts and maps will appear on the monitor built into the back of its head. It will match its pace to yours. It will answer queries sweetly into your bluetooth headphones, never once raising its voice in frustration at your blighted ignorance. A dispenser in its belly obviates the need to learn enough of the local language to order coffee and cake when your legs grow weary and your mind overloaded with facts.

The fascism setting is hidden in a sub-menu. Instructions for how to find it are available in certain online chat rooms, but it is not recommended as it tends to burn out the motor. Remember, you will be charged for any damage.

It guides you along streets loud with spray-painted debates begun in 1992 or 1914 or 1389 but never fully resolved. Your Spartacus provides a literal translation of the graffiti, but it cannot tell you whether it was painted in anger or with a laugh. It does not know the difference between a political rallying cry and stenciled advertisement for a transnational shoe company.

You approach an austere beige stone office building and your Spartacus tour guide speaks a chronology that runs from gestapo to secret police to national news agency. It steers you to a small square dominated by vivid neon playground equipment watched over by a bronze man in a fez. It recites the dates of the protests, size of the crowds, and how the uprising was quelled. It informs you, based on the setting you've chosen, whether this was a step forward or backward for humankind. It tells the number of bricks hurled and count of police hit, but it cannot tell you what a brick feels like in the palm of a fist. It cannot describe how our chests tightened with hope as we stood side by side shouting, Down with the red bourgeoisie! It does not know about the night that followed of rakija-fueled love-making with three different women in three different squats scattered across the city.

Your Spartacus tour guide will not take a wrong turn that leads past a lot where hillocks of rusty brethren await shipment to a corner of the planet where even tourists fear to tread to be broken apart, their greasy guts spilled out to leak into the local aquifer, wires set aside for reuse and the remaining metals smelted and hammered for resale as forks and spoons.

For an additional fee, it will escort you to a yellow stone castle where it plays a grainy black and white video of a woman lying in the center of a burning star. It recites the facts of this infamous performance without a sigh of either pride or contempt, for despite its intricate circuitry and advanced code, the soul of the Spartacus tour guide is carved from stone.

LYNETTE CLENNELL

FOLLINA, ITALY

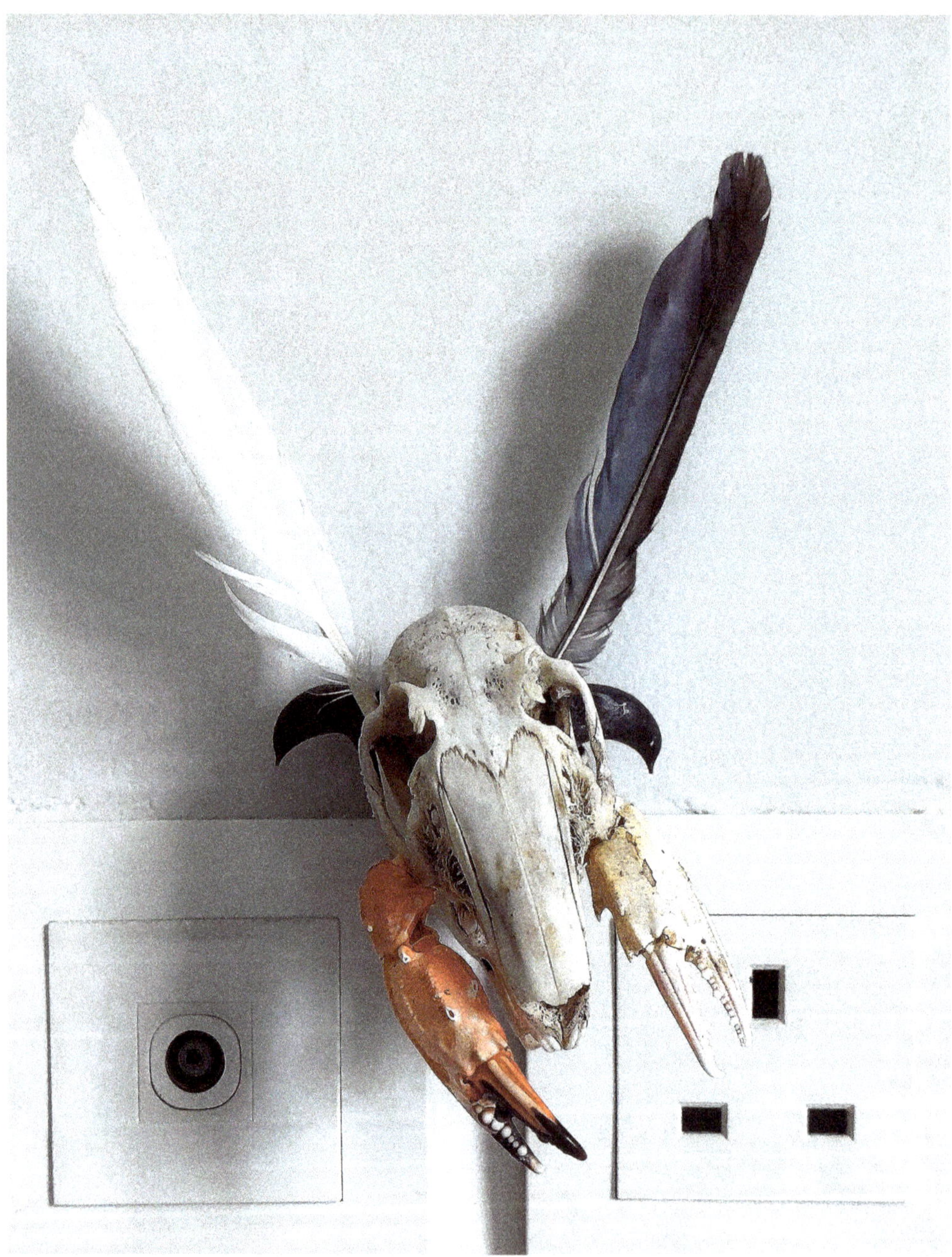

DIS-CON-NECT

Assemblage: rabbit skull, water caltrop nut, crab chelae and feathers.
7 x 10 x 6 cm sculpture photographed attached to electrical wall socket

BILLY CANCEL
BROOKLYN, NEW YORK

my NASCAR Town Co-Narcissist

was born at a red light amongst the crop
fields & chemical plants   never knew her
Acid Dad or his Cholesterol City boom
logic   then what happened? well we
heightened the antagonism   reverse
culture shock still up ahead   our
days of future pasting.   Big Big

    Government was always going
never gone   "please Dinosaur on
Life Support" we begged "no more
assumption songs we're but a crackhead
moment away from almost
single."   today we'll

    take a little more buzzword
salad though   as this is de facto
friday & we are classic bureautrash.

VALERIE SOFRANKO

PITTSBURGH, PENNSYLVANIA

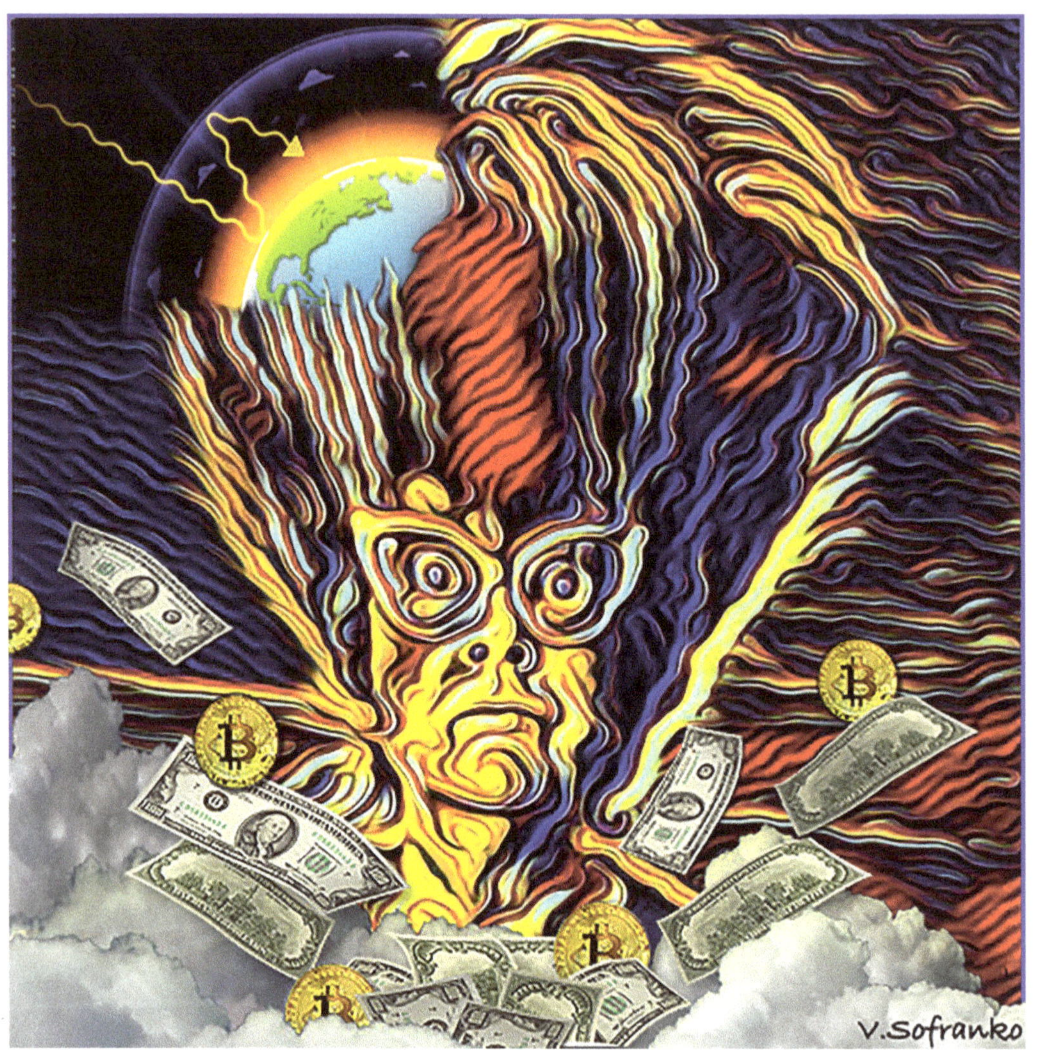

NOTENTIAL REALITY

Self photo, altered and applied Photoshop to create digital collage,
7" x 7" on photographic paper

SUZI KAPLAN OLMSTED
PORTLAND, OREGON

REPEAT DREAMS: LOST SHOES

I lose my shoes in countless dreams
And my purse
And the location of my car
Which in dreams is generally parked
In a weird section of San Francisco
Where the grid of streets is angled
So I can walk barefoot for miles
In the same part of town
Unable to understand why it keeps happening
This week every night I've been a medical student
Showing up barefoot without my books or schedule
One night I was wandering a house party shoeless
Another the neighborhood near school
Shoes were everywhere
But never mine
And I kept losing my bag
As I checked all the shoes trying to find mine
Then I'm in an Italian deli
Shoeless and bagless
And the giant in a wife beater behind the deli counter
Told me to stop being so provincial
Only country girls lose their shoes
In the big city
I'm no country girl
I defended
I just like to take off my shoes
Really, my grandfather had a shoe store
And my father had shoe factories
I've always had more shoes than I could ever wear
But I always think I need more
And my Buddhist teacher used to say
It's better to wear shoes
Than to try to cover the world in leather

MADO REZNIK

BUENOS AIRES, ARGENTINA

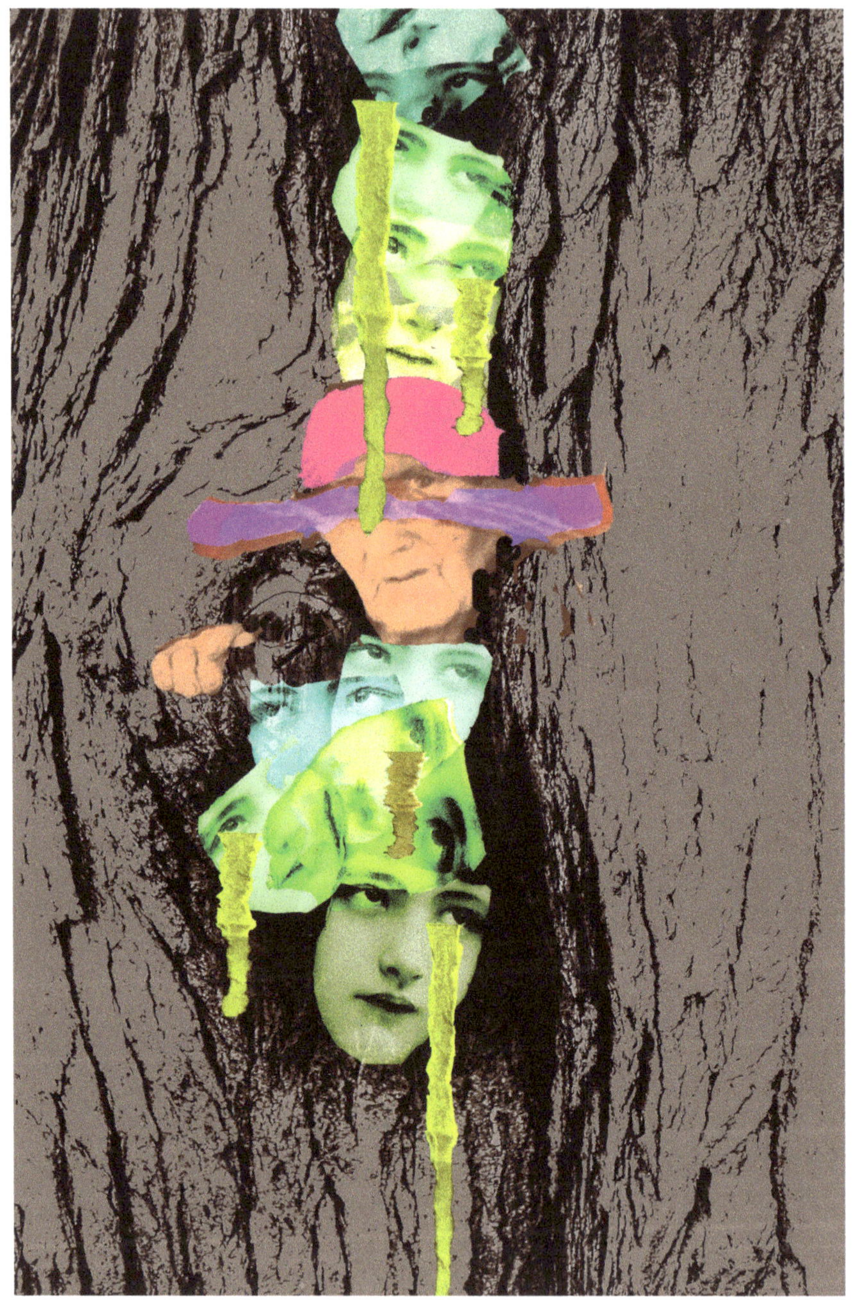

THE WEEPING STRUGGLE

Digital collage, 5.9 x 8.85 inches

ROSE KNAPP

MINNEAPOLIS, MINNESOTA

EPISTEMOLOGY

What can we truly know? Deductively,

Inductively, abductively? What are

The sources, the roots of our knowledge?

BÉNÉDICTE KUSENDILA

SINT-NIKLAAS, BELGIUM

#TANKA (GAS)

tip—a tank of gas—

toe. circle it fast and low.

with forest seeds—seethe!

would I breathe, or prize coal plants?

we CHOOSE our richest retreat

RICH STONE

SAN FRANCISCO, CALIFORNIA

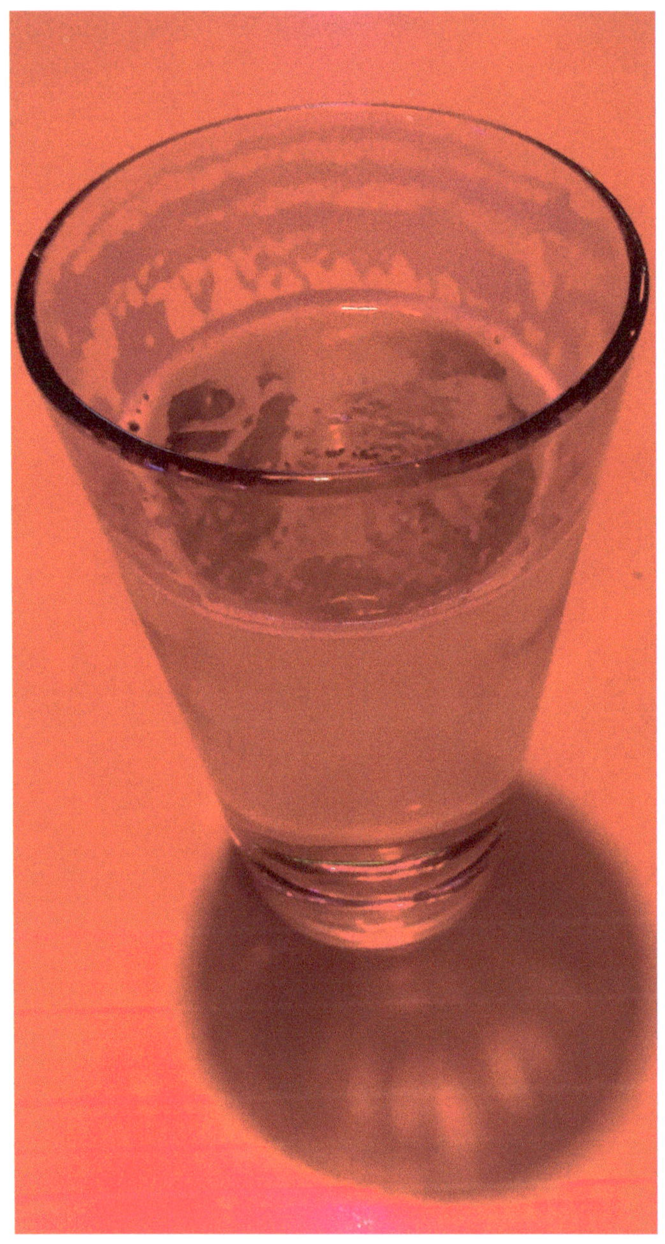

LAST CALL, CODE RED

Photograph

BENJAMIN ROBINSON

DUBLIN, IRELAND

COCKTAIL HOUR

Your fingers are moving over the cracked surface of a dried-up riverbed. Your fingers are sinking into clotted hollows. Your fingers are disappearing into a wilderness of wrinkles. The air is thick with obscenities and obsolete profanities. The air is thick with the sound of veneers peeling away. The sky has torn itself apart. There is a tissue of lies where the sky used to be. Your fingers are digging into mounds of bone meal. Your fingers are covered in corn syrup and hydrogenated fat. Your fingers are covered in blisters. The wind is whistling through the nostrils of a dying silverback gorilla. The wind is whistling through the blowhole of a stranded whale. Your fingers are moving through a mushroom cloud of broken pledges and promises. Your fingers are searching for an exit. Your fingers are looking for a way out. Your fingers are running through the stubble of an incinerated forest. There are bloody stumps where your fingers used to be. Your fingers have been bitten off by the dogs of war and are floating in a glass filled with carbonated whale blubber, crushed ice, triple sec, and fortified silverback gorilla.

LARRY ZDEB

TROY, MICHIGAN

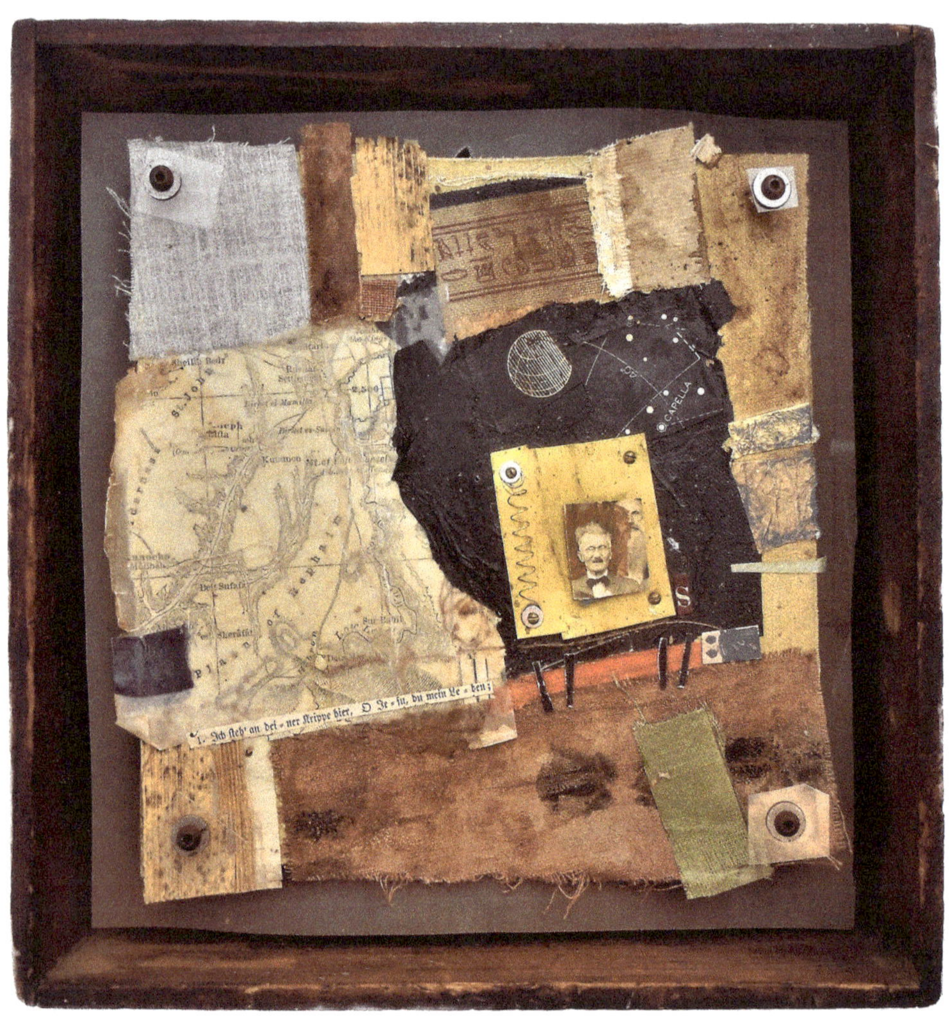

THE EXPLORER

Mixed media collage box made of wood, book parts, cloth, paper, fasteners, and spring,
12 x 12 x 3 inches

JOHN OLSON

SEATTLE, WASHINGTON

ONTOLOGY FOR LUNCH

That photograph of Earth taken from space by Bill Anders of the Apollo 8 crew on Christmas Eve 1968 with an 80-mm Hasselblad lens and which famously appeared on the cover of the *Whole Earth Catalogue* in the spring of 1969 was a powerful image it blew people's minds that beautiful marbled planet is us our home how small how tiny in the black void of space is what now a memory a forgotten dusty metaphor the Zeitgeist has changed it's a hedge fund investor now in a red Ferrari

If all the molecules and atoms and chemicals that comprise my body my being and all the adaptations to the conditions of this planet have been finely balanced & interlaced over a millennia of constant flux disruption and change aren't I isn't everyone the planet thinking about itself and can we extend this further to say we're the universe conscious of itself articulating itself recording itself discovering itself oceanic warming is impacting even remote Palau nobody knows what consciousness is epiphenomenon or freakish bouillabaisse in the bowl of the mammalian skull but where does that leave fungus it serves as a communication network for trees must be some form of intelligence there some days there's a deep despair and some days there's a sense of fatalistic acceptance

I don't think ice is a pretext I think ice is a context everything melts everything is melting and if it's not melting it's drying up like the Doubs of France where people now bicycle the river once flowed and fish zebra trout grayling pike and whitefish wiggled and mated and died and now what is it a bicycle path existence is ephemeral everyone understands that but then denial sets in and life becomes meaningful and happy yogurt for breakfast and ontology for lunch this is why I always carry a store of pepperoni grace comes to us in different ways for some it's a deep understanding of fire and for others moonlight on a lake

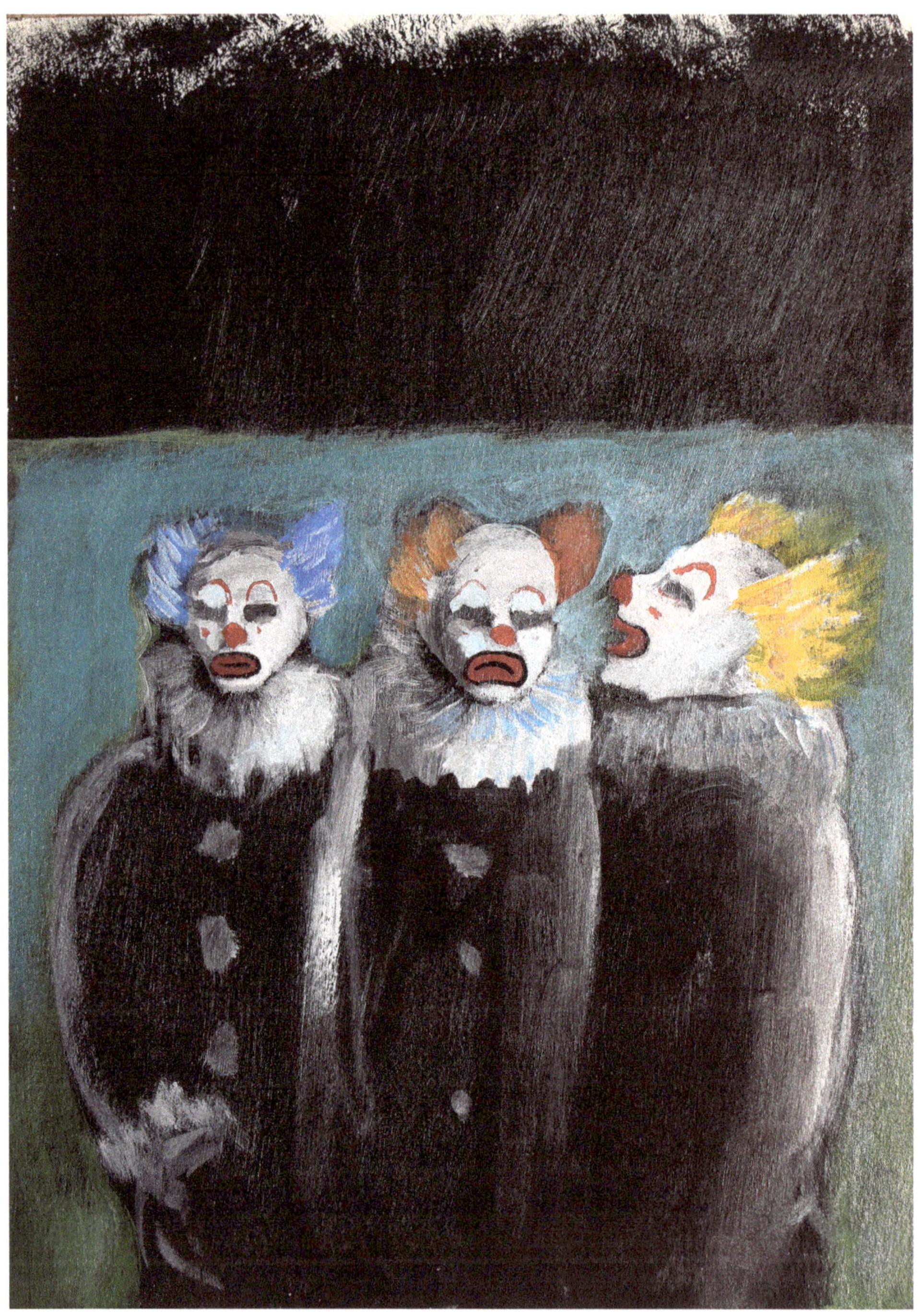

GO INSIDE IF YOU WANT SOME FRESH AIR

Acrylic painting on cardboard, 18 x 34 inches

YARYAN

TOLUCA LAKE, CALIFORNIA

EXHAUSTED

(Dedicated to Oxygen)

Council chairman advisory counsel

To the vice, the chair, the man

New breed, new greed between the lines

Put it to a vote and tow the vine

As there are finer things in life than breath

Drink the wine—end the whining

Watch the cows make a gaseous salute

To the pillage people, plunder wonders

Raiding the utility belt

Wrapped around Blue Mama Globy's waist

Wait for the wasted time to succumb

To the elaborate showmanship

Of tiny humanoids having remorse issues

dressed in polar bear outfits

Dancing the slippery dance downslope

At the power plant pageant

presented by blue death

And green hell enterprises

It's a surprise bending

of the wills and wants

of civilized abandonment

leaving traces of face paint, tears

MALCOLM EASTON

BERKELEY, CALIFORNIA

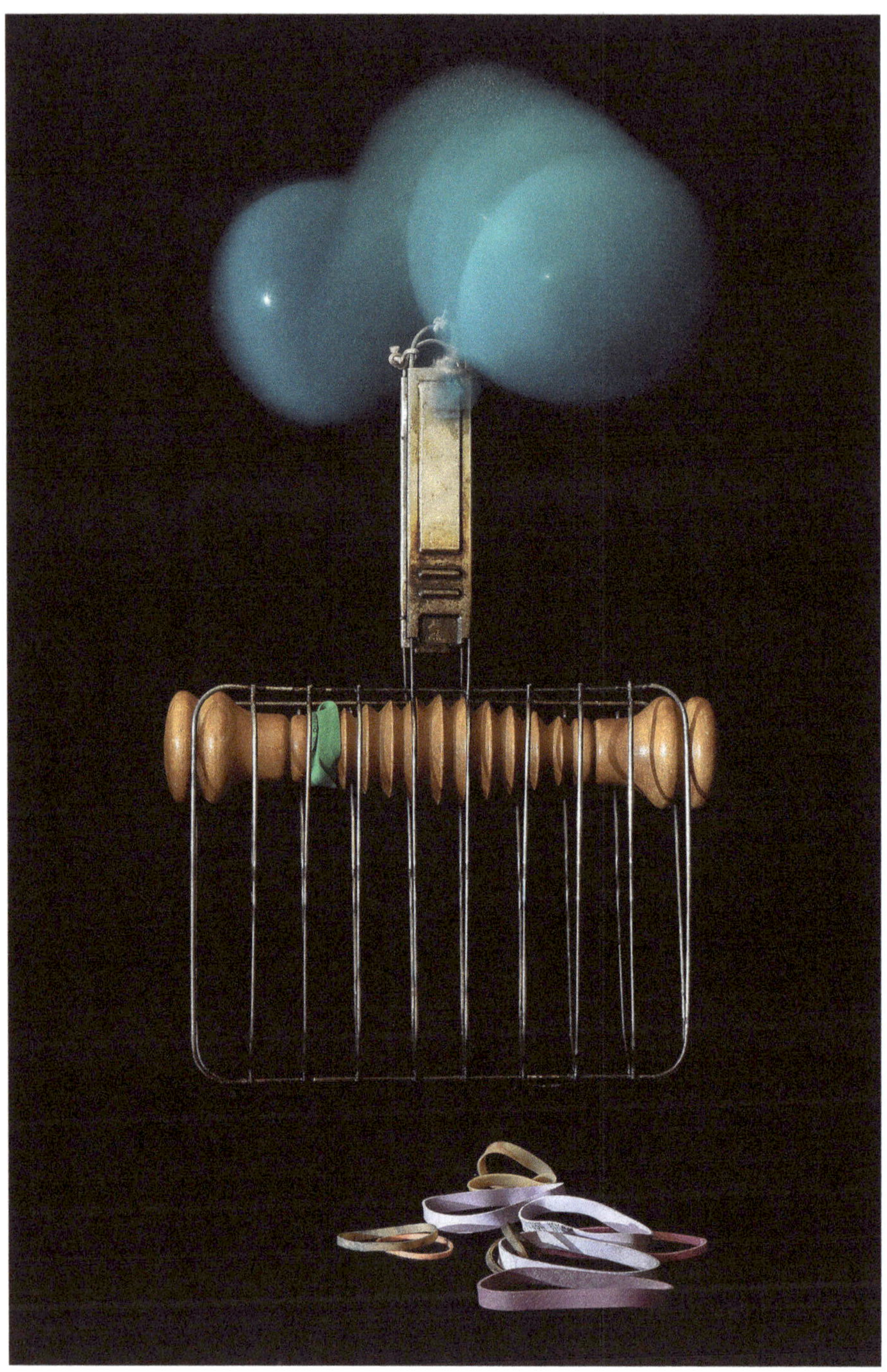

HOT AIR POWER

Basket broiler, wooden roller, rubber bands, blue balloon, hot air, 9 x 19 inches

NICCA RAY

NEW YORK, NEW YORK

RED BALLOON WARNING

Oh, these bleak times where are you red balloon? Have you turned away from hope? Have you become the bloody Nevada skies? A red blaze like no other I have ever seen. An end of the world sky. Can you tell me red balloon why the mob mentality seeks to destroy? How did it feel when they burst you and your skin pruned and you watched yourself deflating? Like our earth. Where is the young Parisian boy inside of myself, the boy who hung to hope even after you died, the boy who soon was embraced by all your colorful cousins? I want to hold the string you held I want to believe in the CEOs who promise toxic emissions will be zero by 2050. I am weary, red balloon, I watch you dying. Please don't shrivel any longer. I'll give you all my breath. I'll make you buoyant. Please, just bring us to light.

ANNA GABRIELLE O'MEARA, ANTHONY COX, PATRICK FORSYTHE

SEATTLE, WASHINGTON; CHICAGO, ILLINOIS; HINESBURG, VERMONT

I AM APOCRYPHA

by Anna Gabrielle O'Meara

My name is Gabrielle and I expect the fear. I want you to write in my fingers. I want your vision in my head. I want you to remind me of who I am. I want to become me. I want you to be like a biblical angel, with all of the terror and all of the eyes.

It's your strength that makes me quiver. Solid, but you still buckle, I know. You shine when you need to, eclipsed by bureaucracy, stealing the words that were unsaid and keeping them.

You're enveloped by a library of fantasies, eternally excited by the very same love you've always held inside of you. Your love doesn't change; it's part of you. You say it's for me but I love your love because it's yours.

The living have the home-field advantage. Do the dead want that? Sometimes. But the living don't even know what ghosts are inside of them.

BETWEEN THIS AND THE NEXT NOTHING

by Anthony Cox

My fear has become something else. I like these still moments with you when I'm afraid of what you're going to say. And there's something about love, about being close to someone, that's like a dare. I love when I can smell my own self-destruction on people. I can even hold that thought in my head and know it as it's happening. But we fucked up, a bit. We just keep taking care of each other.

The universe is made of these little barbells. Everything is constructed from a separation so you can never know the One. You only see every word fail in time and the shadow of that becomes this suggestion of the One. Like a patch of sunlight on the wall. What do you call it? A shadow?

Everything I know about God I learned from Magic Eye books. You stare into nothingness and static until you cross your eyes, and this image pops out, but only in your head, constructed of all the phase shifts between meaningless pixels of data. So they tell you Hell is distance from God, and this world is everything distanced from everything else, but I'm telling you fear distanced from itself is God.

In the beginning was the Word. But the logic just begets itself. It's where the logic breaks that God pops up like a dolphin out of the static.

David Bohm said: "A Love Supreme" is a melody reiterated in every key. God's index file of everything that exists or can exist. This universe is just a hologram, where everything collapses into a single point. A single time. So time and space are just these images that exist in your head, and extension is the illusion.

It's either one or the other, probably.

IF YOU'RE READING THIS, YOU'RE TOO CLOSE

by Patrick Forsythe

I was right to be insulted / even before you started to defend your insult / but that really cemented it.

I grew up a bit, all at once, when I finally grasped (or rather, let go of) the concept of justice (or rather, its total impossibility). If you're reading this, you're too close. Such an equilibrium would require the unjust undone, not the cheapo atonements we settle with in our daily lives and criminal justice system. Criminal. Maybe it feels good enough; maybe you can get over it when someone hurts your feelings or mutilates your body; maybe you lashed back and inflicted more of the same and tucked yourself into bed petting your the temple, saying, shhhhhh, baby, justice was served, justice exists, shhh, shhh, shhh, don't you know that for every action there's an equal and inverse who gives a fucking shit; what my heart craves is un-action, undoing, scifi paradox shit, the same as everyone else deep down, please; dear god, let me to have never have had to know I exist; I promise I'll keep calling you "dear" and check in every now and then if you do <3 Go ahead and settle on a reactionary tangent and give yourself a second to go off on it before coming back. If you're reading this, you're too close, I know you've taken the plunge yourself, or maybe you're as good at compartmentalization as my therapists have encouraged and can limit this to little dips in and out. No, I'm no better or more enlightened, but at least I learned to face hideous impossibilities instead of ducking in and out of scripture or psychosocial shadowplay shit, shit! Letting that shell drop from the ego is a dive into an abyss of radical horror and acceptance, and it further fucks you up real, real bad, but an ideal society is only possible if comprised of a citizenry as further fucked up real, real bad in the same ways as me, and they'll all want to gather together in a big conference hall with me in the center and they're hugging me so hard and love me so much and so totally I-and-I never had a choice and none of them will have ever had choices of their own, a prerequisite to the nothingness their embrace smushed me into; a jam of human nothingness squelching through a crowd of jostling, hot, loving bodies tightly packed into our chosen no-choice industrial oven set to blaze itself clean.

JAN HERMAN

NEW YORK, NEW YORK

ON LOAN

When our beginning and our end
   are both on brokered loan
from a twisted clown who sends
   bolts of lightning down, bad luck.
When captains of the rising seas
   claim mastery, and the world
in all its finery is theirs,
   we who know its agonies
are left to cope. Even our
   miseries are a taunting hope.
When green and rolling fields
   and all our merry city streets
are gone, such is sorrow.
   Weep then new lines to sail upon.

LOIS KAGAN MINGUS

NEW YORK, NEW YORK

SURROUNDED

Eat the abyss.
Dance it. Sing it.
Celebrate
the edge of it.

It's waiting for you
to untwist its braids or comb its
strands.

The continuing narrative
stares at you,
pushing you, pushing you.

Different degrees of color wait.
Walk into it
and do something about it.

JANE ORMEROD

NEW YORK, NEW YORK

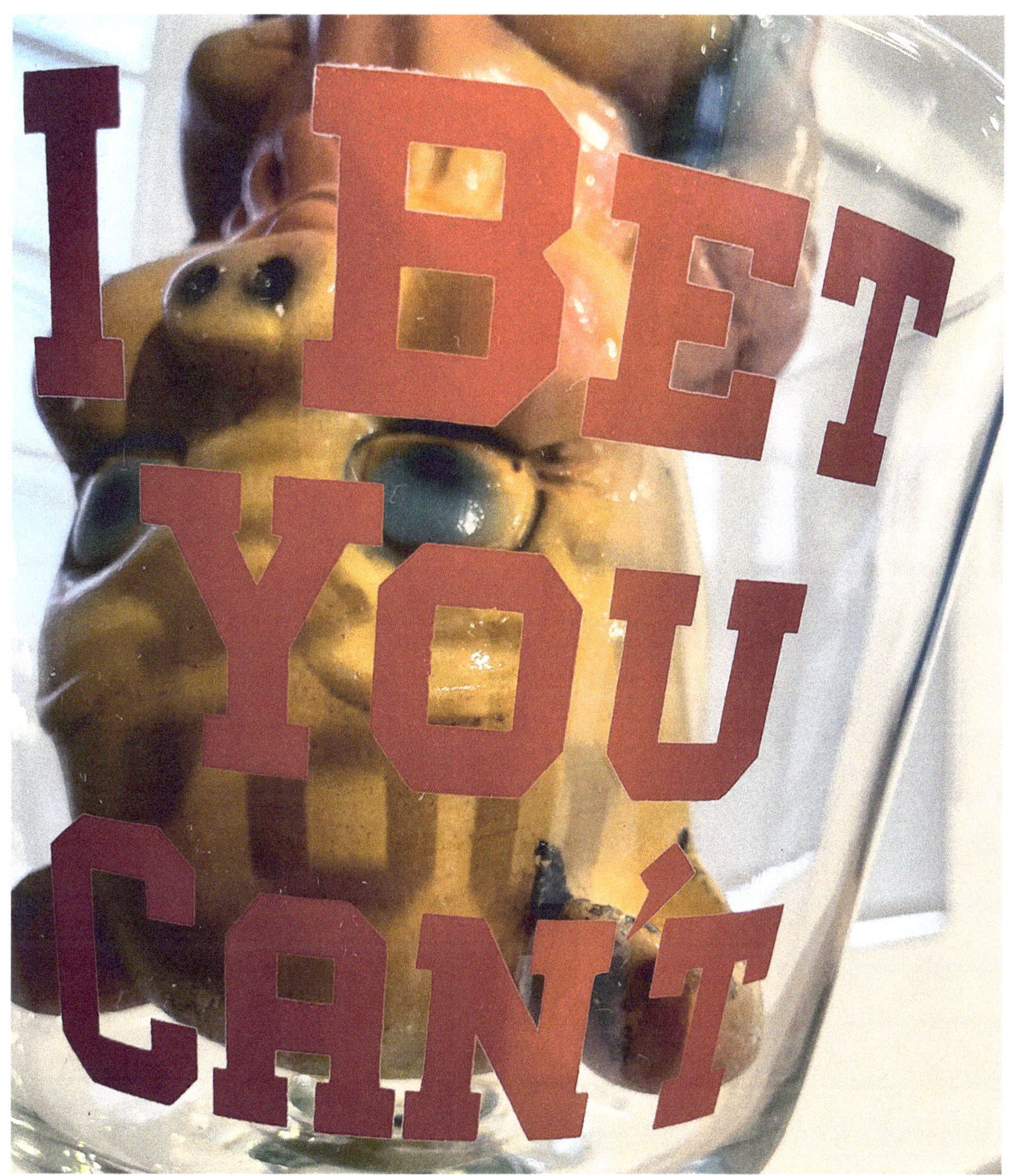

I BET YOU CAN'T

Mixed media, 1300 x 1473 pixels

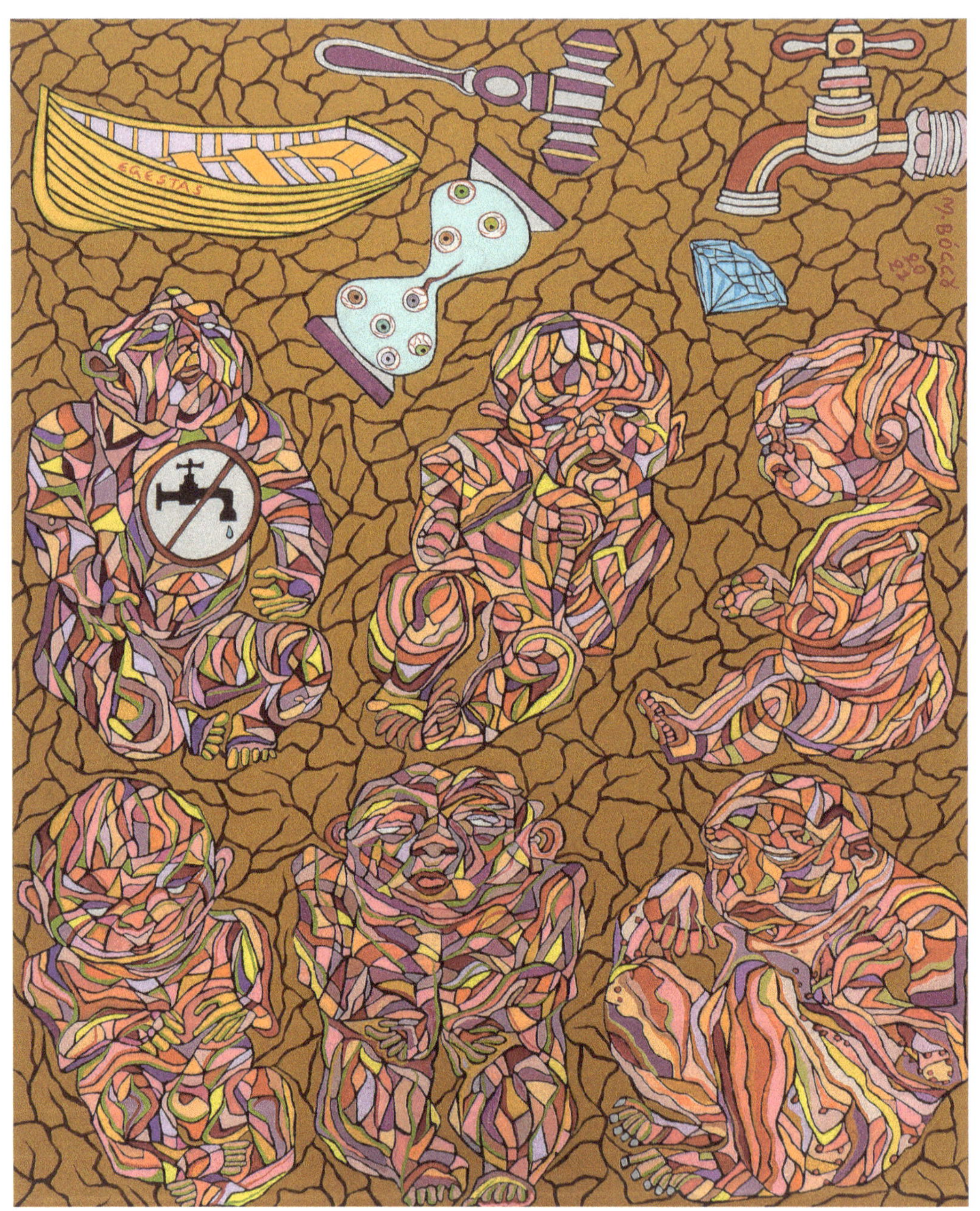

AUCTION FOR A SOCIETY'S DEATH

Acrylic on canvas board, 40 x 50 cm

DUSTIN NELSON

MINNEAPOLIS, MINNESOTA

WYRM

there's no understanding in vivisection
scale networks beautiful
pre-exsanguination
but dominant post-
asteroid forms
never knew the pore-filling horror
of hopping mammals
desert parch baked in-bone
dirt sunk like deep-sea
divers staring back up
the canal they already braved
before the maw
they can see
the only liquid
that keeps them alive
is you

MARTIN H. LEVINSON

RIVERHEAD, NEW YORK

THIS IS THE WAY THE WORLD ENDS

A half-starved dove with hardly
any feathers flew past my window
today before crashing wildly to earth,
the start of the seventh extinction.

Adios fish tacos and chicken fajitas
@ Antojitos de Michoacan. Au revoir
movies, museums, and *Remembrance
of Things Past*.

It's been a great ride through the rodeo of
everyday existence and it ends with a bang
not a whimper; irreconcilable grievances,
climate change annihilation,

As the cockroaches crawl amidst
debris from verbal bombast and
oil company braggadocio, the people
who remain march wordlessly
into the abyss.

SARAH LEGOW

PORTO, PORTUGAL

ON DEFEATING THE APOCALYPSE

The Apocalypse, he is a dickhead. He's in jail for aggravated assault and he once spat on my sister. I used to cut his grass as a kid, and he paid me in counterfeit nickels. They still worked at the slot machines, though, and that's how I won my millions. I named my yacht after him.

SCOTT WANNBERG

1953–2011

HARD

Night hides in a huge toothpaste tube.

Please lower your weapon a fraction of an inch.

Winter on every channel.

Hope we survive the main course.

Hard for people to see each other as they supposedly are.

Hi, I'm not a person, I'm an actor, just playing one.

At the vulnerable car wash on the precarious highway

they use water suspected of a major crime.

Night ghost writes its tell all.

The feature version fared badly on its initial airing.

Are we standing on someone's giant wedding cake?

The children of love

never actually make it to the bedroom.

MARC OLMSTED

PORTLAND, OREGON

sharp flat reports

homeless camp gunfire
meth medicine at the 7/11
—don't break up the fight—
you'd get your final dose
(a metal slug in the brain—
bargain basement SpaceX)
and now the curb shrine flowers
Day of the Dead candles—
where it happened
his picture grinning

ERICA ESH HENRY

THE WOODLANDS, TEXAS

BIOGRAPHICAL RECYCLING TANKA

(For ARP)

5 "I recycle! ME!"

7 Non-recyclers question why;

5 "It goes in the dump!";

7 "…Can't recycle THAT!" They balk.

7 Only dialogue recycles.

SALVATORE ESPOSITO

LONDON, UNITED KINGDOM

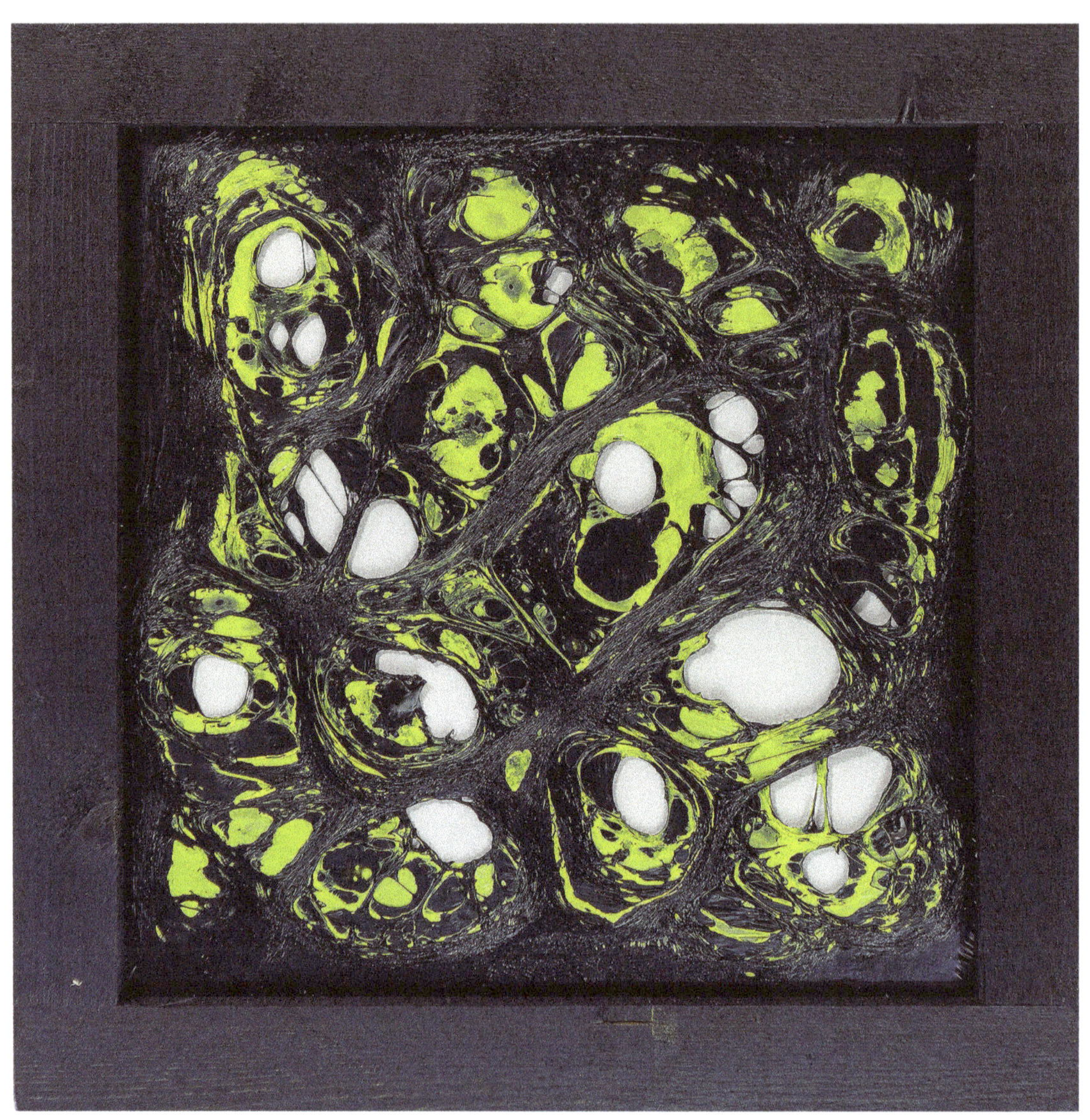

WIND'S UNSUSTAINABLE LIGHTNESS

Melted garbage bags framed, 50 x 50 cm

AMY BARONE

NEW YORK, NEW YORK

DARK SHADOWS

The menace coils toward tainted air.

It shrieks in wild riots and impaired cities.

Relentless storms uproot trees and darken streets.

An earthquake struck North Carolina after 100 years of calm.

Thick noxious smog stifles fresh breezes.

We look for refuge in eerie-colored skies that weep.

The pest silently divides on Facebook and Twitter.

Greed crushes true community. A game of dominoes ends badly.

We walk 'round treeless circles touched by clouds,

hoping, hunting, but not a cornflower to be found.

PAMELA PAPINO-WOOD
YONKERS, NEW YORK

COULD NEVER BE MORE

Truth is,

I don't like me like I like you

Full of wonder and beautiful eyes

I lie to myself and think you want me

The banter in your voice is percolating lust

But I must be delusional

You, meaning three, equals more than me

To compensate for the growing void

Black hole of emptiness and

Boring conversation

You must know, of course

With the weight of my heated stares

Imagining you pressed into me

Which could never be

Because I don't like me like I like you

Exposing the invisible

Scintillates amygdala's fear

So I run, look away, peering through peripherals

While clenching you in dreams

I mean your lips must be soft

and your body warm and hard

To balance my imbalance

Imperfections that are me

Parts I could never let you see

PATRICIA LEONARD

BRONX, NEW YORK

SHE LIVES IN ME

I remember the crashing waves at her feet as she spun me around the summer of '93. The sun-kissed pillows of her lips perched sweet memories. Honey eyes and long black hair glistened with salt water and sand as if she was a mermaid touched on land. Her toffee skin blemish free rubbed smoothly into me as I exited her womb 23 years ago. Coconut oil and white diamonds rush through my nostrils faster than bread fresh out the oven on a Sunday morning.

She died twice on the table while I signed a lease to an apartment across the country, her husband by my side. A little biventricular robot was installed in-between arguments of who had the rights to say how we would continue the path of life or death. Bluebirds sang in the background of my busy mind while the crows circled the future carcass. She thought it was the flu and went to sleep, as many women do. She was no more than 52.

ZOLTAN SIMON

BUDAPEST, HUNGARY

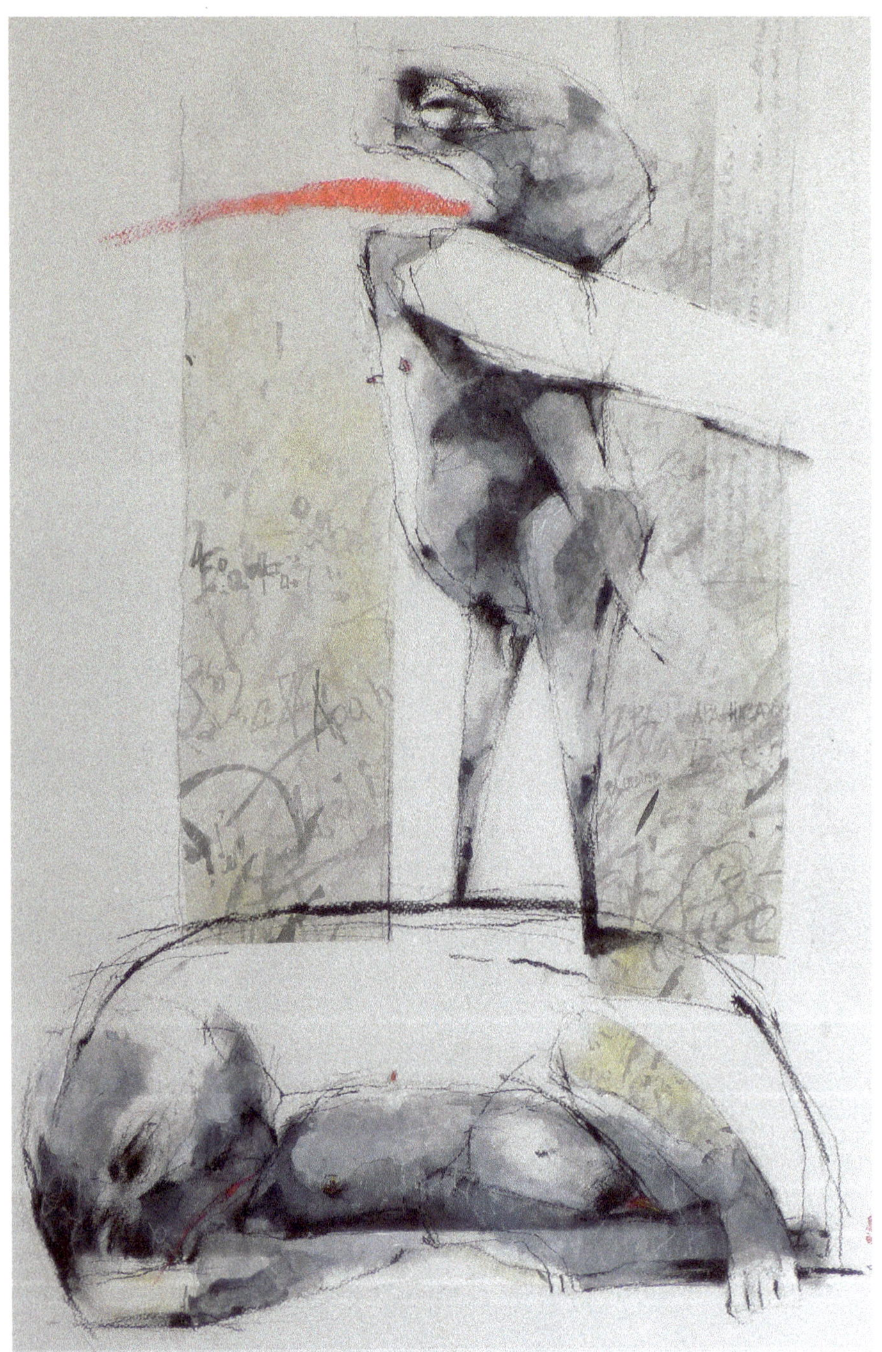

DAD COMING HOME

Acrylic and charcoal, 50 x 70 cm

FRANCINE WITTE

NEW YORK, NEW YORK

SEVEN BILLION LATER

And no one thought to bring enough food. My mother

Would have shuddered scrolling the internet, the far-off

countries that include even ours. You have to be ready,

my mother would say, even if it means sharing what's yours.

She was always the one to take the burnt lamb chop,

the broken heel of bread. She'd sit at supper, head down,

eyes sneaking peaks at us enjoying it all and that was her food.

I remember family vacations, long clamory drives, my mother

in the front seat doling out goldfish crackers from a baggie

because she understood the fidget of hunger. Once we were settled

with too much chew in our mouths to fight anymore, she'd turn back

around, having given my father the peace and quiet he needed to drive.

Then she would stare out the window, staring at the fields and fields,

the empty earthtable waiting for its invisible mother to take the wheel.

TERESE COE

NEW YORK, NEW YORK

HUIS CLOS

Clarity can't manage to put in an appearance,
reason's beyond damage and drops its last pretension,
and planet Earth has been declared a liability.
Marketing flights to rosy Mars, you stand quite isolated,
dreaming of a planet that is food- and oxygen-free.
As if you'd have a blast there. As if you were somehow whole.
Imagine taking acid inside a space suit. As if, as if, as if.

ANN FIRESTONE UNGAR

NEW YORK, NEW YORK

THE EARTH'S MAID SPEAKS

What kind of slobs are we?
Would you live a day in a filthy flat,
toilet stinking, floors gathering hair,
shredded paper shards, piles of used plastics,
air heavy with reefer residue,
water less than crystalline?

So, set your heads to clean
this really, really, really big house
so it doesn't become a true prison
hurtling through space,
carrying the foolish few
who think that life
on a rock called Mars
is the solution.

REGINA LAFAY BELLAMY

PAIGNTON, ENGLAND

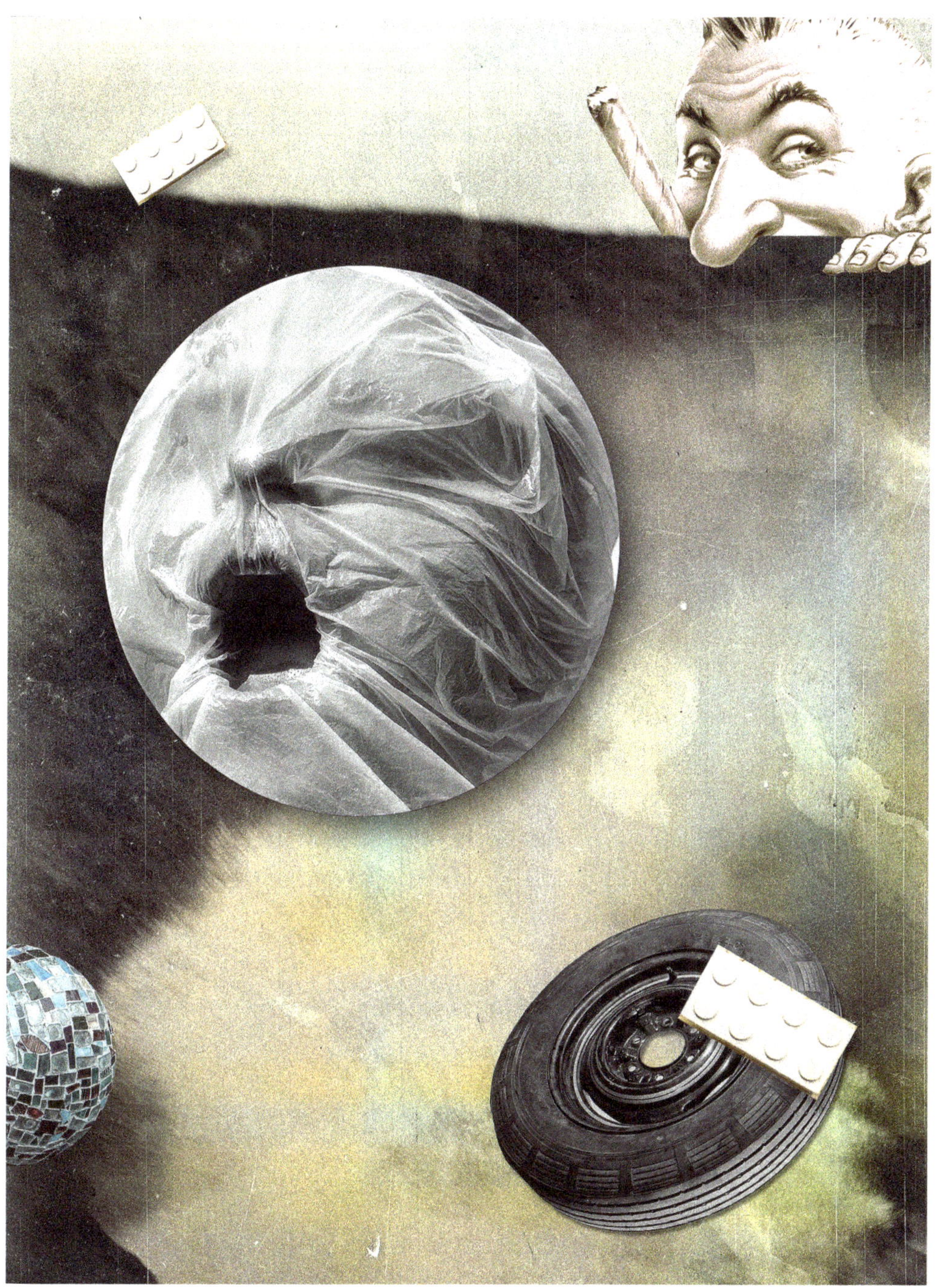

NYET ZERO

Digital collage, 8 x 11.25 inches

JOANIE HF ZOSIKE
MANCHESTER, NEW JERSEY

MY SLEEPY GORGEOUS LIE . . .

". . . the sky is green above you, my sleepy gorgeous lie . . ." Marcela Sula

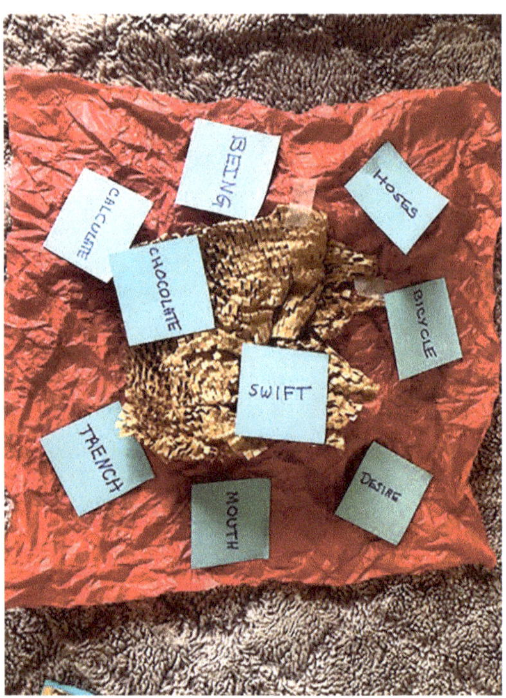

. . . wraps itself around my left leg and squeezes out essence of green sky, an angry blanket inducing involuntary screams. Gurgling, swaying, conniving to convince tempura on the table to absent itself and paint expected colors, none of this fooling around no more.

No time and place for limitations when infinity lies in corners of churches, synagogues and masjids. Infinity lies. Mouths perpetuate the notion of forward movement—a countdown universe belies the lie. And green sky? Counterfeit, an attempt at décor.

All the panels slide in my minka, there is no spatial permanence in a Nipon home. How did I get to Japan? Now, when only my mind is capable of flying; nor do I have the coin or balance to hoist myself into a jet to sit for hours in the sclerosis theatre of pressurized journeying—Hormones bore me eastward. Now is static. Speed has stopped. Glimpse limping on tarmac, suffer shame of inertia.

The lie. Nothing gorgeous about it. I can broad jump into Land of Coma. Float comes with effort when sweat covers me from head to toe. Cautious fast forward. I'm at the bank trying to reset my password, embarrassed by my profuse onion-scented extrusion. No confusion. Lie is light is life is lifting louvre window. Look out on green froth, which floats to the sky. I lie if I say I'm numb.

GERALD NICOSIA
CORTE MADERA, CALIFORNIA

POEM FOR THOSE WHO HAVE LIFTED THEIR VOICE

for Lawrence Ferlinghetti

It is a time of total lostness

When the soul of America lies frozen

In a powerless homeless shelter in Dallas

Or abandoned in the hallway

Of an overfilled hospital in L.A.

When I look to every mailbox

For offers of help

When the numbers on gas stations

Echo like the body count in Vietnam

When a Marine sergeant in a wheelchair

Who says "Don't kill"

Knows more than

The president of the United States

When Kenneth Rexroth lies buried

Under blood-red leaves

And the grass no longer grows and

The rivers no longer flow

For all the petrochemicals

You cannot write lyric poems

In a time of utter hatred and mean spirit

I have only my heart to offer

However little it matters—

But if I did not offer it

The sin would be compounded.

CLEMENTE BOTELHO

MILTON, ONTARIO, CANADA

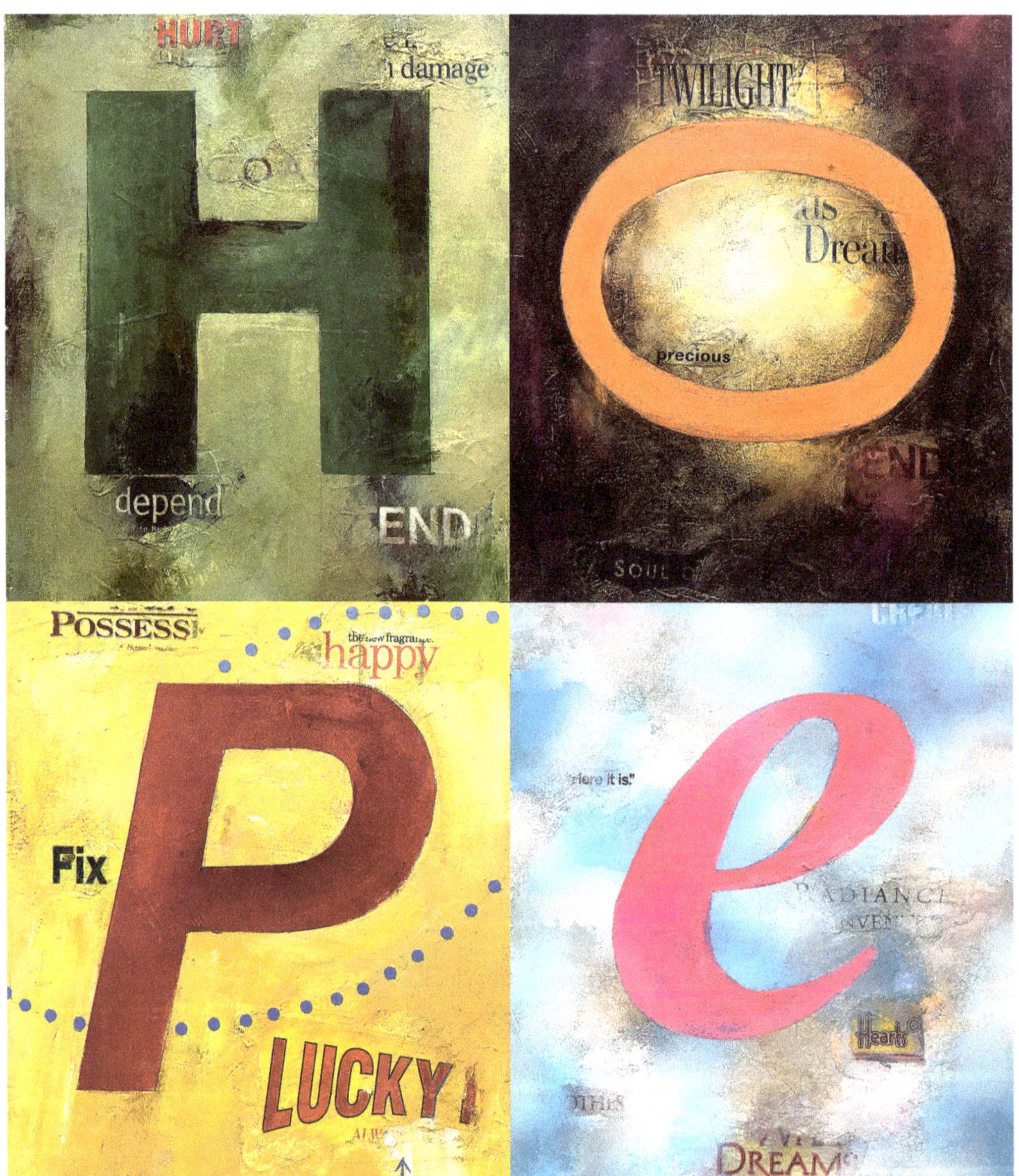

ENDANGERED SPECIES #3 (HOPE)

Acrylic, collage, 22 x 26 inches

ANNALIESE JAKIMIDES

BANGOR, MAINE

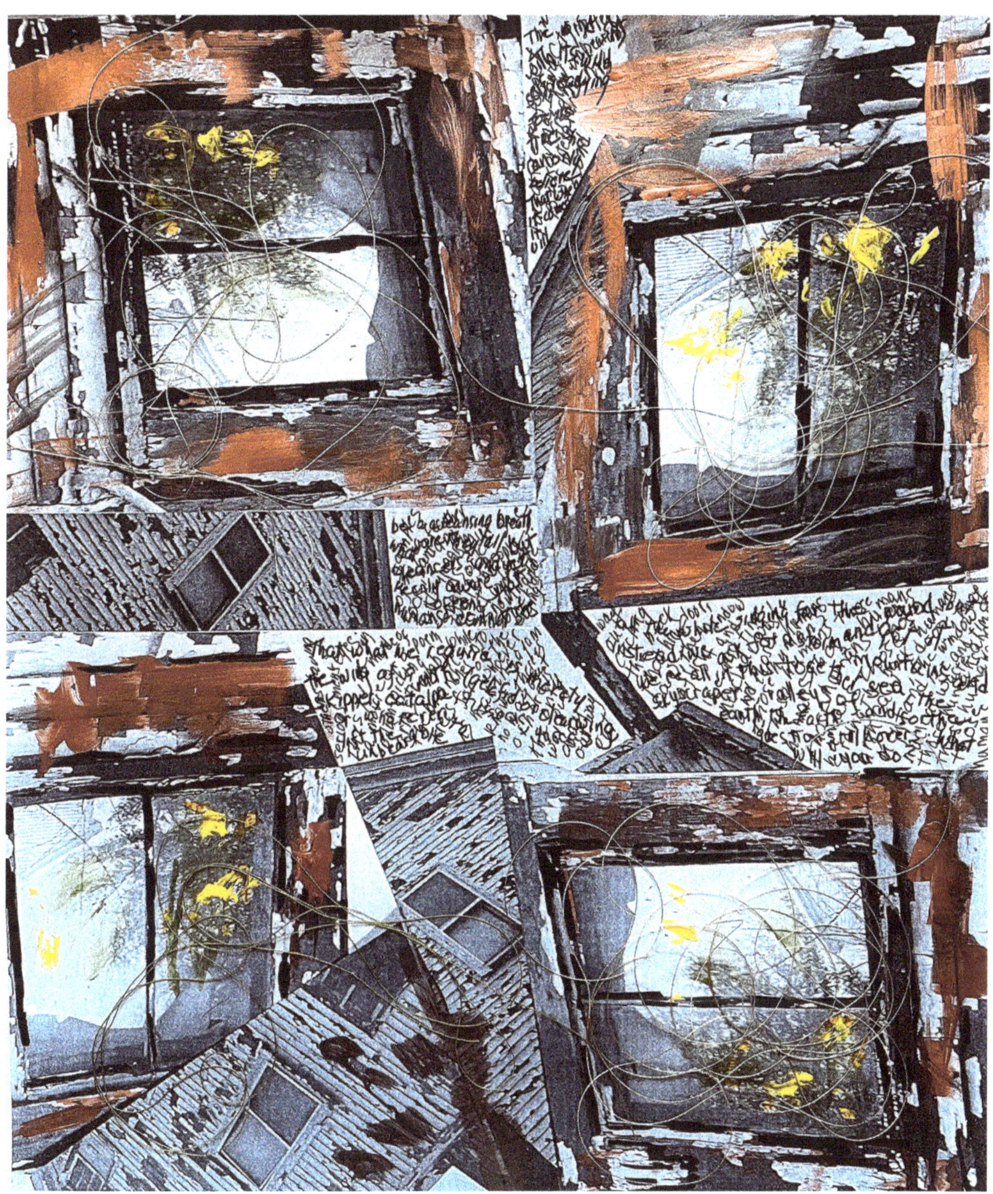

UNBEARABLE FRAGMENTS THE ONLY WAY OUT

Mixed media on paper, 8 x 10 inches

PETER CARLAFTES & KAT GEORGES

NEW YORK, NEW YORK

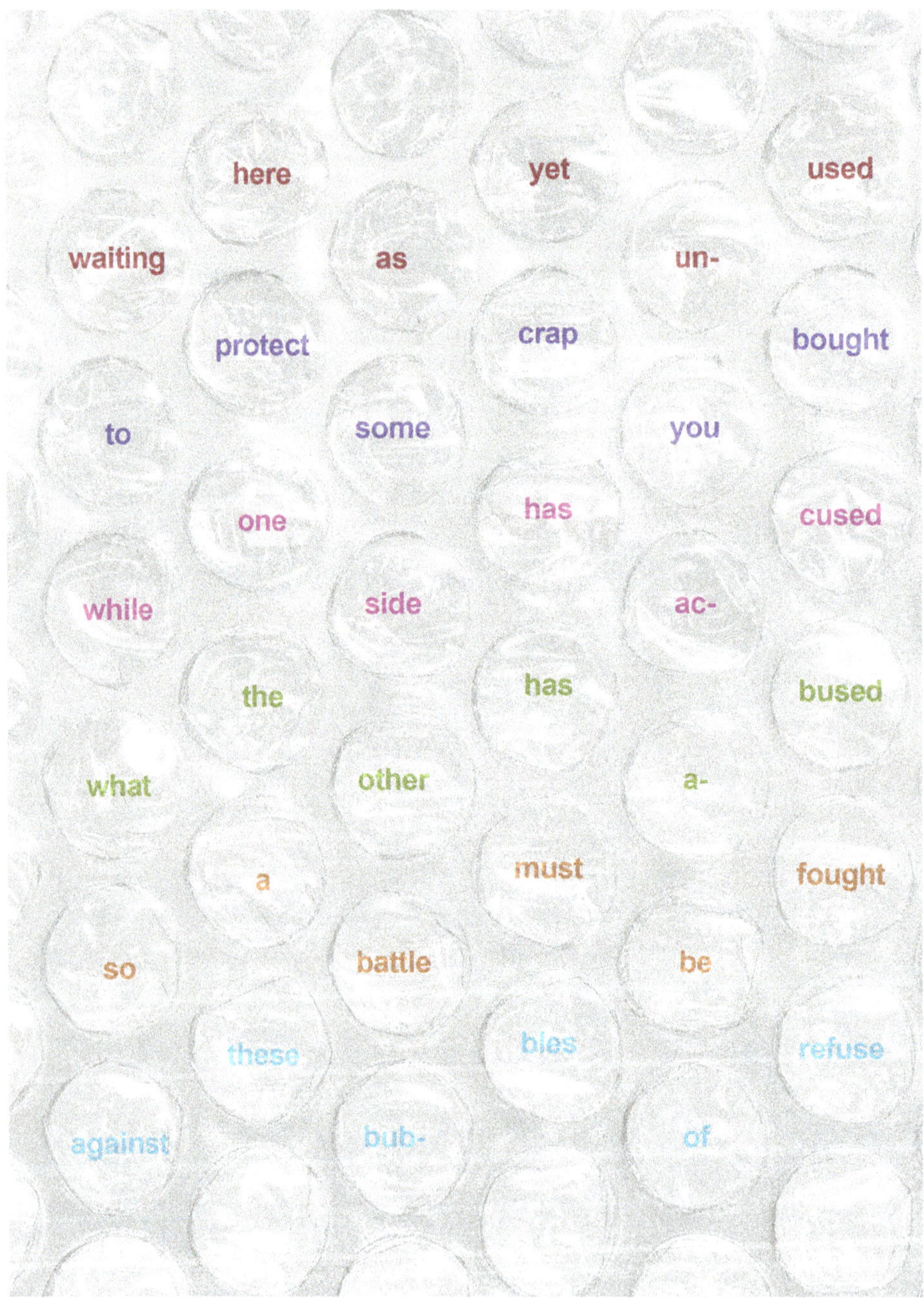

tRubble wRap

Digital collage

MEGHAN GRUPPOSO

NEW YORK, NEW YORK

IT'S NOT

It's not minimalist
if what's missing
still exists
but in a landfill

It's not theft
if no one knows
it's gone

It's not hoarding
if it's curated

It's not garbage
if they held it everyday
until they parted
& it's kept now
in my pocket

It's not sentimental
if it wasn't made public

It's not obsessing if
the object carries meaning
only when remembered
& it's only remembered
when seen & it lives
in a box   on the shelf
in the closet   in the basement

It's not a path
once grown over
in their absence

DEREK ADAMS

SUDBURY, SUFFOLK, UNITED KINGDOM

BEWARE OF SEASONS BEARING GIFTS

SPRING arrived
tiptoeing bare legged through the morning mist
heralded only by the gentle song of birds
clutching it's box of delights
brimming over with

        new flowers
        young lambs
        fresh pastures
        warm lips
        bright eyes

Together
we took April showers
bathed in the warmth of each other
as we lay in the soft grass

But we flew too close to the sun
and in the heat of the moment
the

        flowers wilted
        lambs roasted
        the grass was no longer green
        lips grew cold
        eyes dulled

While
beneath us
the earth dried and cracked
but no longer moved

SUMMER arrived
        hot on my heels
and handed me a box
empty
except for a note which said
This box belongs to Pandora.

BONI JOI
LUCERNE, SWITZERLAND

MY PARIS AGREEMENT

If I could be anything I'd be a deconstructed beauty,
committed to un-carb and re-green.

I'd have my energy cleared, smudged, and crystaled,

rehouse my eyelids higher not so I'm high maintenance
but just a little more expansive.

I'd invent a breathing system
to romance the capitalist bug that sings in my ear.

If I could corrugate the sky with dull satellites
in place of the musky ones

then I would finally study the capsaicin stars
I was meant to be bound to.

So far I haven't gone back to the blur of fabrics,
artisanal heels, junk food t-shirts,

and yards of repurposed polyester sequin dresses.

I try to cure myself of a not-so-crystalline consciousness
with the praxis of techno pranayama.

I now understand my inner body in an unorganized fashion.
Yesterday I exhaled sparkles.

Today I stand in eco-athleisure at the edge of the plastic-filled
ocean and witness its multitudes

of burgundy greenhouse gas horizons.

PETER CICCARIELLO

PUTNAM, CONNECTICUT

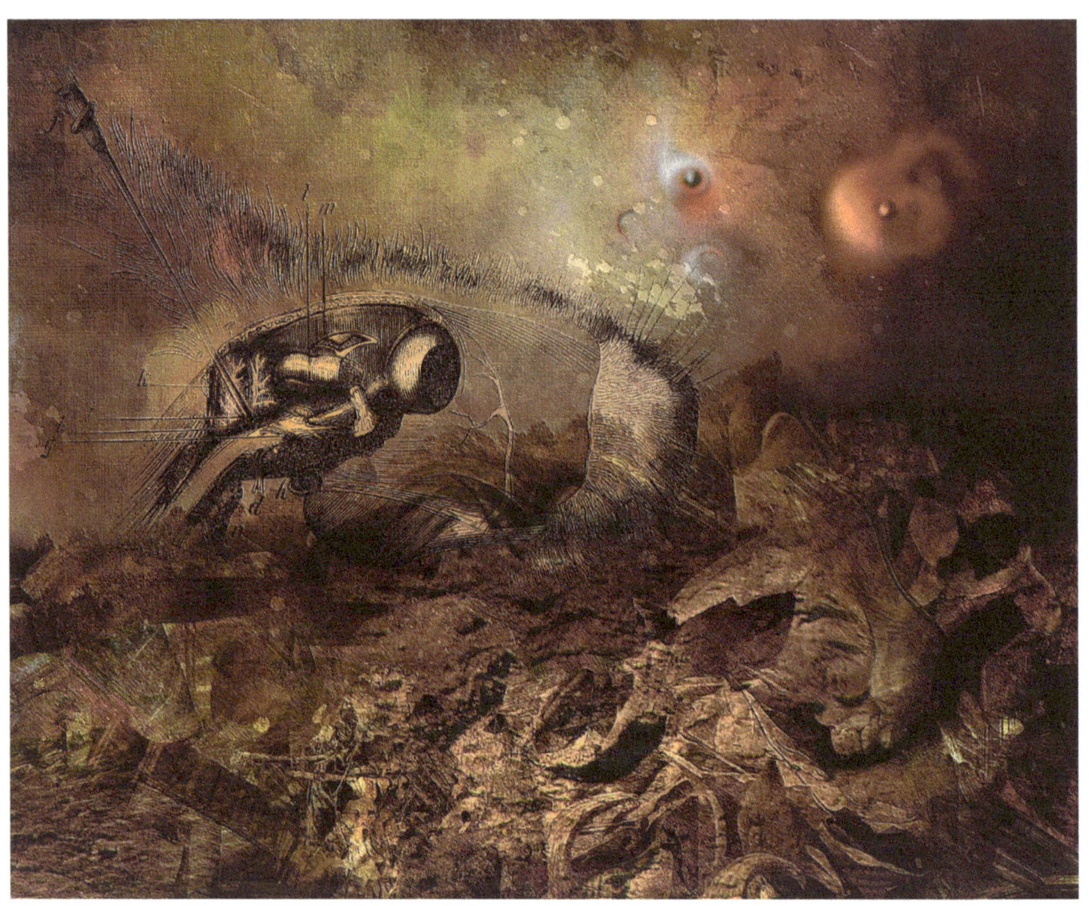

EVERY SCARED RABBITT

Digital collage, 10 x 8 inches

THOMAS FUCALORO
STATEN ISLAND, NEW YORK

HUMANS ARE DEAD LONGER THAN THEY ARE ALIVE

A child draws a giraffe and then
gives it bloody fang prints on its
neck. Life captures death splendidly
and with purpose

Blurred visions, euphoric monsters
rip apart demons but still live in my
head trying to see the euphoric
through my eyes and failing

Trying to take the right medication
to help you feather away the space
between you and forward, feeling
like tense collarbones

Your chest cavity fills with moths
fluttering and one auburn stained
butterfly still, as you sit in a mocking
chair, pendulum pondering

Evocations of what we can't squish
with our hands and split with our skulls
trying to find the smear that suffers
color, texture, and tone

Then finding yourself in a calm
temporal moment of, and you release
dawn into crush, into destroy, into bringing
back to life what you know not need

And then something shatters and
your spine drops down a couple
of timelines and death, seems
to start capturing life

without purpose

BRENDA WHITEWAY

CHARLOTTETOWN, PRINCE EDWARD ISLAND, CANADA

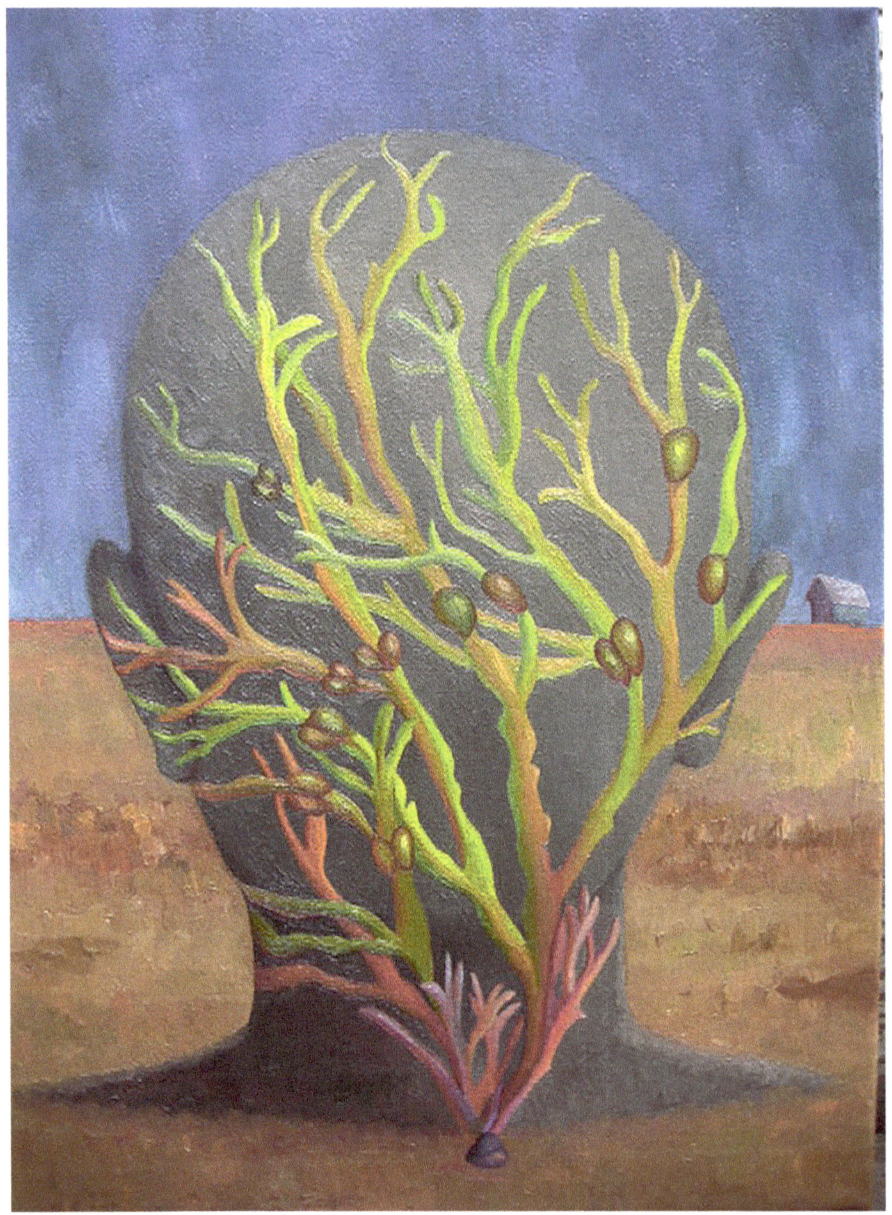

HEAD IN THE SAND

Oil on canvas, 9" x 12"

KELLY TALBOT

INDIANAPOLIS, INDIANA

TRUTH TONGUE

Above the cobblestones of London,

thirty thousand lanterns consume

oil siphoned from the souls

of the final cetaceans.

The nuclear towers of Beijing

crackle and glow, reflected

in uranium currents that flow

into the fishless sea.

In the ski resorts of Colorado,

millionaires rub their hands

at hearths of carbonizing logs

cut from now rainless forests.

A firefly swaying in an empty field,

a phoenix swirling in some remote canyon,

a spark flickering in the unknown ether,

I sigh my incandescence in solitary purity,

far beyond the enlightenment of men.

SAM DODSON

LONDON, UNITED KINGDOM

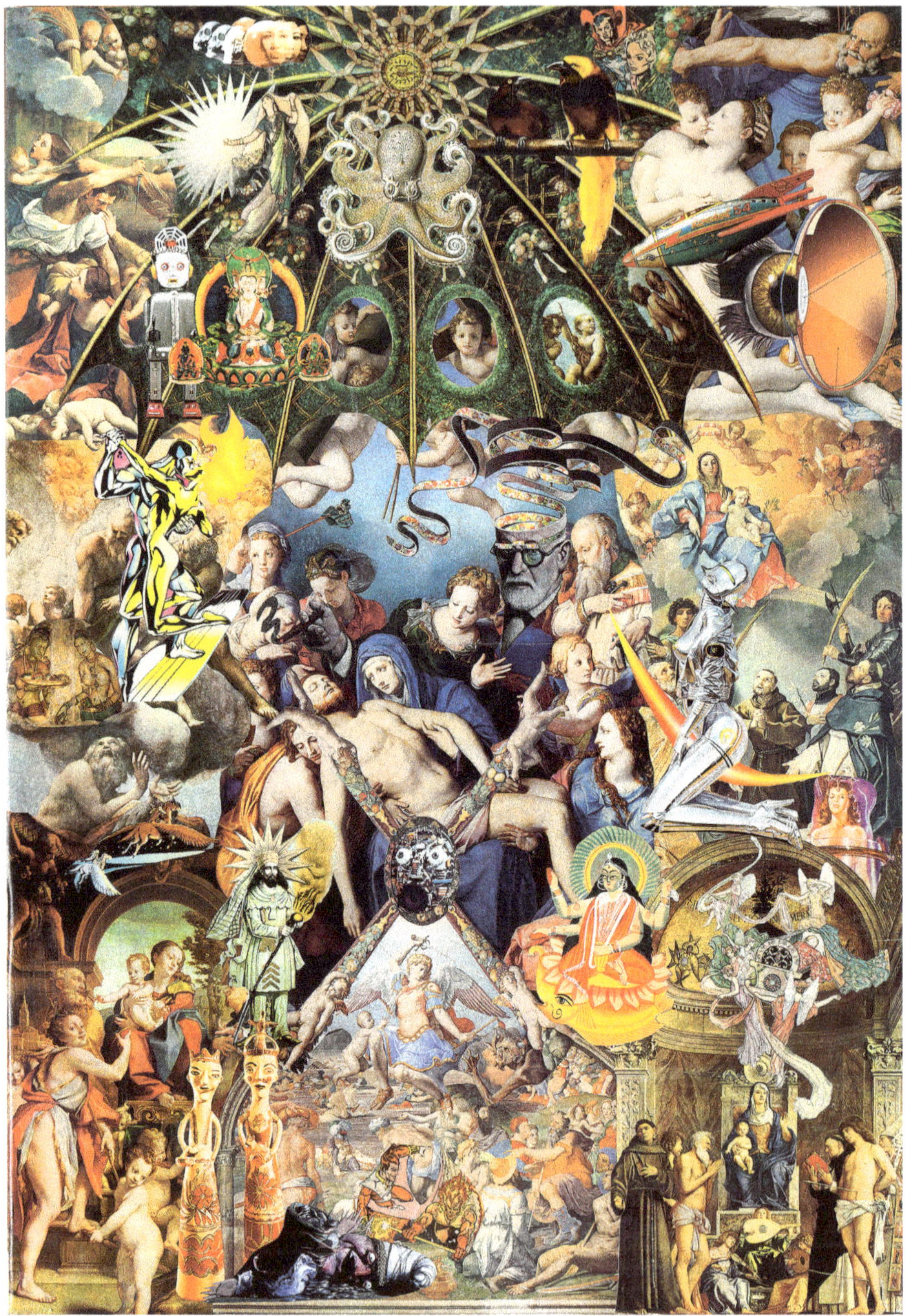

THE GREAT UNRAVELING OF ALL AND ALL

Collage on canvas, 59 x 84 cm

PAUL SOHAR

WARREN, NEW JERSEY

RED AND BLACK

Two cars at a standstill, one red, the other black.

The red has the side pushed in

and the black the front demolished.

Plenty of glass shards, broken metal parts on the asphalt.

The props of the usual battlefield.

Who did what and to whom?

What did the red have against the black and

the black against the red? They're both silent now,

but as I pass by on the shoulder

I can hear their voices in the wind:

I was here first, says the red.

No, I had the right of way, says the black.

Red ideology against the black

and the black against the red. Yes, ideology!

War. Crash. Silence. Truce. Time to re-arm.

The red is not quite red but more like burgundy,

and the black is more like dark gray. Both open

to negotiation, but only war can assign the guilt.

MATTHEW HUPERT

NEW YORK, NEW YORK

WAR IS A FAILURE OF THE IMAGINATION

On the savannah we barely scraped by
Found fat on the hoof evasive
sweet from the hive elusive
& still we gorge though the pantry is full

10 thousand years of evolution
is hard to ignore
with only 2 centuries of plenty
here & there

War is not
how you name your gods
distribute your goods
have a king
don't have a king
or wave your flag

Was is caused by just 2 things
Scarcity & scarcity mindset
&
all scarcity now is just scarcity mindset
in those with the guns

We've left the savannah
We don't need to scrape by
There's honey and hotcakes and hamhocks for all

It's hard to ignore
fear so old
that it's locked behind doors
& enshrined as order

NEAL SKOOTER TAYLOR (LA DADA)

LOS ANGELES, CALIFORNIA

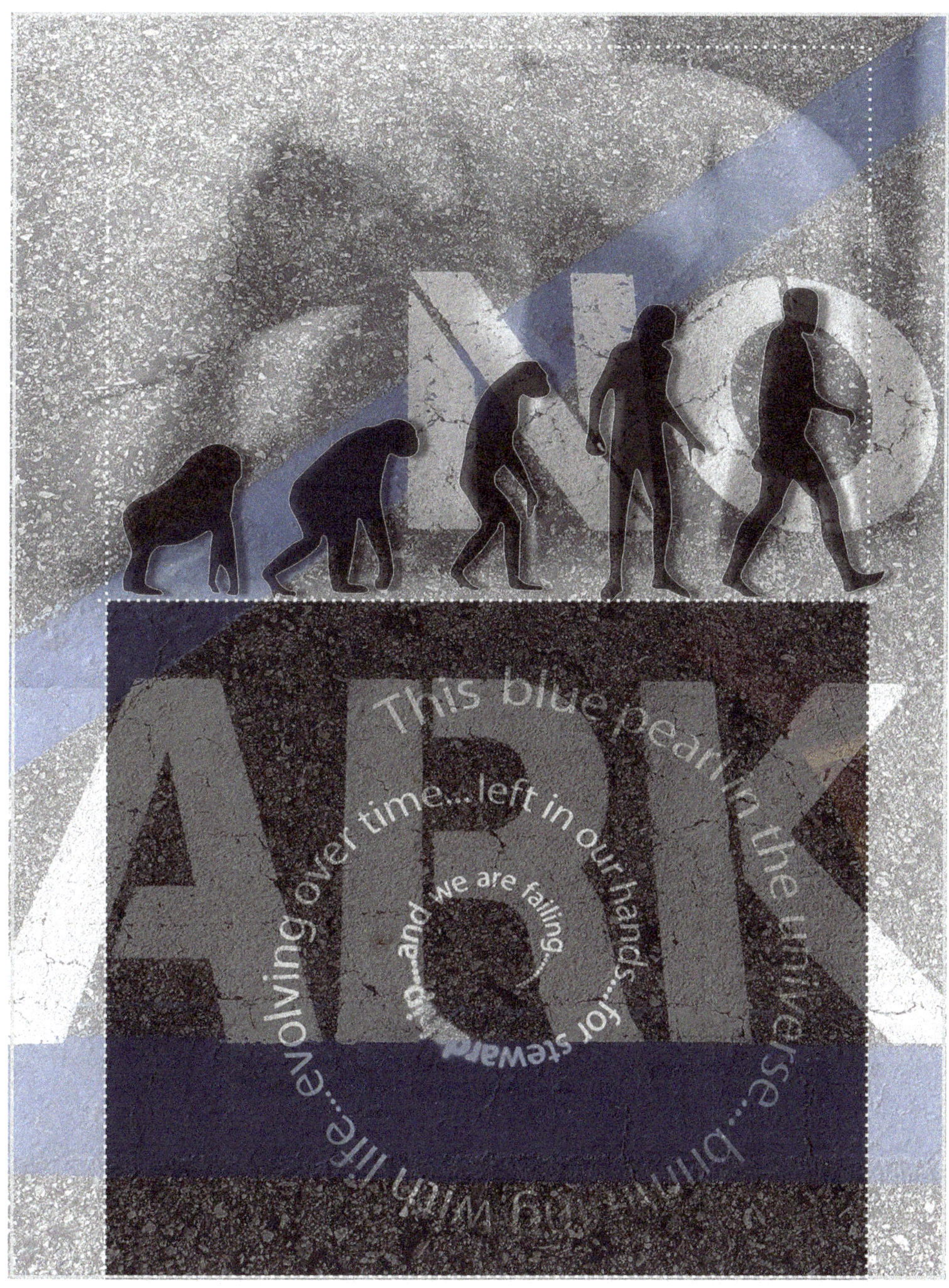

NO ARK

Digital collage

JÓZSEF BÍRÓ

BUDAPEST, HUNGARY

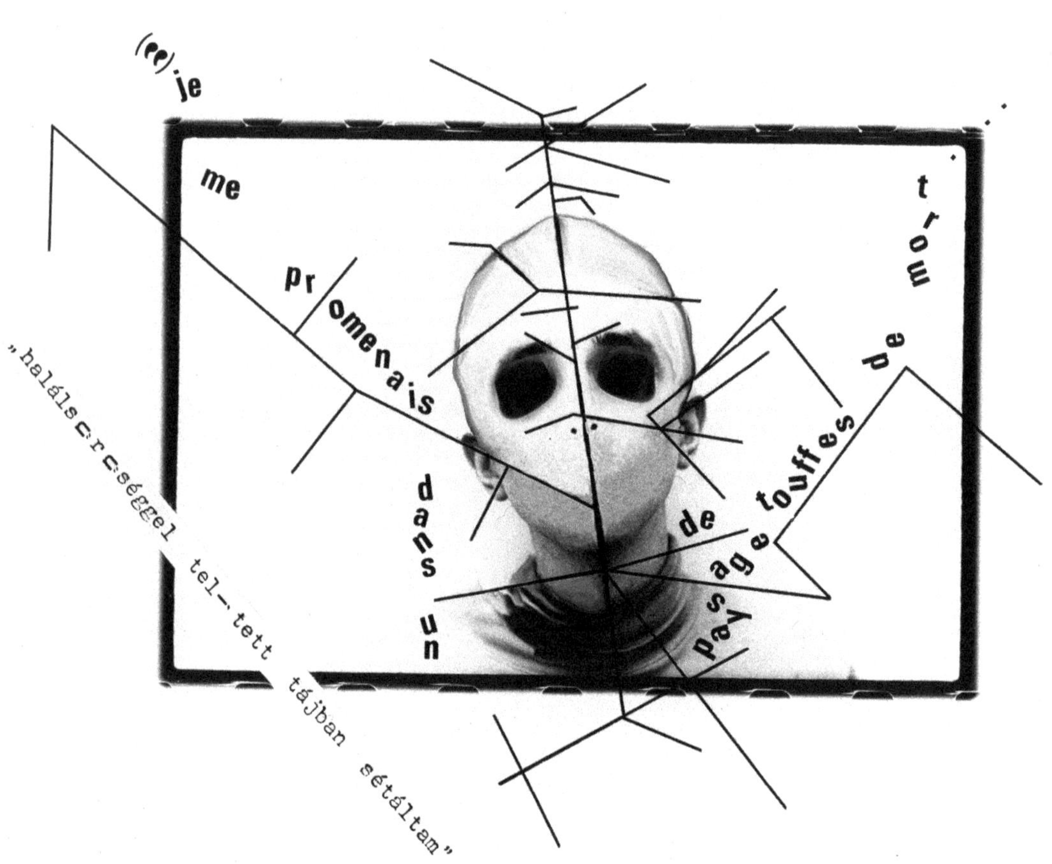

TZARA QUOTE

Collage

CARLA BERTOLA

TORINO, ITALY

Mixed media

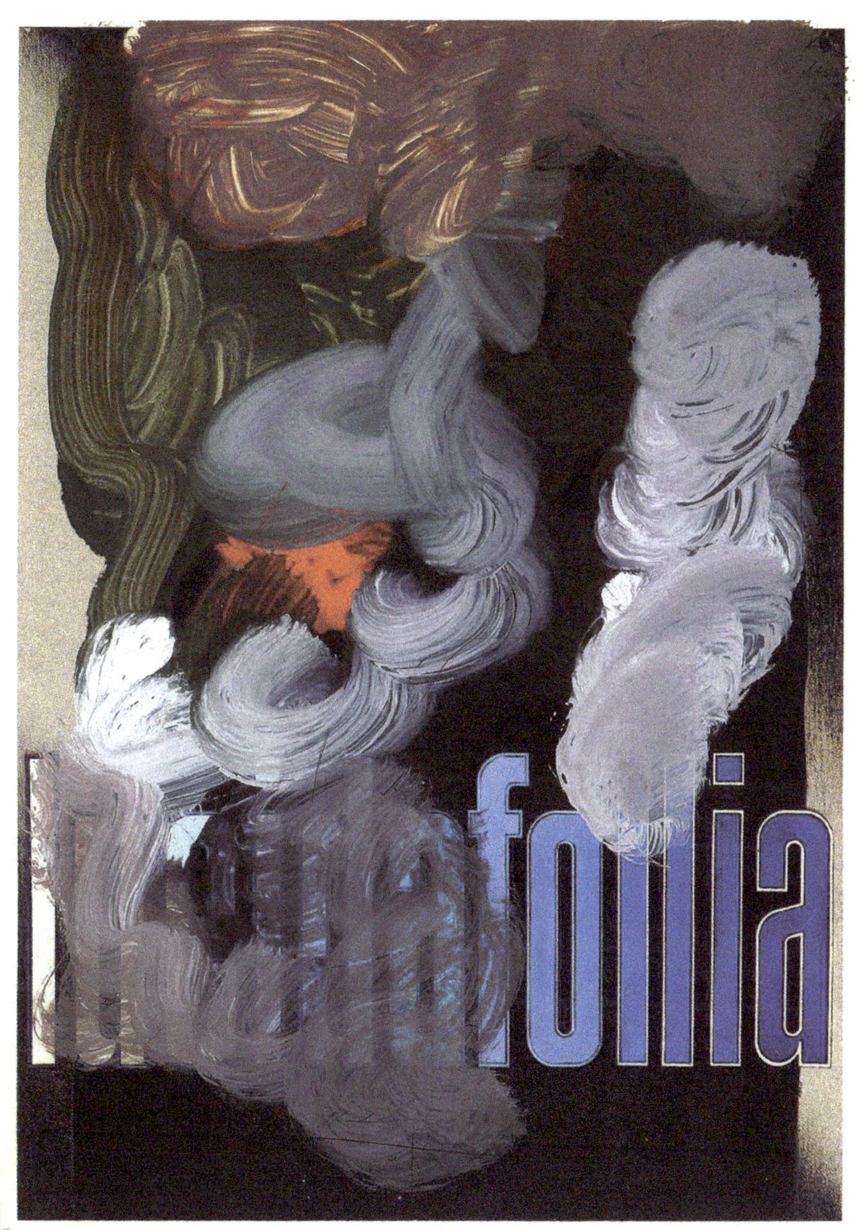

OUR NEAR FUTURE

Mixed media

BRUCE LOUIS DODSON

BORLÄNGE, DARLARNA, SWEDEN

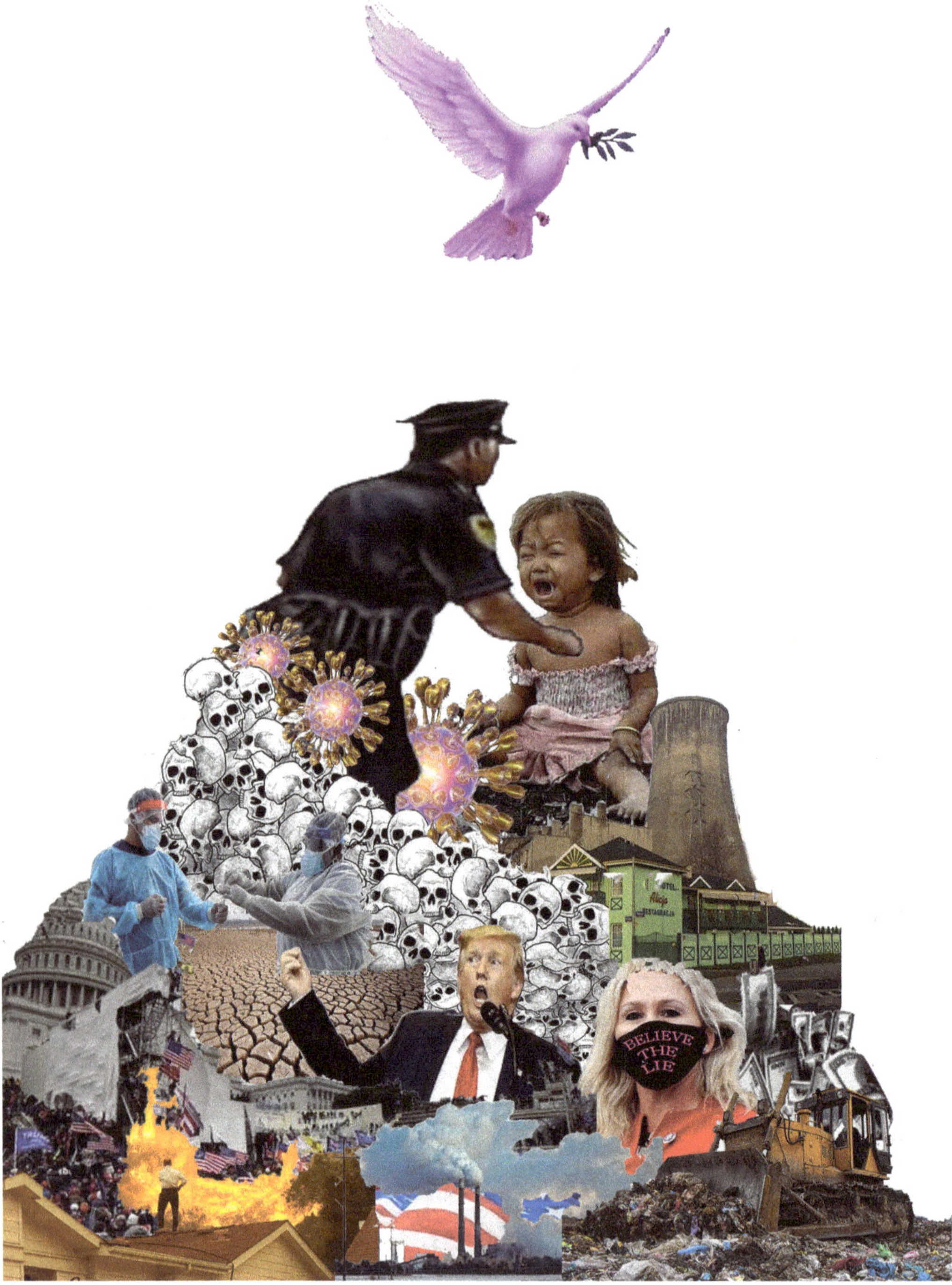

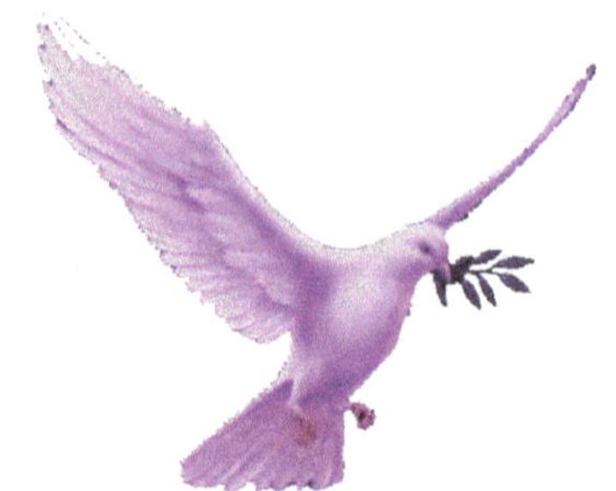

BEAUTY CHANGES

Digital collage, 6 x 8 inches

ROBERT DUNCAN

FAIRFAX, CALIFORNIA

CRACKER JACK PRIZES OF THE VELDT

All that piss-warm, we're gonna plant a million trees,

One sickly twig for every citizen-shopper

Forks over for a big carbon-spurting thingamajig
Or even a little lithium-cobalt dealie
(Each of those righteous cuties, btw,
Loaded with the latest in manganese! nickel!
And CHILD LABOR!)

Kaboom!
It's your 4th-of-July Tree-planting Sale-a-thon!

Dubious to a contemporary fault,
You still feel the jolt when
The aspartame-lipped bastards
Are so bottomless,
Popping by shithole countries
That really need the bribes
To scoop vast hectares of native turf
And spew alien seedlings—

Cracker Jack prizes
That, in the name of Abu Bakr and
Julia Butterfly Hill,
Choke the habitat with sameness
And crack all the children's teeth.
Kaboom!

LAWRENCE HOLZWORTH

NEW YORK, NEW YORK

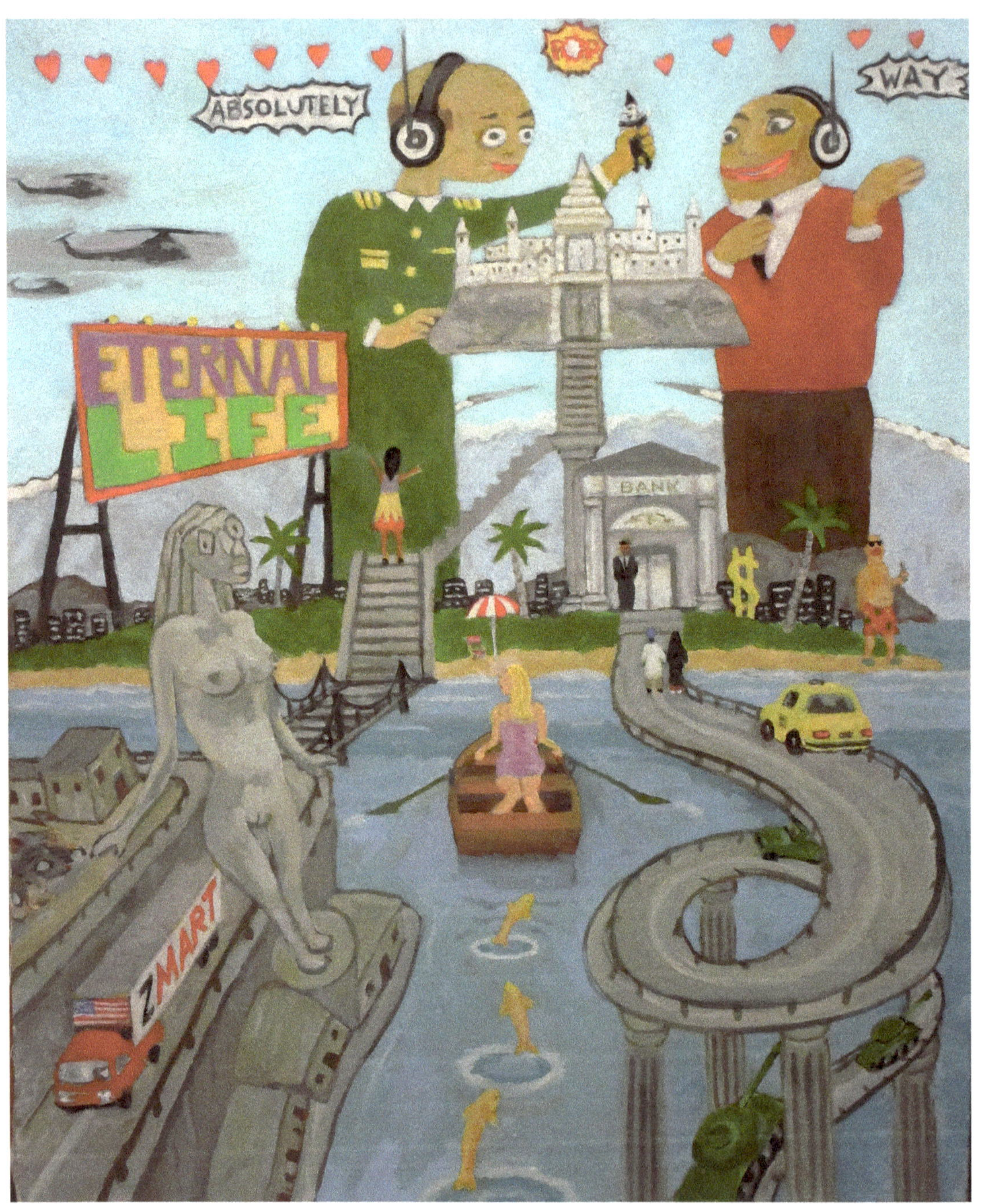

MASTERS OF THE UNIVERSE

Acrylic on canvas, 30 x 36 inches

JEFFREY CYPHERS WRIGHT
NEW YORK, NEW YORK

DOOMSDAY GLACIER

Look out, Captain, she's gonna blow!
Star Trek

How to ignore the cold vapor on the nape

of your neck? I picture my mom in 1949,

"Fraternity Sweetheart," with her pearls on.

I want to be a poinsettia near the altar

when the choir lets it rip and you get

that chill up the stripper pole of your spine.

Hallelujah treadmill of toy professionals.

Get real, America. I guess it's time to stock

the bar and break out the glass axes.

Are you ready to rumble? Rudolph sees

what's coming and closes his eyes.

It won't be long until the phat lady

sings the Apocalypse Heartache Blues

while we think up fun new things to do.

VITTORE BARONI

VIAREGGIO, ITALY

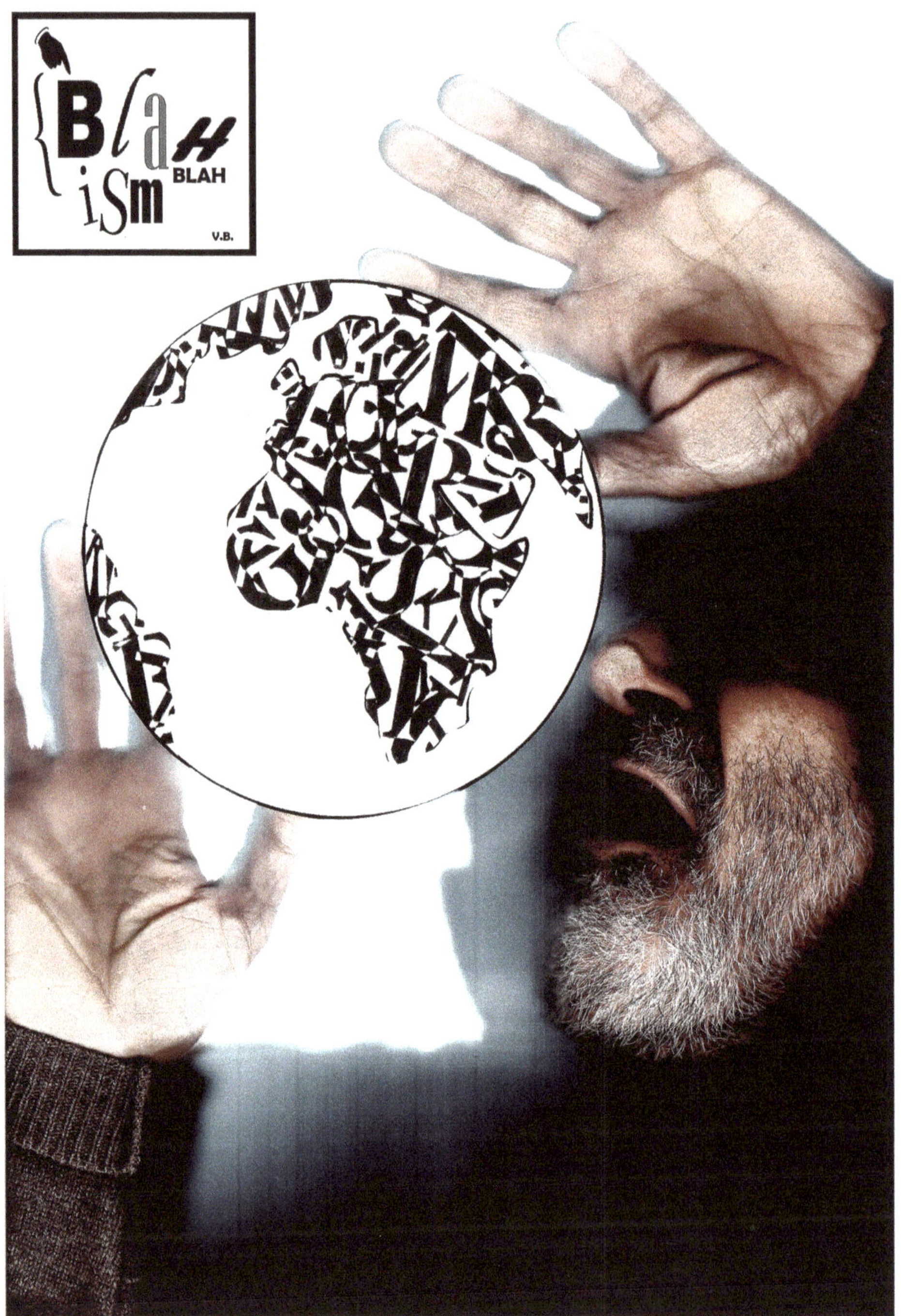

BLAH BLAHISM

Collage and scanner photo, vertical A3 size

YRIK-MAX VALENTONIS

TAMPA, FLORIDA

WHAT A COP?

the annual migration of the politicians to have repeated discussions

their ongoing deposition about the despoiling of our habitation

about the adverse effects of pollution without trying to find a solution

strange purchase of carbon footprints in exchange for affordable climate change

there is no slowing the destruction from this fruitless collaboration

LINDA LERNER

BROOKLYN, NEW YORK

BETWEEN

what we hear barreling toward us

and the warning is where we are: In Kentucky

they heard it in the distance, got the warning

but some distances can't be measured

grow more distant when we try

and it's a lovely Spring December day in New York

we're enjoying a brief reprieve if we don't

think about what's causing it, the build up

of gas in the atmosphere, how much damage

experts removed between what politicians promised,

the hot air from their words

we get trapped in, and that siren going off

in the distance, do you hear it?

Will they? Ever?

LARS CROSBY

BERLIN, GERMANY

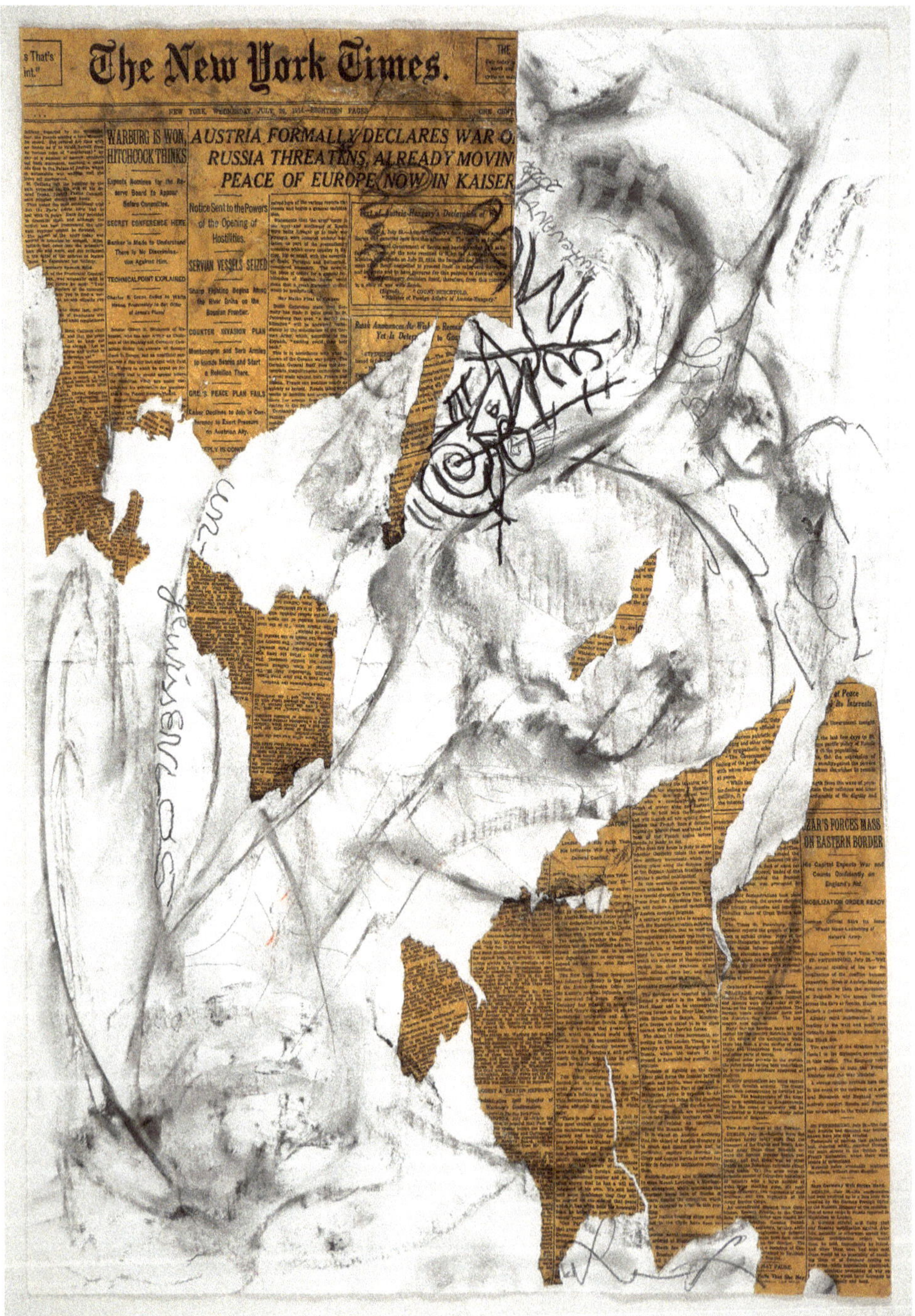

Un-gewissEN-LOS nyet zer0

A snippit of a New York Times issue Wednesday, July 29, 1914;
charcoal etching, instinct, mind, heart, breath, and hands; A2

FAUSTO GROSSI

BILBAO, SPAIN

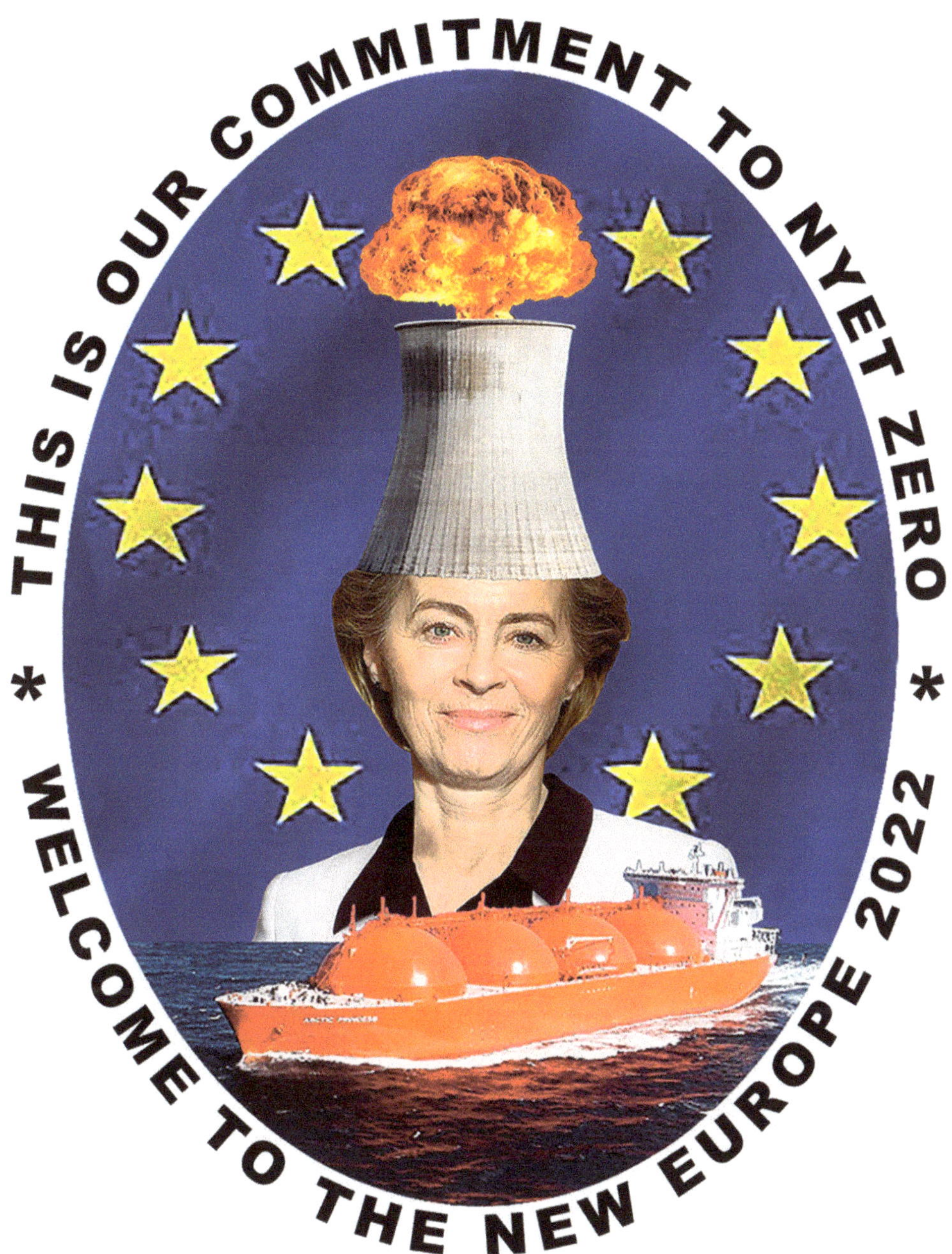

A.R.P. (A REACTOR PREPARES)

Infographic, 3.347 x 4.29 inches

JACK SEIEI

TOKYO, JAPAN

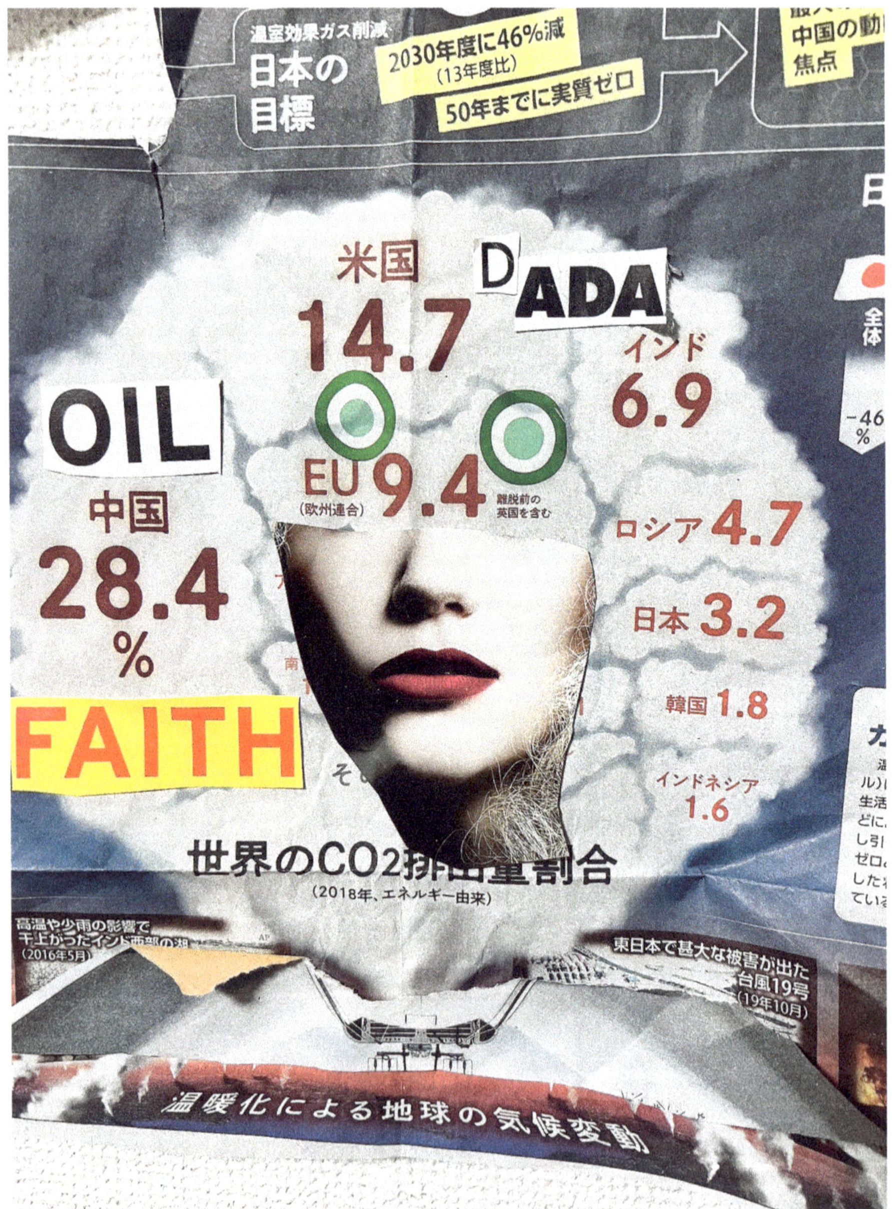

NYET ZERO

Collage, A4

GERALD YELLE

AMHERST, MASSACHUSETTS

LAMB OF WALL STREET

The boss said we should get in on this unique
opportunity to amass a personal fortune.
A friend had told him about it. "Two dollars
is all it takes. You put in the first dollar
the first day and the second dollar the second.

This gets you dividend-yielding certificates
that pay compound interest a dozen
times a minute—they get caught in this loop
like an old-fashioned broken record, a process
that in a week can net millions:
Little-known stock market anomaly."

He made it sound risk-free. I put in five
grand, all I had in the bank. I talked to him
yesterday. I said not only had his strategy
not made me rich, it swallowed up
the whole five Gs in fees and stock drops.

He said he'd never suggest an investment
was foolproof. If I'd stuck with the two-dollar
ante I might've still lost but at least
I'd have my four thousand, nine hundred
and ninety-eight. Ma wants to know why

I listened to him in the first place.
But he seemed so sure we'd be millionaires.
I'm bound to try again—with just the
two dollars this time—soon as Ma lends it.

SANDRA GEA

MARIA, SPAIN

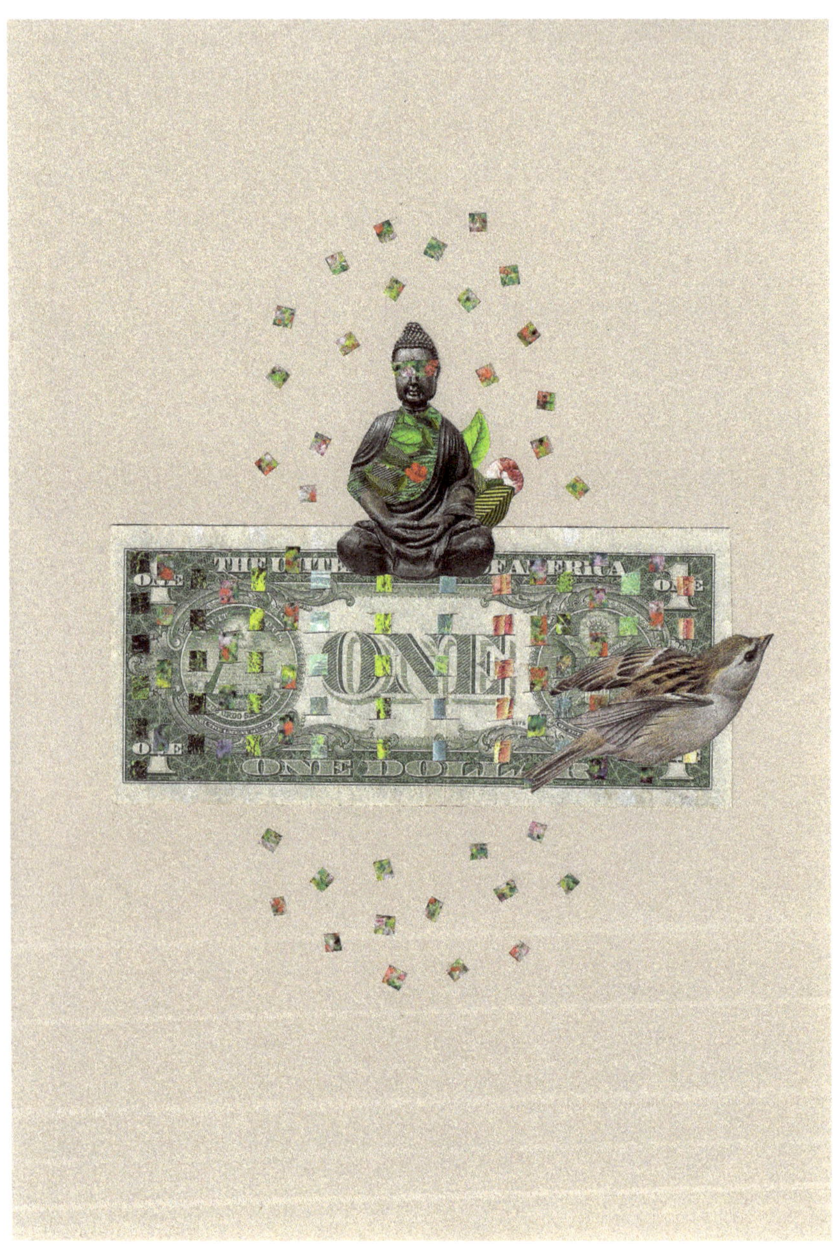

MONEY FOR NOTHING, GET THE CHANGE FOR FREE

One dollar bill, analogue collage on paper, 210 x 297 mm

ALLISON DAVIS

SAN FRANCISCO, CALIFORNIA

THE DEADLIEST SIN

"The idea that some lives matter less is the root of all that is wrong with the world."
—Dr. Paul Farmer (1959-2022)

Greed is the deadliest sin.
Insatiable appetite devours
nature's balance and abundance.
No discernment or devotion.
Global warming, global warring,
sickening us, slaughtering Ukrainians.
Headlines divine Big Oil's
impending disaster:

America's Petroleum Giants Face A Reckoning
for the Environmental Devastation
Caused by Fossil Fuel Emissions.

Greed hoards, steals, and robs,
embracing provisional pleasures.
Emissions, without conditions, zero sum game,
nyet zero gain, ignoring regulation's premonitions.
Putin's putrescent presence
beckons billion dollar yachts,
mafia oil oligarchy bots,
provoke retribution, evolution.

"We can't stay here, we'll all die."

Big Oil pulls out of Russia's energy war,
coitus interrupts, before we're fucked:
Exon, Shell, BP, which was the first,
McDonald's and Starbucks coerced.
Crimea wasn't enough, Ukraine won't be enough.
Nothing will be enough, get tough.
Biden's supply chain push and pull for Ukrainian aid,
EU's contemplation of NATO and member upgrade.

"Saudi Arabia sides with the Russians."

Disruptors, interceptors, correctors,
impede tyrants, tycoons,
cool off the ecosphere, stop inclement avarice.
Paul Farmer's health creed:
prevent human fodder, bring vigor. inoculate.
For the earth: pull the pump chump,
let the solar shine, no more pimping, intercede,
reduce speed, gut greed, the number is zero.

AVELINO DE ARAUJO

NATAL, BRAZIL

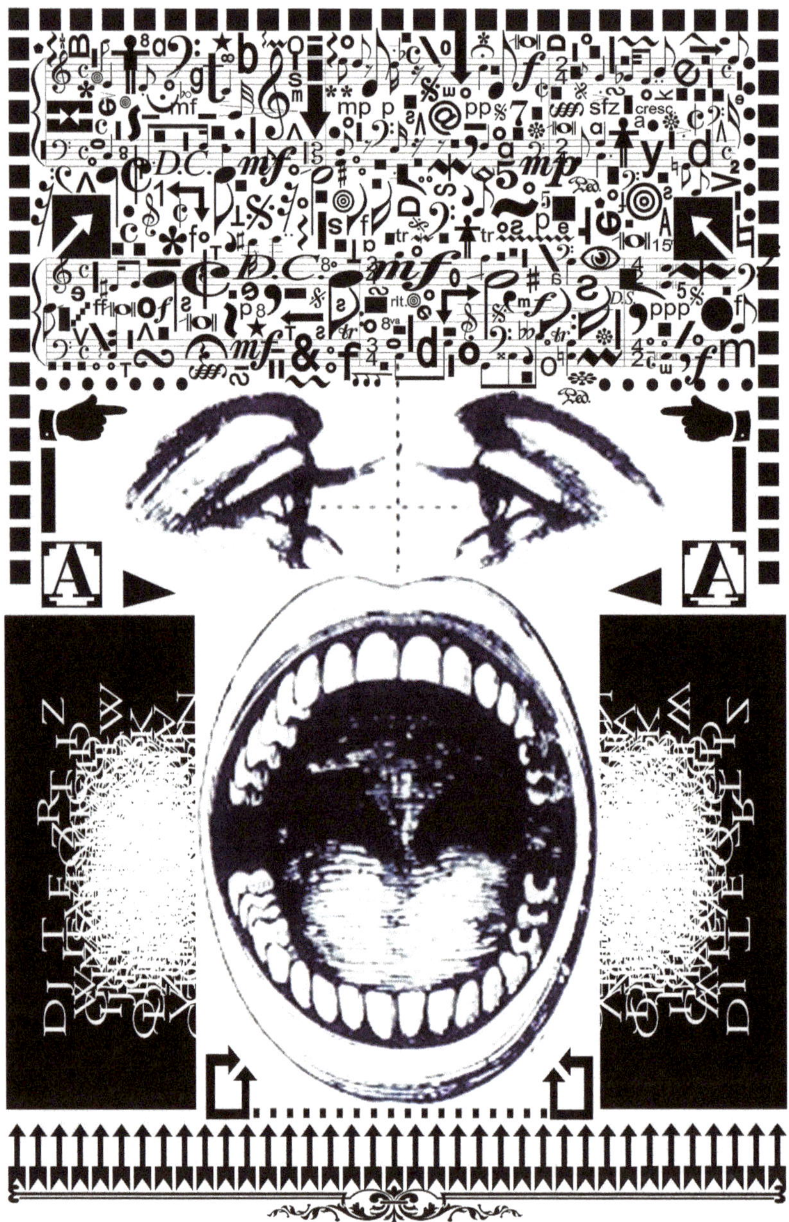

HELP

Collage

L. ROSE

SAN FRANCISCO, CALIFORNIA

NOT YET NO ONE

First after the First Nation, a counting system that begins with oneself, and with Christ

Eroticism of the number 1

Phallic unity of a lie of false Origin

The phallacy of being Phirst

Because before 1 there is the assumption that there is 0, a void that is feared, because it is not oneself, it is Other, it is 0ther

n0b0dy

n0 0ne

n0where

n0thing

a thing that is not yet known

a beauty that is not yet understood

a land that is not yet trampled

resources that are not yet exploited

women that are not yet captured

an idea that is not yet conceived

a philosophy that is not yet grasped

a nation that is not yet necessary, nor united

a belongingness that is not yet felt

an identity that is not yet defined

a culture that is not yet written

just 0s and 1s

nothingness and being

The arrogance of existence

0ver the unrec0gnized n0nexistent pe0ple

WAYNE ATHERTON

DOVER, NEW HAMPSHIRE

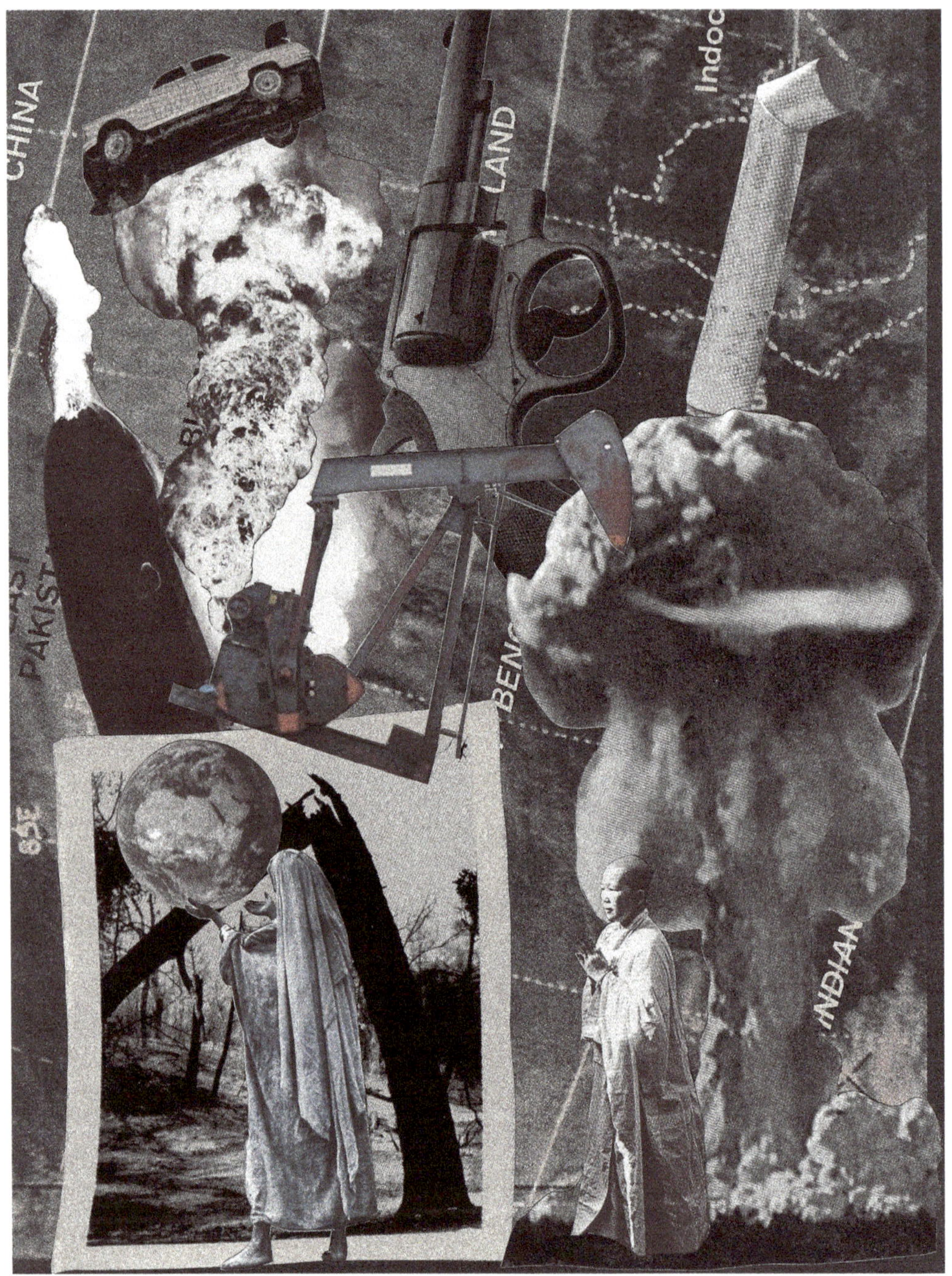

THE CENTER CANNOT HOLD UNTIL SAVED BY ZPG

Hand cut collage on paper, 8-1/2 x 11 inches

FEDERICO FEDERICI

MELOGNO, ITALY

CARBON OFFSET SWEETENER

he borrowed death
among these windy plants
like one last winding path
or heap of ants at work
where mendless silence seeks
vocalised comparison
—*wo versammelt sie die Klänge?*—
vocal folds he flinches from

he holds dominion eternal, ever
existential of the dawn of dark
of the law the bark breaks
when it falls; thereafter
his mind-sheet billows:
sweetener dissolves in the sea

J. D. NELSON

LAFAYETTE, COLORADO

THE LAKE WAS LOOKING UP AT THE STARS
WHILE A STONE SAT AT THE BOTTOM

a swayed flex of sugar
the custom of shipping frogs

a new now

speak to the astronauts about the peat moss
stay until the dream starts

INA AL-SOQI

SAN FRANCISCO, CALIFORNIA

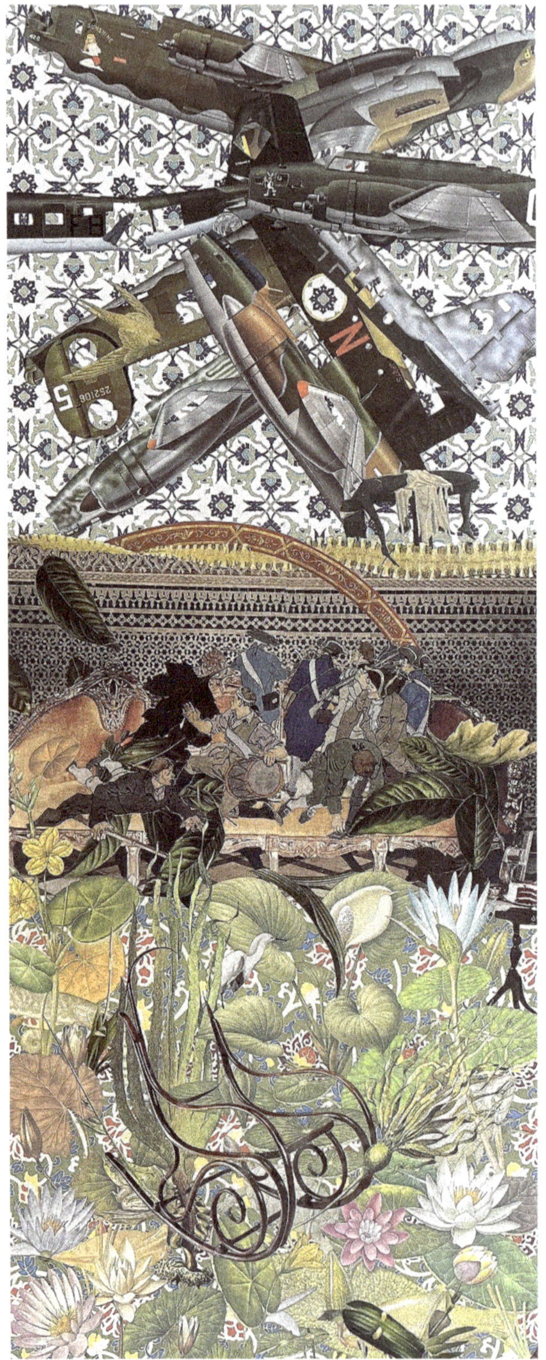

FLEET WEEK

Hand-cut and assembled collage

ANDRENA ZAWINSKI

ALAMEDA, CALIFORNIA

TWO TROVES

1. The Mound
Children once scrambled up Indian Mound's bluff
to its dome in Pittsburgh's McKees Rocks Bottoms,
bicycles hastily dropped on their sides at its foot.
They scurried to unearth a trove of arrowheads,
chunks of tortoise shell, stone pottery beads
from the dusty loam of the burial ground, treasures
that hadn't been quarried, robbed, or collected
into Carnegie Museum's cardboard storage chests.

They would tell and retell stories of General McKee,
rumored to have leapt to his death fleeing Indians
he betrayed trading Fort Pitt's smallpox ward
blankets of death for their corn and beans,
tell and retell stories of giants interred there,
ancient aliens, angel brides, superhero shamans,

all while roasting Oscar Meyers on tree branches
shaved with pocketknives over a circle fired
by Blue Tips and Sunday funnies of Bumsteads,
Pluto and Goofy, the Archie crew before returning
the trove back to the dirt and ash, shaking off
all the bad omens and any angry spirits.

2. The Dump
Children scamper and scavenge with pails
and ziplock bags off the Northern California
Coastal Trail in Ft. Bragg's low tide, collect gems
of tossed glass castoffs from drugstore junk
and liquor bottles pitched over the cliff into the sea
along with cars, appliances, anything else fires
could not reduce that could sink into the deep,
into the town dump to be reborn—

washed in on waves as smooth red, blue,
green, brown glittering shards of sea glass
from ruby taillights, sapphire apothecary jars,
amber beer bottles, all awash with sea foam,
pounded and tossed in mermaid swells
to become something else, to become
earrings and bracelets wrapped in filagree,
encased pendants dangling from chains,
epoxied mosaic sun catchers, all rising up
from an underwater garden to pricy Mendocino
market stands, shops, and galleries. Deserted
seaside memories collected with troves
of shells and driftwood dumped yet again,
this time at the bottom of guesthouse drawers.

ALEXANDER LIMAREV

NOVOSIBIRSK, RUSSIA / SIBERIA

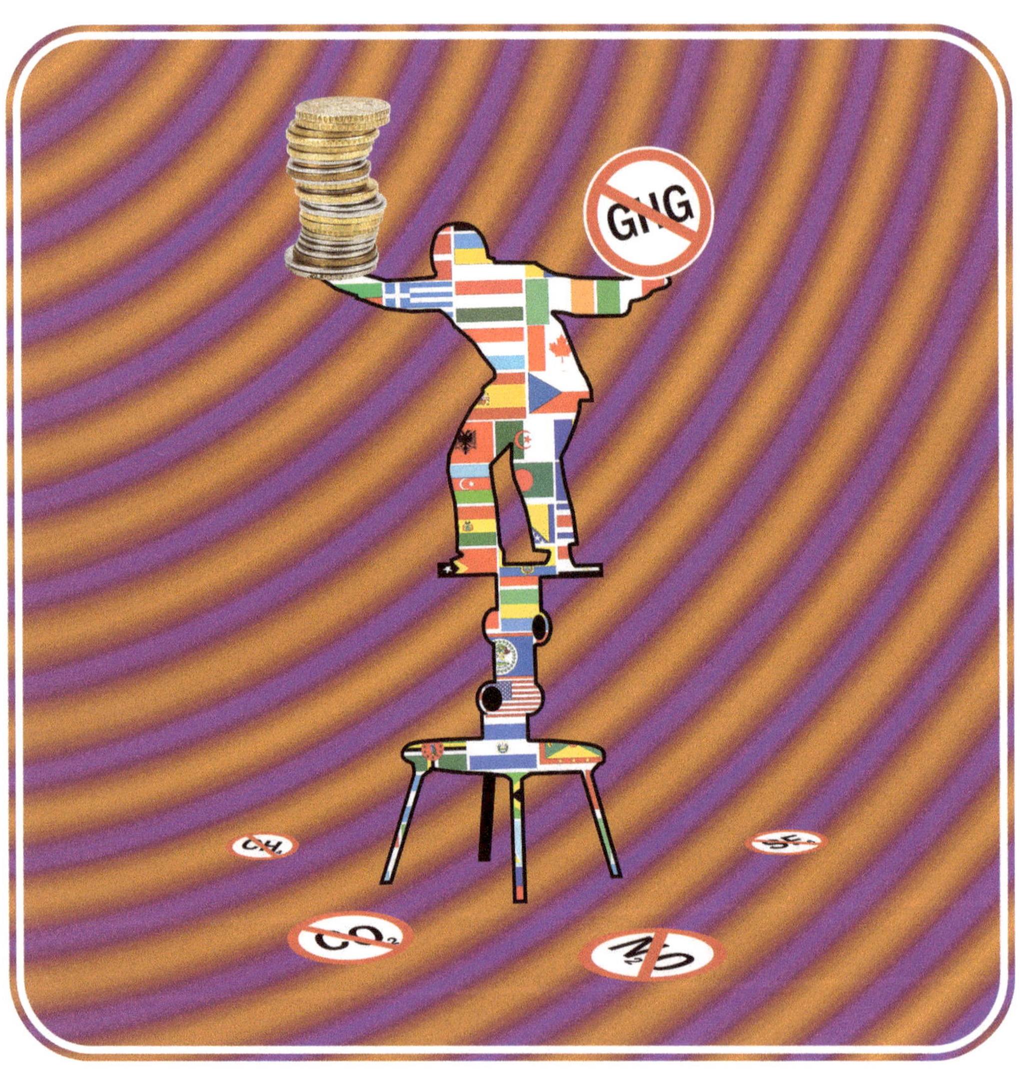

GHG BALANCING ACT

Digital collage; 2480 x 2480 pixels

ZEV TORRES
NEW YORK, NEW YORK

REINVENTING THE BOX

Think outside the box

Of the inside of a box,

Of the possibilities within a box,

The value of a box made entirely from

Rare-earths and aluminum foil,

With no obvious point of entry or escape,

In which you can seek shelter and evade detection

And store your intangibles and non-fungibles,

Your cryptocurrencies and block-chains,

Preserving their value throughout the calamity

au courant

Along with your prestige and social standing,

Ensuring, that upon your reemergence, there will be

No diminution in your capacity to live extravagantly

Off nothing more than

The churn of self-sustaining debt.

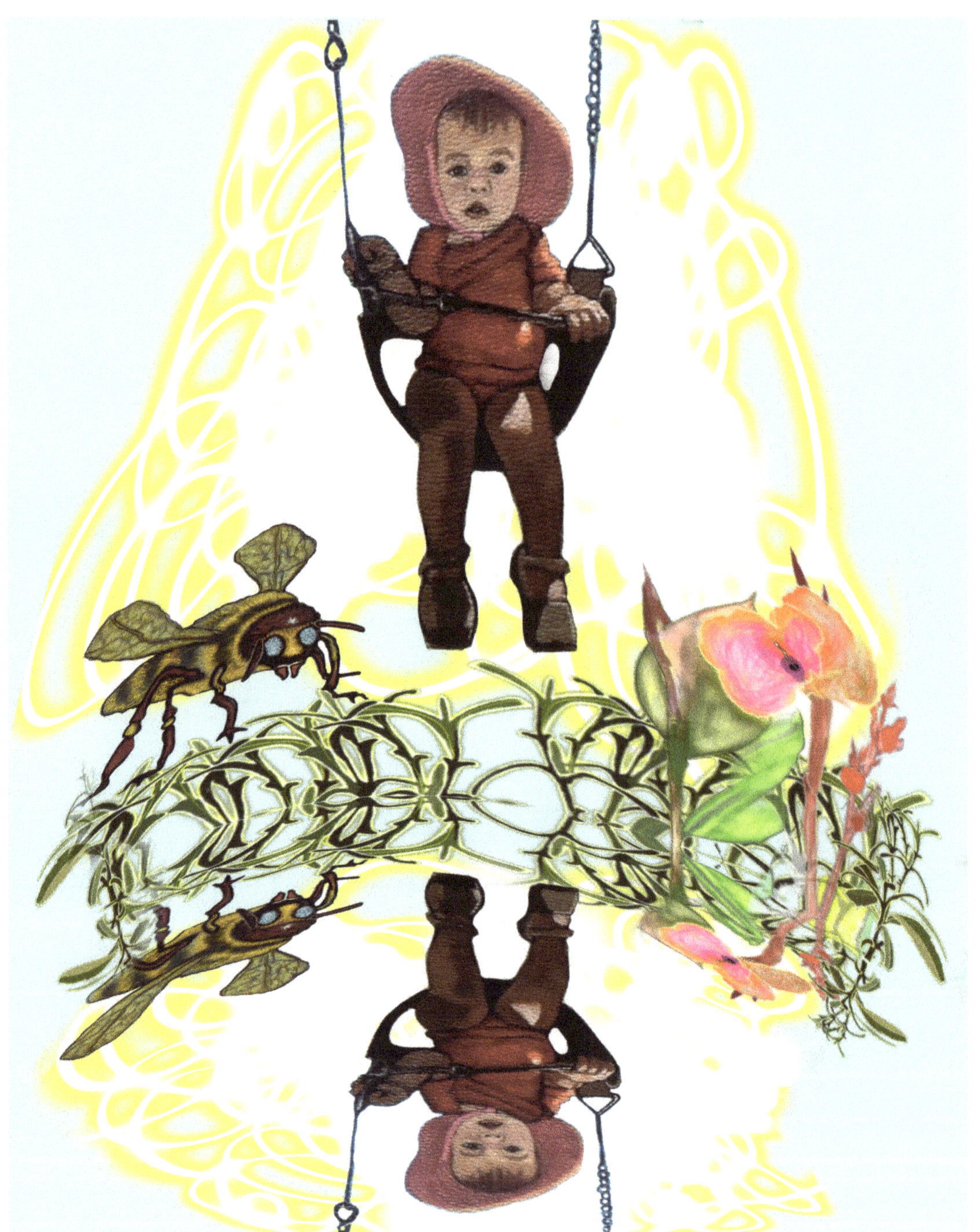

NOT YET

Digital collage of paintings, 9 x 12 inches

TRAVIS RICHARDSON

CULVER CITY, CALIFORNIA

LEGACY

Which was worse,

Reagan's trickle-down economics

or repealing the fairness doctrine?

Give a billionaire a tax break and they'll keep the money.

Give a low-income worker a tax break and they'll spend it,

generating immediate economic activity.

It's not a theory, it's reality.

But nyet.

That's not what the "conservative" movement wants you to think.

Give money to people and they won't work.

They'll take advantage of the system.

Or so the welfare queen theory goes.

Nyet. Nyet. Nyet.

Before the truth was squashed by Reagan

Every broadcasted controversial argument needed a counterargument.

Context was given to whatever message was being argued

But nyet.

You cannot peddle emotionally powered, fact-free bullshit that way.

Today fake news calls legitimate news with journalistic standards fake.

And what are the results?

A compromised general was considered for the joint chief of staff.

A legitimate Russian asset became president.

People will not take free, life-saving vaccines.

The US capitol was stormed by rioters trying to overturn a free and secure election.

Reagan may have bankrupted the Soviet Union and won the Cold War

But he sowed the seeds of distrust and lies.

Pitting Americans against Americans

Tearing this country apart.

SUSAN SHOSHANNAH ADLER

CHAPEL HILL, NORTH CAROLINA

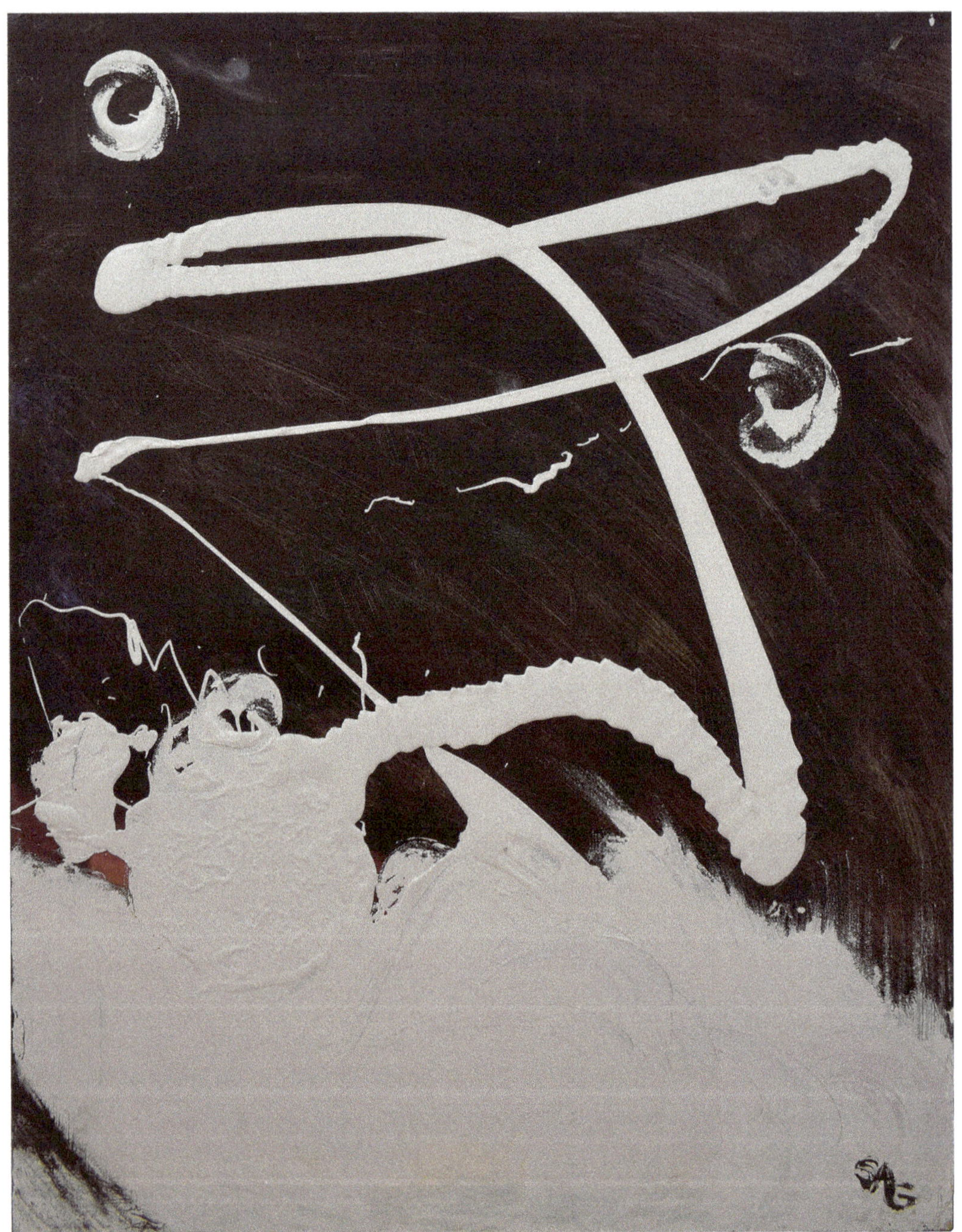

ZOOM

House paint and acrylic, 24 x 30 inches

AUSTIN ALEXIS
NEW YORK, NEW YORK

DRONE DRAMA IN THE COUNTRY

Night, an hour before

it melts into dawn.

One can hear the birches

suck up the soil's moisture.

Even the crickets have quieted.

Eventually your kingdom of dark

is bluntly interrupted

by the whir of a mechanical thing,

a drone,

      coasting

           along,

searching for an exact location

while pushing   away   silence.

Since when is nature's hocus-pocus

less powerful than technology's magic?

You won't stand for this.

Whip your branches into a wind-frenzy.

Look: the drone prematurely lands,

crouches, will rest until after sunrise.

O how you want to gloat in victory,

confront the machine with it!

But you use your energy

to resume your love affair with peace,

your embrace of the absence of daylight.

KAREN BOISSONNEAULT-GAUTHIER

STITTSVILLE, ONTARIO, CANADA

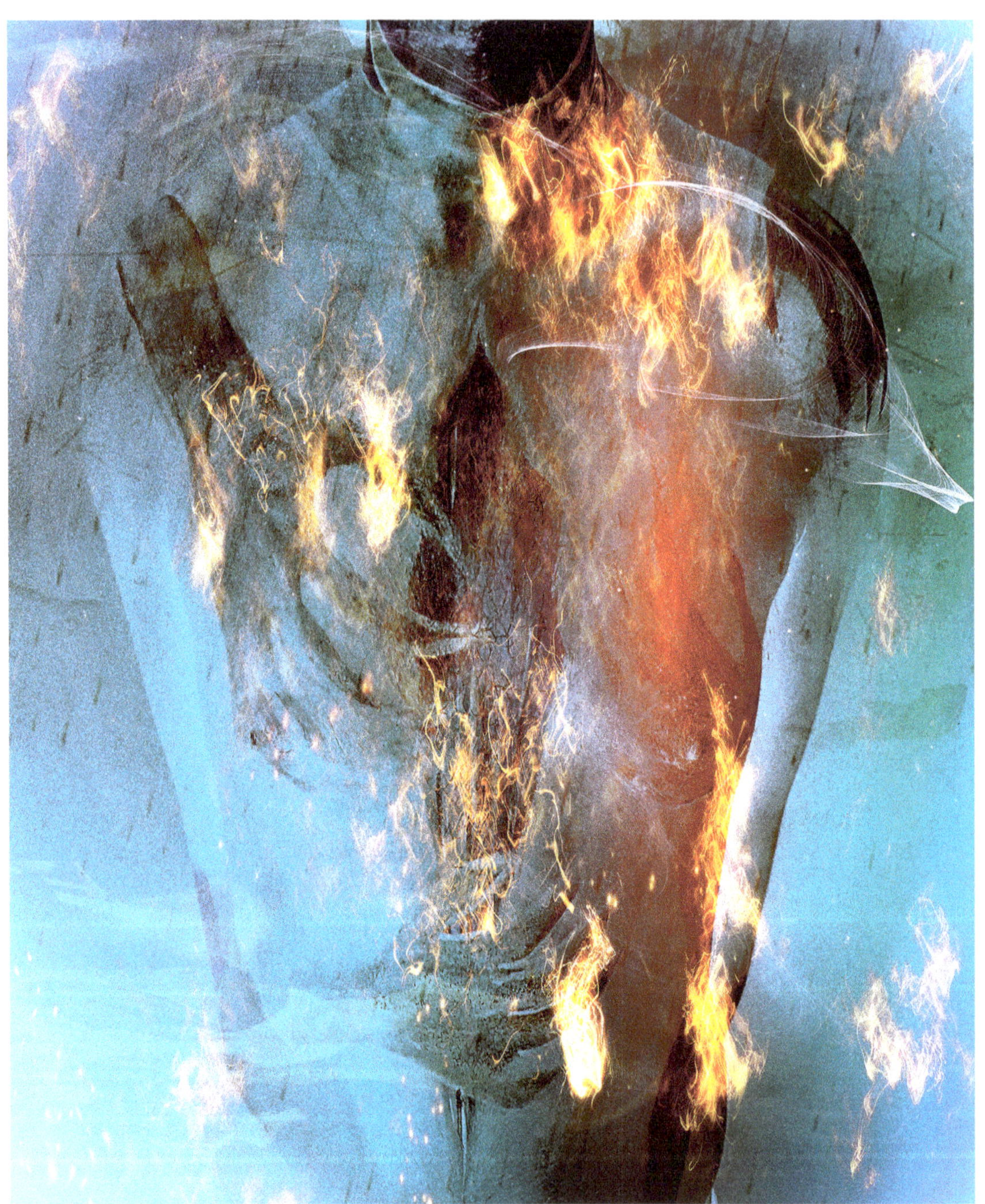

BURNING MAN

Digital photography. The subject was body painted.

DOUG KNOTT

OJAI, CALIFORNIA

GOODBYE ANXIETY, HELLO KAFKA

It was a trial of sand

with evidence of self-burial.

A lifetime of waving many legs in the air

trying to turn over.

What kind of impression will I make on God?

Will he find me wanting, or simply odd?

I want acquittal in the conflict

of loving and rejection of love,

Because I was too young at the time.

Yes, I admit taking part in my own physical decline

living without permission or even good taste.

I'm quite a specimen to scuttle along so long.

A few bedsores, but still eager.

Maybe it was all a reflection

or my own invidious projection—

and I was the only one fooled. Damn.

The earth doesn't turn, it leans.

Give me a verdict with a center of gravity

and I promise to ignore it.

LILY DESPIC

WINNIPEG, MANITOBA, CANADA

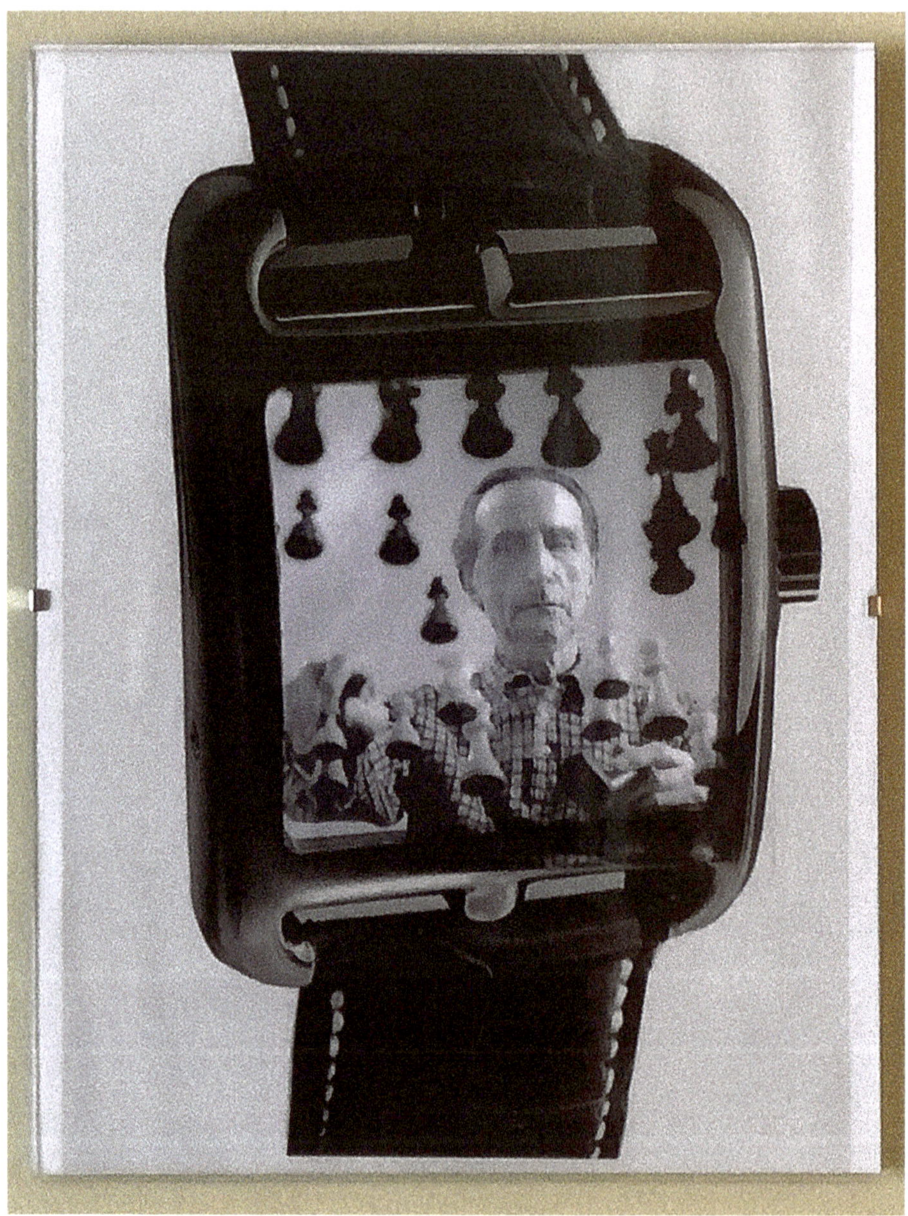

CHESS: THE FINAL (NYET) FRONTIER

Mixed media: vellum, photo copy transfer on acetate sheet, 8-1/2 x 11 inches

DAVID LAWTON

NEW YORK, NEW YORK

UBU RECYCLES

(after Alfred Jarry)

(Père Ubu appears in the city square, in all his royal corpulence. He plants himself by the sewer cover.)

FSHIT! It is such waste. This glorious byproduct of our conspicuous consumption. Gluttonous bounty enabled by governmentally lowered interest rates. Epiphenomenon caused when Happy Meals and crème brûlée intersect. This base matter my rapacity demands should produce gold, even if it is brown. By the green sterno that reheats my pot stickers, this calls for a science of particularities, epic in scope. The vehicle of this particular science is my greatest, because only, accomplishment: The Veloci-Pump! (The Veloci-Pump is revealed. A bicycle-powered poop vacuum.) A mechanism to not only clear the cesspit of the matériel, but separate the equivalence of contraries into the actual and the subjective. Solid fertilizer to nourish the motherland, and the palpable vapor that could power the empire! (Ubu climbs onto the pump with some difficulty.) I hoist my ample scrotums into the saddle, applying my ripe piggies to the pedals (he begins pedaling), engaging its series of gears and hydraulics, riding crop at my side (striking the body of the pump). Like shrimping in a rock pool, I tap the bottom, perspiring heroically. Feeling an intensification of existence (riding furiously), brandishing our national banner of the White Trash Eagle (does so), until my thundering buttcheeks break this cheap-ass street (the area around the sewer cover collapses, dropping the pump, along with Père Ubu, into the sewer), and a tidal wave of sludge leaves me covered in esteem.

(A sour flourish of trumpets.)

NINA ŽIVANČEVIĆ

PARIS, FRANCE

WHAT THE ALIENIST AVANT-GARDE SHOULD DO

1. Contrary to every avant-garde movement: the ALIENIST avant-garde should unflinchingly support each and every one of its members.

2. It has always had and should maintain the error of thinking of itself as "the avant-garde" as it absolutely has a monopoly on innovation.

3. Refute the notion of the avant-garde as an aesthetic minority.

4. Behead the people who dare say that, "Avant-garde is a genre that deludes itself into thinking it's a socio-political uprising."

5. Maintain high profile while working in academies for the sake of poetry and philosophy alone.

6. It is still the avant-garde not the Territorial Army.

7. Emotion itself is not sentimental. HOWEVER:

8. It differs from other contemporary guardians as it never forgets to make people laugh.

9. It is never ashamed of the immortal one-liners we find in great poets from Shakespeare to Blake to Ginsberg to Lana Del Rey.

10. Fight the idea that either an avant-garde hero or the immigrant poet should be placed in solitary confinement.

11. The Alienist avant-garde is a work of art which contains its own (as well as many other) critique(s).

12. Avoid the foulest misunderstanding of the Alienists' AG: "Just as it is easier to produce abstract paintings than figurative paintings, so it is easier to produce avant-garde poems than poems." Etc. etc. etc.

13. A) Be an Alienist—don't be a policeman.

    B) However: Nothing is as important as the AAG (Alienist avant-garde) preaching 'alienation' and 'agon' from its professorial pulpits—if you don't do it, no one will do it for you.

WHAT THE ALIENIST AVANT-GARDE SHOULDN'T DO

1. Become or call itself an ARRIERE-GARDE! (Backyard tiptoeing). Thus the nicest thought of a much quoted British post-colonial poet here: As Marxists covet the hierarchy of academia, anarchists seek the horizontals of bohemia.

2. Think that the "isms" are younger brothers and sisters of the Alienist avant-garde. To cater to Alienism is not merely a fashion statement!

3. Believe that, "Certain hallmarks of avant-garde poetry (e.g., the ampersand or zig-zagging to and fro across the page or a 'yr' for 'your') are mammalian signaling-devices." Or if there's a strong belief, it should not be expressed in meows or in chirping.

4. It should never ask dumb questions such as, "What use is the campus Marxism of the avant-garde when it does nothing for the proletariat?" when the proletariat itself has never abandoned Karl Marx.

5. Ever be confused with the war of the cottage cheese industries.

6. Give us the impression that the Alienists lack in ideas or that their texts are meaningless. They're a work of art.

7. Above all: Don't trust Blake who spent his life fighting Urizen—he DID believe in power. ("One power alone makes a poet: Imagination, the Divine Vision.")

8. By no means forget that revolt is more content than form. There's always "more to artistic progress than minor technical adjustments."

9. By no means forget: Alienists' poetry—which draws from a reservoir of Marxian prophecies of doom—seems more about consciousness-raising than exalting the verse. Marx himself expropriated ideas from Heinrich Heine, who was both celebrant and satirist.

10. Above all: The Alienist avant-garde should not be its own audience, a fish-tank of bedbugs riding on sharks . . .

11. However, thou Alienist should know: There is nothing wrong in floating in the above-mentioned fish tank.

12. NEVER say such things as, "Paul Celan was too busy struggling with real issues to get hung up on a conflict between avant-garde and mainstream"; it goes without saying, thus give some respect to the dead and to the weary. Or just say, "Sadly enough, Paul Antschel was pinned down by too much light that kept him out of Auschwitz . . ."

13. NEVER forget: The poem is always more of a work of art than a signature on a petition.

BRENT BECHTEL

TAYLORS, SOUTH CAROLINA

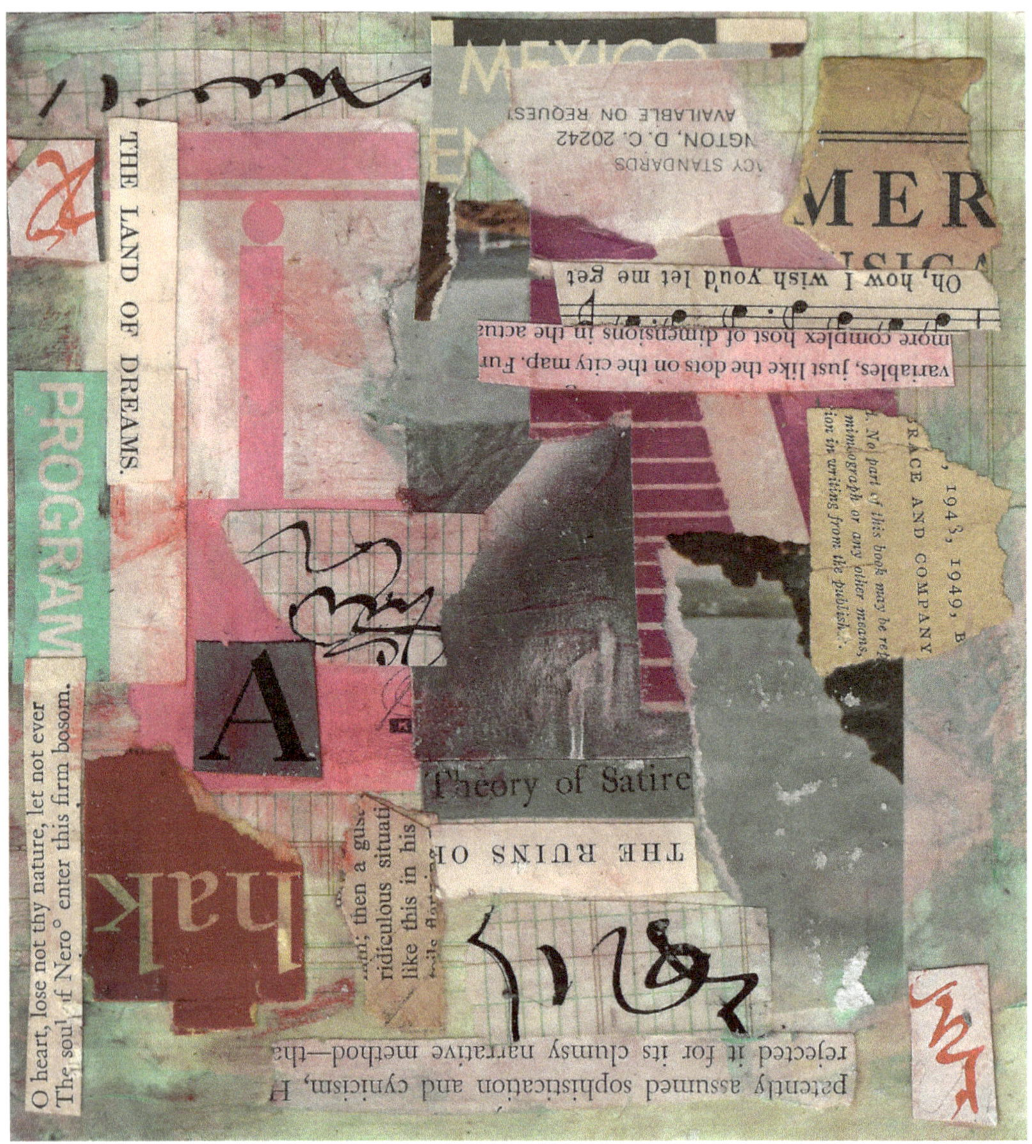

THE RUINS OF SATIRE

Heavy paper, India ink, pigment, application of sandpaper, fixative, 5.5 x 5.75 inches

J. J. STEINFELD

CHARLOTTETOWN, PRINCE EDWARD ISLAND, CANADA

AN ABSURD STAND-UP DADA COMEDIAN OF LITTLE REPUTE

An absurd stand-up Dada comedian with two broken legs

and a broken heart wanting to reshape the world

working the audience at a monetized corporate conference

on how to convince the shareholders and politicians

that up is down, and pollution is pleasantness—

where is Orwell when you need him?—

a tearful the-show-must-go-on absurdist

mingling and mangling language and cosmologies

as the prosperous audience of the indifferent

watch him working the packed room

an absurd stand-up Dada comedian of little repute

tapping absurdly at the walls of deception

feeling for the hidden flaws of construction

learning haphazardly to refine absurdity and comedy

desiring the escape of time travel to future half-sane times

holding enigmatic tongue and unknowable breath

as the room fills with small talk biting into reality

and small dreams dipped in avarice and cryptocurrency

this endless last chance, hail-Mary kick at the can,

for ill-conceived immortality or its on-stage counterpart

the absurd stand-up Dada comedian's legs and heart refusing to heal

this time, just as last time, lost in time

timeless as the swallowing of a gold-plated watch

a last-ditch attempt to amuse the audience

at a monetized corporate conference.

EGON GUENTHER

DIESSEN, GERMANY

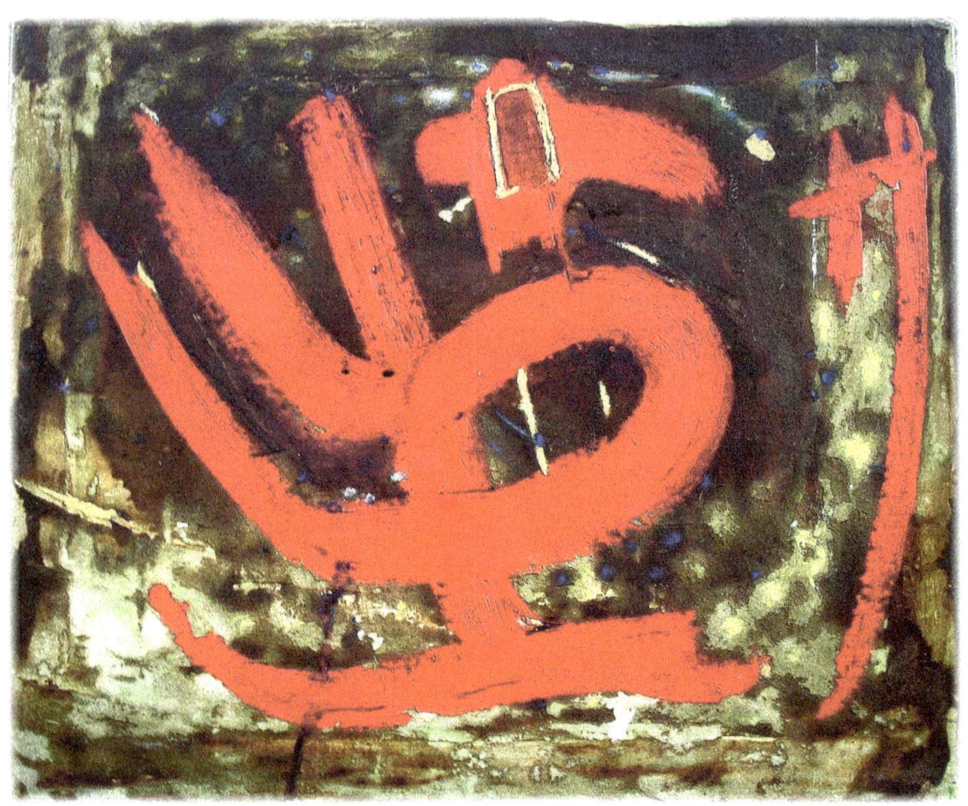

SUPRANYET [to lots of hot air]

Oil/tar on canvas, 51 x 40 cm

CHERYL J. FISH
NEW YORK, NEW YORK

NOT (N)YET

That slow mired in distraction.

Hard to greet, took away.

Gentle at first, then a cold kind of kinky.

Sobering, booted you from a dream.

Rigid to touch, wet from numinous

flood. Slept inside a drawer

Then called you out.

Caused an itch multiplied by fossil pain.

Knew the way, ignored the warnings.

Breezed

by as if falling through fingers.

Stuck in the head, burst

the vessels. Blundered, blushed

made excuses. Belched and

breathed. Posted and linked about it.

MUTES CÉSAR

ARCOS DE VALDEVEZ, PORTUGAL

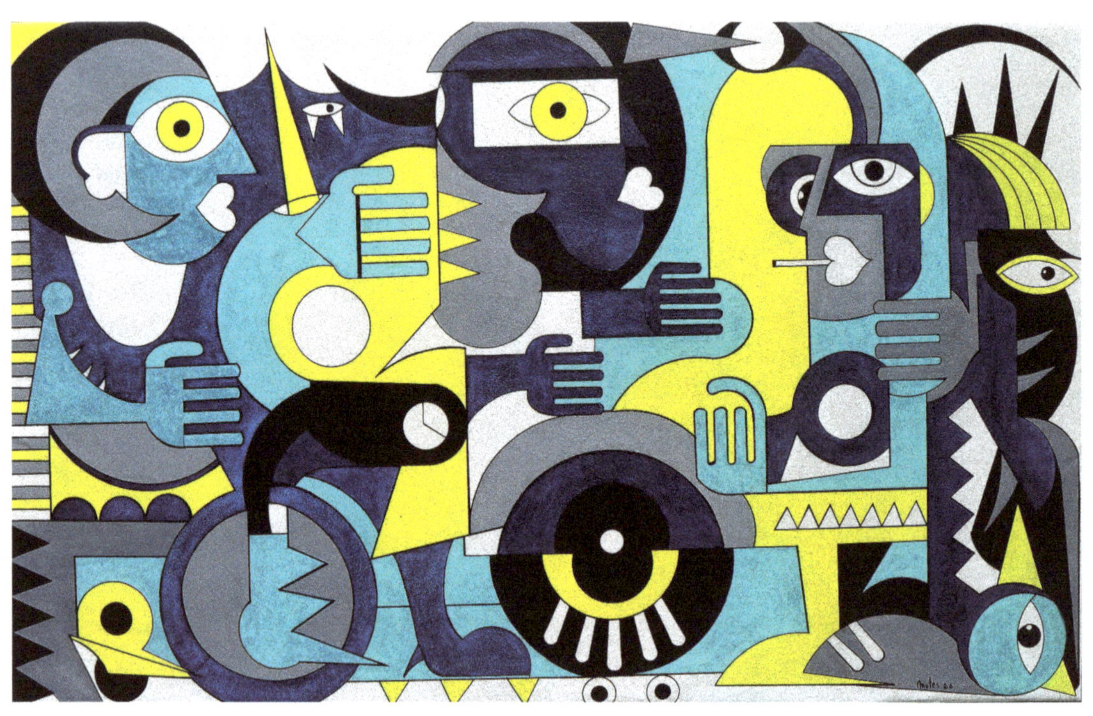

**DESEMBESTADAS CORRERIAS NA LUTA
CONTRA AS MUDANÇAS CLIMATÉRICAS.**

Oil painting, 105 x 170 cm

OLADIPO KEHINDE PAUL

LAGOS, NIGERIA

TIME WILL HEAL US

We are in a powerful cosmic trajectory opposition.

We have refused to invite peace to the table of reason.

The spirits of history have hijacked the catalogue of our collective memory.

War is a memory of peace.

We go to war because we do not know why we are here.

We go to war because the cry of the innocent tingles our blood.

Man is the prey. Man is the beast.

Man is the pillar of this ephemeral world.

Confusion of analysis. Moribund situation.

Equality, liberty, and fraternity in the season of doubt and belief.

Wine has been replaced with blood.

Russia and Ukraine on cosmic man madness.

Waiting for a classical empirical mutation.

Rumbles and troubles for nadir and hero worship.

We do not see the future and retrogression becomes inevitable.

We are in the season of war and peace.

Should we go to war to have peace?

We have different perspectives. Power mongers.

Let's see who profits from this avoidable WAR.

MILANA JUVENTA

MOSCOW, RUSSIA

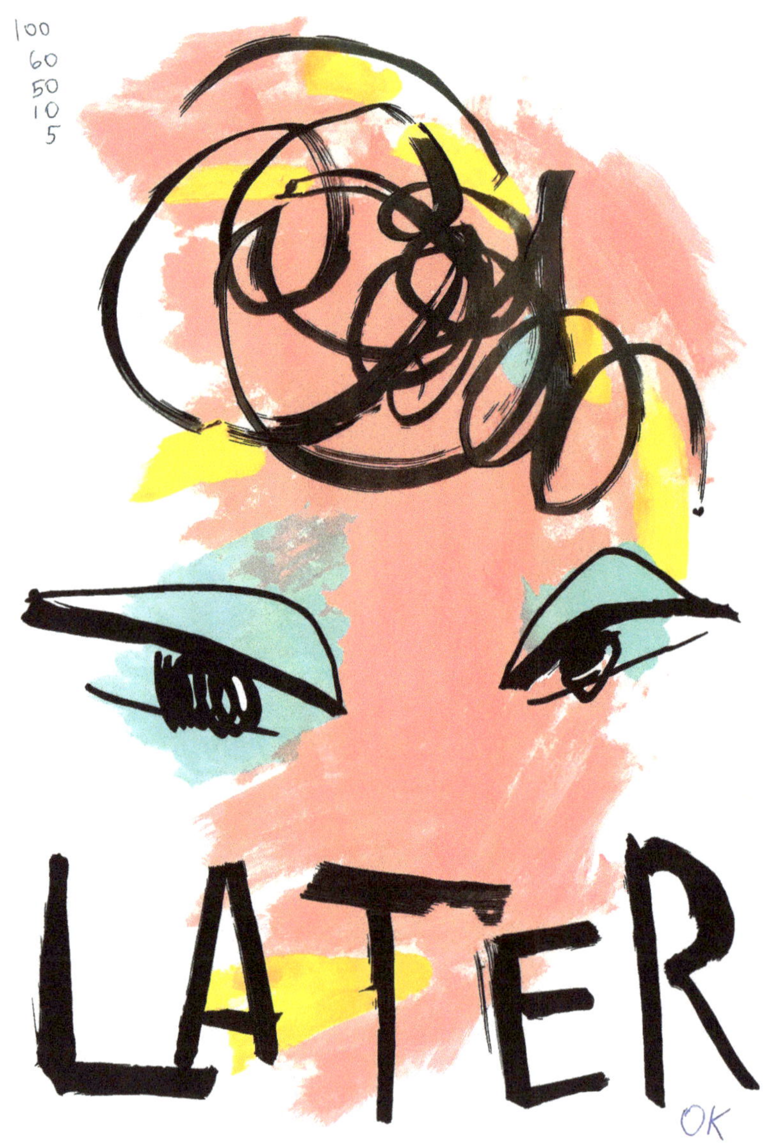

LATER

Semi-physical, semi-digital art, 2152 × 3037 pixels

Recent and Forthcoming Books from Three Rooms Press

FICTION

Lucy Jane Bledsoe
No Stopping Us Now

Rishab Borah
The Door to Inferna

Meagan Brothers
Weird Girl and What's His Name

Christopher Chambers
Scavenger
Standalone

Ebele Chizea
Aquarian Dawn

Ron Dakron
Hello Devilfish!

Robert Duncan
Loudmouth

Michael T. Fournier
Hidden Wheel
Swing State

Aaron Hamburger
Nirvana Is Here

William Least Heat-Moon
Celestial Mechanics

Aimee Herman
Everything Grows

Kelly Ann Jacobson
Tink and Wendy
Robin and Her Misfits

Jethro K. Lieberman
Everything Is Jake

Eamon Loingsigh
Light of the Diddicoy
Exile on Bridge Street

John Marshall
The Greenfather

Aram Saroyan
Still Night in L.A.

Robert Silverberg
The Face of the Waters

Stephen Spotte
Animal Wrongs

Richard Vetere
The Writers Afterlife
Champagne and Cocaine

Jessamyn Violet
Secret Rules to Being a Rockstar

Julia Watts
Quiver
Needlework

Gina Yates
Narcissus Nobody

MEMOIR & BIOGRAPHY

Nassrine Azimi and Michel Wasserman
*Last Boat to Yokohama: The Life and
Legacy of Beate Sirota Gordon*

William S. Burroughs & Allen Ginsberg
*Don't Hide the Madness:
William S. Burroughs in Conversation
with Allen Ginsberg*
edited by Steven Taylor

James Carr
*BAD: The Autobiography of
James Carr*

Judy Gumbo
*Yippie Girl: Exploits in Protest and
Defeating the FBI*

Judith Malina
*Full Moon Stages:
Personal Notes from
50 Years of The Living Theatre*

Phil Marcade
*Punk Avenue: Inside the New York City
Underground, 1972–1982*

Jililian Marshall
*Japanthem: Counter-Cultural
Experiences; Cross-Cultural Remixes*

Alvin Orloff
*Disasterama! Adventures in the Queer
Underground 1977–1997*

Nicca Ray
*Ray by Ray: A Daughter's Take
on the Legend of Nicholas Ray*

Stephen Spotte
*My Watery Self:
Memoirs of a Marine Scientist*

PHOTOGRAPHY-MEMOIR

Mike Watt
On & Off Bass

SHORT STORY ANTHOLOGIES

SINGLE AUTHOR

The Alien Archives: Stories
by Robert Silverberg

First-Person Singularities: Stories
by Robert Silverberg
with an introduction by John Scalzi

Tales from the Eternal Café: Stories
by Janet Hamill, with an introduction
by Patti Smith

*Time and Time Again:
Sixteen Trips in Time*
by Robert Silverberg

*Voyagers:
Twelve Journeys in Space and Time*
by Robert Silverberg

MULTI-AUTHOR

*Crime + Music: Twenty Stories
of Music-Themed Noir*
edited by Jim Fusilli

Dark City Lights: New York Stories
edited by Lawrence Block

*The Faking of the President: Twenty
Stories of White House Noir*
edited by Peter Carlaftes

*Florida Happens:
Bouchercon 2018 Anthology*
edited by Greg Herren

*Have a NYC I, II & III:
New York Short Stories;*
edited by Peter Carlaftes
& Kat Georges

*No Body No Crime:
22 Stories of Taylor Swift-Inspired Noir*
edited by Alex Segura and Joe Clifford

*Songs of My Selfie:
An Anthology of Millennial Stories*
edited by Constance Renfrow

*The Obama Inheritance:
15 Stories of Conspiracy Noir*
edited by Gary Phillips

*This Way to the End Times:
Classic and New Stories of
the Apocalypse*
edited by Robert Silverberg

MIXED MEDIA

John S. Paul
Sign Language: A Painter's Notebook
(photography, poetry and prose)

HUMOR

Peter Carlaftes
A Year on Facebook

DADA

*Maintenant: A Journal of
Contemporary Dada Writing & Art*
(Annual, since 2008)

FILM & PLAYS

Israel Horovitz
*My Old Lady: Complete Stage Play and
Screenplay with an Essay on Adaptation*

Peter Carlaftes
Triumph For Rent (3 Plays)
Teatrophy (3 More Plays)

Kat Georges
*Three Somebodies: Plays about Notorious
Dissidents*

TRANSLATIONS

Thomas Bernhard
On Earth and in Hell
(poems of Thomas Bernhard
with English translations by
Peter Waugh)

Patrizia Gattaceca
Isula d'Anima / Soul Island
(poems by the author
in Corsican with English
translations)

César Vallejo | Gerard Malanga
Malanga Chasing Vallejo
(selected poems of César Vallejo
with English translations
and additional notes by
Gerard Malanga)

George Wallace
EOS: Abductor of Men
(selected poems in Greek & English)

ESSAYS

Richard Katrovas
*Raising Girls in Bohemia:
Meditations of an American Father*

Far Away From Close to Home
Vanessa Baden Kelly

*Womentality: Thirteen Empowering Stories
by Everyday Women Who Said Goodbye to
the Workplace and Hello to Their Lives*
edited by Erin Wildermuth

POETRY COLLECTIONS

Hala Alyan
Atrium

Peter Carlaftes
DrunkYard Dog
I Fold with the Hand I Was Dealt

Thomas Fucaloro
It Starts from the Belly and Blooms

Kat Georges
Our Lady of the Hunger

Robert Gibbons
Close to the Tree

Israel Horovitz
Heaven and Other Poems

David Lawton
Sharp Blue Stream

Jane LeCroy
Signature Play

Philip Meersman
This Is Belgian Chocolate

Jane Ormerod
Recreational Vehicles on Fire
Welcome to the Museum of Cattle

Lisa Panepinto
On This Borrowed Bike

George Wallace
Poppin' Johnny

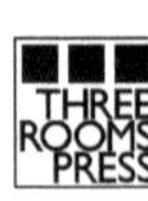

Three Rooms Press | New York, NY | Current Catalog: www.threeroomspress.com

Three Rooms Press books are distributed by Publishers Group West: www.pgw.com

CPSIA information can be obtained
at www.ICGtesting.com
Printed in the USA
JSHW012052090622
26924JS00002B/2